DESIGNER PROFILE
2012—2013
VOL.2
GRAPHIC & CORPORATE & MULTIMEDIA DESIGN

FORM BOOKS

BIRKHÄUSER
BASEL

FORM BOOKS

DESIGNER PROFILE
2012—2013 VOL.2

GRAPHIC & CORPORATE & MULTIMEDIA DESIGN

BIRKHÄUSER
BASEL

6 FOREWORD

ESSAYS

8 **SPRECHENDE BILDER** THE GRAPHIC NOVEL BOOM
Barbara Schär

18 **BAURS CRESCENDO** THE SOUND OF TYPOGRAPHY
Rahel Ueding

24 **DESIGNER IM NETZ** WHAT THE WEB CAN DO FOR YOU
Karianne Fogelberg

PROFILES

34 **GRAPHIC** DESIGN
100 **CORPORATE** DESIGN
132 **MULTIMEDIA** DESIGN

INDEX

140 ALPHABETICAL
144 FIELDS OF ACTIVITY
158 AWARDS

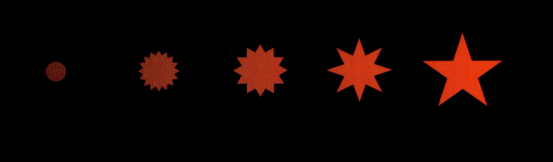

FOREWORD

Seit 1998 sind die Designer Profile eine feste Größe: Wenn es darum geht, den richtigen Kreativpartner für einen bestimmten Auftrag zu wählen, führt für Entscheider kein Weg an diesem Kompendium vorbei. Hier zeigen Gestalter aus den Bereichen Produktdesign, Messe- und Ausstellungsdesign sowie Corporate Identity und Webdesign ihre aktuellen Projekte. Somit erschließen sich Kompetenzen und Stärken der einzelnen Büros und man ist auf einen Blick informiert über den neuesten Stand der Dinge. Flankiert von unserer Website designer-profile.de, auf der die dort vorgestellten Designer ihre Profile permanent aktualisieren und neuste Arbeitsbeispiele präsentieren, bietet der Birkhäuser Verlag mit der Marke „Designer Profile" eine starke Informationsplattform.

Jeder weiß: Die New-Business-Akquise ist ein hartes Geschäft. Man kann dabei nicht allein auf die eigene Website bauen und hoffen, dass neue Kunden dort zufällig vorbeischauen. Man muss als Designer vielmehr diverse Kommunikationskanäle nutzen, um sein Ziel zu erreichen und auf das eigene Dienstleistungsspektrum aufmerksam zu machen. Die Designer Profile sind dabei ein wichtiger Baustein. Ein anderer ist die Zeitschrift form, die seit zehn Jahren ebenfalls im Birkhäuser Verlag erscheint. Das traditionsreiche Magazin wird schon immer gern von Entscheidern gelesen, um mehr über Design-Trends zu erfahren und junge Talente zu entdecken. Auf unserer Website www.form.de kann man übrigens nicht nur täglich News aus der Designszene finden oder ins Auge springende Banner schalten, sondern auch unsere Mediadaten herunterladen – besuchen Sie uns im Netz!

Aus der form bringen wir in dieser Ausgabe der Designer Profile ausgewählte Beiträge, die Sie interessieren werden: Hier berichtet etwa der Münchner Industriedesigner Peter Naumann, wie er mit Bleistift, Spachtel und Computer der fast vergessenen Motorradmarke Horex neues Leben eingehaucht hat. Das Ergebnis ist zeitlos, formschön und wird bald für Furore sorgen!

Viel Freude bei der Lektüre wünscht Ihnen

Dr. Ulrich Schmidt, Verlagsleiter, Birkhäuser GmbH

These designer profiles have been a fixed entity since 1998: When looking for the right creative partner for a particular job this compendium is absolutely indispensable to decision-makers. Here, designers in product design, trade fair and exhibition design, corporate identity and web design present their current projects, thus demonstrating the expertise and strengths of their individual studios and enabling readers to keep abreast with cutting-edge trends at a glance. Flanked by our website, designer-profile.de where the designers portrayed constantly update their profiles and present the latest examples of their work, with its brand „Designer Profiles", Birkhäuser Verlag has a strong information platform to offer.

Everybody knows: Nowadays, acquiring business is a tough job. Relying on your own website and hoping that new customers will just happen upon them by chance is simply not enough. Indeed, as a designer, to achieve your objectives and to advertise the range of services you have on offer, you need to use various different communications channels. The designer profiles are an important element of this. Another is the periodical form that Birkhäuser Verlag has also published for the past ten years. Decision-makers have always liked to read this long-established magazine to find out more about the latest trends in design and to discover young talents. Incidentally, not only does our website www.form.de offer news about the design scene on a daily basis and allow you to take out banner ads that really jump out at you, in fact, you can even download our media data – why not visit us online!

In this issue of the designer profiles we bring you selected articles from form that will interest you. For example, Munich-based industrial designer Peter Naumann reports how he used pencils, palette knives and computers to breathe new life into Horex, a motorbike brand that had almost faded into oblivion. The result is timeless, elegant and will soon be causing a sensation!

Enjoy!

Dr. Ulrich Schmidt, Chief Unit Manager, Birkhäuser GmbH

GRAPHIC DESIGN

SPRECHENDE BILDER
THE GRAPHIC NOVEL BOOM

Text: Barbara Schär
(redaktion@form.de)

Stetig steigende Absatzzahlen belegen den Erfolg der Graphic Novel. Wiederauflagen, Neuerscheinungen und Übersetzungen schießen aus den Verlagshäusern hervor. Doch dieser Aufschwung hat auch Nachteile. Denn Bildsprache und Erzählstruktur verlieren immer häufiger an Qualität. Wir stellen sieben neue Titel vor, die sich von der Masse abheben.

Der US-amerikanische Zeichner Will Eisner war der Erste, der den Begriff Graphic Novel 1978 auf ein Cover druckte. Eisner wollte sich mit dem Buch „Ein Vertrag mit Gott" („A Contract with God") von klassischen Comicheften distanzieren. Doch war die Bezeichnung auch ein verkaufstechnischer Trick, aus der Hoffnung entstanden, einen belletristischen Verlag für sein Buch zu finden. Sein illustrierter

Continually rising sales figures point to the graphic novel's success. A veritable avalanche of re-editions, new publications and translations is issuing forth from publishers. But there is also a downside to this boom. A frequent aspect: the inferior quality of imagery and narrative structure. We present seven new titles that stand out from the mass.

American illustrator Will Eisner was the first to use the term graphic novel on a book cover in 1978. With "A Contract with God" Eisner sought to distance himself from the classic comic magazines. But the designation was also a sales-related move prompted by the hope of finding a belles-lettres publisher for his book. His illustrated novel is a collection of short stories describing Eisner's memories

✭✭
ABBILDUNGEN, ZEICHEN UND SYMBOLE SIND IN DER REGEL LÄNDER- UND KULTURÜBERGREIFEND VERSTÄNDLICH. SPRACHBARRIEREN LASSEN SICH DURCH BILDER ÜBERBRÜCKEN.
✭✭

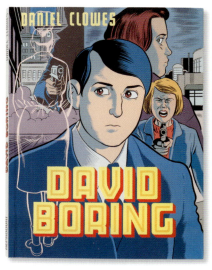
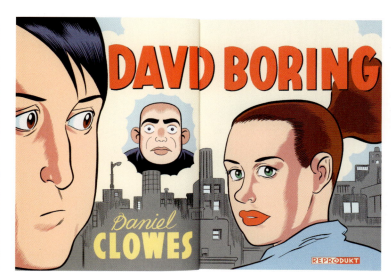

© Daniel Clowes / Reprodukt 2010, Berlin

Daniel Clowes' Erzählungen sind genaue Gesellschaftsstudien mit sarkastisch-tragischen Protagonisten. „David Boring" (oben) findet sich nach seiner ersten großen Liebe in einem surrealen Weltuntergangszenario wieder. Dem melancholischen „Wilson" (unten) begegnet der Leser auf einseitigen Strips, die von seinen alltäglichen Zweifeln erzählen.

Daniel Clowes' stories, with their sarcastic-cum-tragic protagonists, take a very detailed look at society. When the first great love of his live is over, "David Boring" (above) finds himself immersed in a surreal end-of-the-world scenario. The melancholic "Wilson" (below) features in one-page strips that tell of his daily doubts.

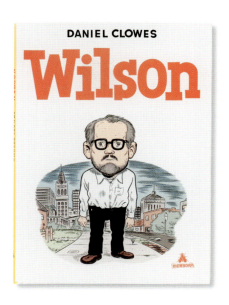

© Eichborn AG 2011, Frankfurt am Main

GRAPHIC DESIGN

★★
ILLUSTRATIONS, SIGNS AND SYMBOLS ARE GENERALLY UNDERSTANDABLE ACROSS NATIONS AND CULTURES. LANGUAGE BARRIERS CAN BE BRIDGED USING IMAGES.
★★

Roman ist eine Sammlung von Kurzgeschichten, die Eisners Kindheitserinnerungen in der New Yorker Bronx, kurz vor dem Zweiten Weltkrieg, schildern. Noch heute verblüfft sein Umgang mit Licht und Schatten, die charakterstarken Gesichter und die Einflechtung des Textes ins Bild. Autobiografische Berichte von Kindheit und Krieg bis zur Reisereportage sind weit verbreitete Themen der grafischen Novellen. Vielleicht, weil Erinnerungen im Gedächtnis als Bilder gespeichert und als solche direkt abrufbar sind. Besonders im Kindesalter ist die visuelle Wahrnehmung der sprachlichen noch weit überlegen. Abbildungen, Zeichen und Symbole sind in der Regel länder- und kulturübergreifend verständlich. Sprachbarrieren lassen sich durch Bilder überbrücken – umgekehrt kann die Sprachlosigkeit angesichts eines Krieges in der Zeichnung Ausdruck finden.

    Historische Ereignisse finden sich nicht nur als persönliche Schilderung, sondern vermehrt auch als penibel recherchierter Bericht in der Graphic Novel. Das äußerste Beispiel hierfür ist Jens Harders Buch „Alpha ... directions". Es komprimiert die Erdentstehungsgeschichte vom Urknall bis zum ersten Menschen. Auf 360 Seiten. 14 Milliarden Jahre auf grob geschätzt 2.000 Zeichnungen – das macht etwa ein Bild alle sieben Millionen Jahre! In kleinen Panels und doppelseitigen Illustrationen verbindet Harder bildliche Anspielungen auf Tim und Struppi, Donald Duck, Van Gogh, Jules Verne, Steinzeitillustrationen und frühzeitliche Weltbilder. „Mit Alpha möchte ich alle visuellen Vorstellungen über die Entwicklungen ab

of his childhood in New York's Bronx shortly before World War II. Today, people continue to be amazed at his handling of light and shadow, strong faces and the weaving of the text into the image. Autobiographic reports of childhood and war through to travel reporting are common topics of graphic novels. Perhaps because recollections are stored in the memory as images and as such are directly retrievable. And especially as children our visual perception is far superior to our linguistic perception. Illustrations, signs and symbols are generally understandable across nations and cultures. Language barriers can be bridged using images – conversely, speechlessness in the face of war can be expressed in drawing.

    Historical events not only feature as personal descriptions but increasingly also as painstakingly researched reports in the graphic novel. The most extreme example of this is Jens Harder's book "Alpha ... directions." It condenses the story of how the earth was created from the big bang to the first human-being. On 360 pages. 14 billion years in roughly 2,000 drawings – that is one image for every seven million years! In small panels and double-page illustrations Harder unites visual allusions to The Adventures of Tintin, Donald Duck, Van Gogh, Stone Age illustrations and archaic images of the world. "With Alpha I would like to bundle all the visual conceptions about developments from the supposed zero through to the creation of the universe as we know it," explains the illustrator. For example, a billiard game explains atom collisions; the spark of a match stands as

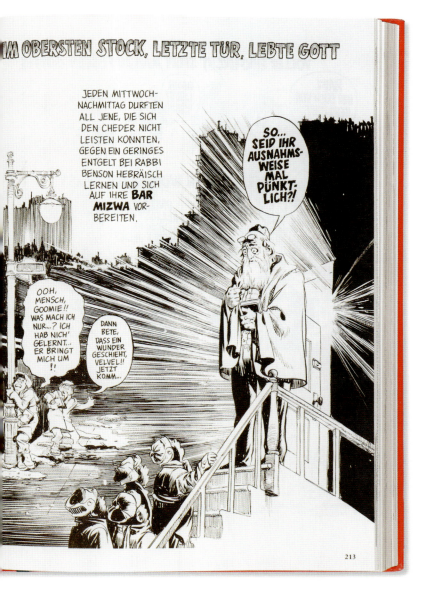

© Carlsen Verlag 2010, Hamburg

dem angenommenen Nullpunkt zur Entstehung des uns bekannten Universums bündeln", so der Illustrator. Ein Billardspiel erklärt zum Beispiel Atomkollisionen; ein Streichholzfunken steht als Auslöser für das Aufglühen eines Sterns. Mit Ideenreichtum und Assoziationskraft fügt Harder unterschiedlichste Stile zu einer Einheit zusammen. Das Buch legt den Gedanken nahe, dass der Mensch sich schon immer stark am Bild orientierte.

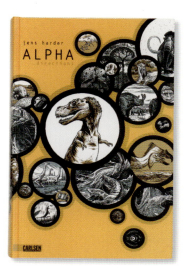

Eine Dokumentation mit kleinerem Radius ist „The Beats" von Harvey Pekar und Paul Buhle – sie erzählt faktenreich die Geschichte der Beat-Literaten. Pekar und Buhle sind dabei nur Autoren, gezeichnet haben mehrere Illustratoren mit jeweils eigenem Strich. Anders als in „Alpha ... directions", das ohne viel Text auskommt, ist „The Beats" reich an konkreten Informationen. Im Zweiseitentakt reihen sich Biografien aneinander und machen es dem Leser teilweise schwer, die Protagonisten zu unterscheiden – hatte nun Kerouac toupierte Haare oder war das Burroughs? Von der Beat-Generation zur Beat-Musik und zur Biografie „Baby's in Black" von Arne Bellstorf: Das Buch erzählt die Liebesgeschichte der Fotografin Astrid Kirchherr aus Hamburg und dem „fünften Beatle", dem Bassisten Stuart Sutcliffe. Sie beginnt mit ihrem ersten Blickkontakt und endet mit Sutcliffes frühem Tod. Bellstorf hat die Story nach Erinnerungen und Fotos Kirchherrs gezeichnet. Die Gesichter sind treffsicher gestaltet, die Mimik der Dargestellten wirkt jedoch oftmals wenig nuanciert. Kaum Text, abwechselnd in englischer und deutscher Sprache, verweist auf die Sprachbarrieren des Paares und endet, als Sutcliffe stirbt, in der Sprachlosigkeit.

Zwei Medien wissen, zeigen, erklären besser als eines. Bilder können einen Text verdeutlichen, unterstützen und positiv auf den Lesefluss sowie die Aufmerksamkeit einwirken. Bestes Beispiel: die illustrierte Bibel. Satz für Satz hat Robert Crumb, seit über 40 Jahren Meister der schrägen Helden und Gewaltfantasien, die Kapitel der Genesis illustriert. Ein Buch, das ich ohne Crumb womöglich nicht zur Hand genommen hätte.

Per Definition ist die Graphic Novel ein einbändiger Comic im Buchformat, der sich an erwachsene Leser richtet und komplexe,

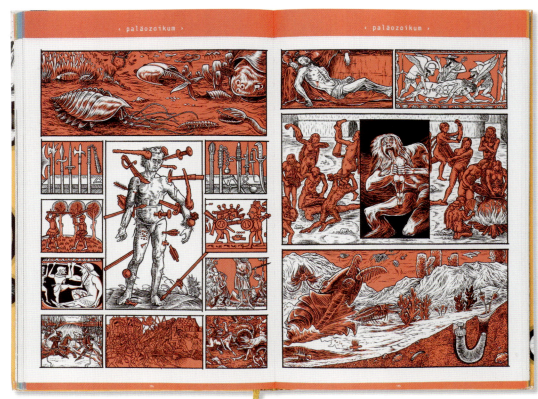

© Jens Harder / Carlsen Verlag 2010, Hamburg

ernsthafte Geschichten erzählt. Vom herkömmlichen Comicstrip unterscheidet sie sich maßgeblich durch kleineres Format, Umfang, hochwertige Herstellung und den meist schwarz-weißen Strich. Viele Gestalter sehen sich durch eine derartige Kategorisierung jedoch eingeengt, manche Illustratoren wähnen hinter der Bezeichnung Graphic Novel rein verkaufsstrategische Motive. So auch Daniel Clowes, dessen Werke als Graphic Novels vertrieben werden, obwohl er selbst der Bezeichnung kritisch gegenüber steht. Sein kürzlich erschienener „Wilson" ist das ironisch-tragische Porträt eines melancholischen Eigenbrötlers in der Midlife-Crisis. Zynisch und selbstvergessen beobachtet er seine Alltagswelt. Der amerikanische Illustrator zeigt ihn auf einseitigen und farbigen Comicstrips. Sein „David Boring" wiederum ist die Geschichte eines jungen Außenseiters

ZWEI MEDIEN WISSEN, ZEIGEN, ERKLÄREN BESSER ALS EINES. BILDER KÖNNEN EINEN TEXT VERDEUTLICHEN, UNTERSTÜTZEN UND POSITIV AUF DEN LESEFLUSS SOWIE DIE AUFMERKSAMKEIT EINWIRKEN.

trigger for the lighting up of a star. Drawing on imaginativeness and the power of association Harder combines a wide variety of styles to form a whole. The book suggests that human beings have always been strongly inspired by images.

"The Beats" by Harvey Pekar and Paul Buhle is a documentation with less of a reach, but brimming with facts. It relates the story of the Beat literary figures, and Pekar and Buhle are only the authors, the drawings were executed by several illustrators, each with their own style. While "Alpha … directions" manages without much text "The Beats" is rich in detailed information. Biographies follow thick and fast every two pages and this occasionally makes it difficult for the reader to keep the protagonists apart – did Kerouac wear teased hair or was it Burroughs? From the Beat generation to Beat music and the biography "Baby's in Black" by Arne Bellstorf: The book tells the love story between Hamburg photographer Astrid Kirchherr and the "Fifth Beatle", bass guitarist Stuart Sutcliffe. It begins with their first glance and ends with Sutcliffe's early death. Bellstorf drew the story after Kirchherr's recollections and photographs. Though the faces are drawn accurately the facial expressions of the characters often lack subtlety. Sparse text, alternately in English and German, refers to the couple's language barriers and ends when Sutcliffe dies, in speechlessness.

Two different media show and explain more than one. Images can clarify a text, support and positively influence the flow of reading and attention. The best example: the illustrated Bible. Robert Crumb, the master of weird heroes and violent fantasies, illustrated the Genesis

© Walde+Graf Verlag AG 2010, Zürich

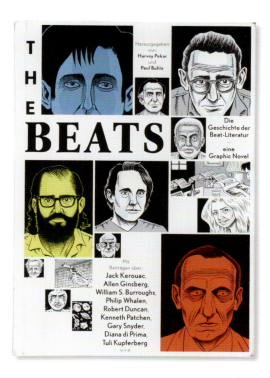

chapters, sentence for sentence. A book I might never have picked up if not for Robert Crumb.

By definition the graphic novel is a one-volume comic in book format, which addresses adult readers and relates complex, serious stories. It differs decisively from the customary comic strip in its smaller format, scope, high-quality production and the typically black-and-white style. However, many designers feel restricted by such a categorization, some illustrators perceive purely sales tactics behind the term graphic novel. For example Daniel Clowes, whose works are marketed as graphic novels although he himself is critical of the designation. His recently published "Wilson" is the ironic-tragic portrait of a melancholy brooder in mid-life crisis. Cynically and absent-mindedly he observes his everyday world. Clowes depicts him in one-page, colored comic strips. By contrast, his "David Boring" is the story of a young outsider in three acts. His publications are

TWO DIFFERENT MEDIA SHOW AND EXPLAIN MORE THAN ONE. IMAGES CAN CLARIFY A TEXT, SUPPORT AND POSITIVELY INFLUENCE THE FLOW OF READING AND ATTENTION.

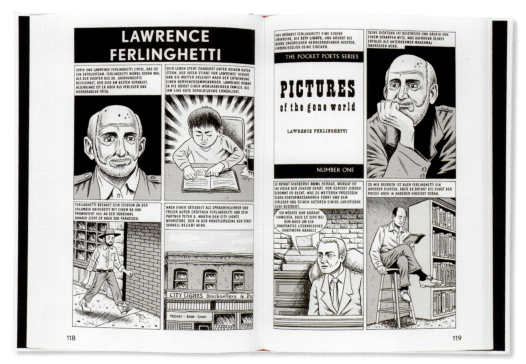
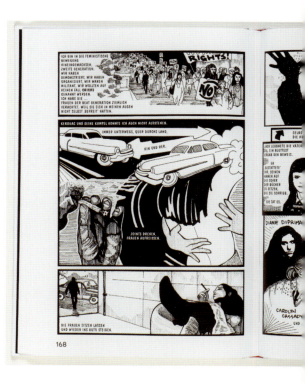

„The Beats" von Harvey Pekar und Paul Buhle ist ein informationsreiches Buch zur Beat-Literatur. Es umfasst mehrheitlich Biografien, aber auch wichtige Episoden dieser Literatur-Generation. Ein Dutzend Zeichner haben illustriert, somit ergibt sich im Buch eine visuelle Vielfalt.

"The Beats" by Harvey Pekar and Paul Buhle is a book packed with information on Beat literature. The majority of texts are biographies, but they are interspersed with key episodes of this literary generation. The illustrations are from a dozen different graphic artists, lending the book great visual diversity.

© Arne Bellstorf / Reprodukt 2010, Berlin

in drei Akten. Clowes' Veröffentlichungen zeichnen sich durch den klaren Strich im Stil der fünfziger und sechziger Jahre, einen analytischen Blickwinkel und das gekonnte Lettering aus. Auch wenn Clowes gegenüber dem Label Graphic Novel Vorbehalte hat: Seine Arbeiten gehören zu den Höhepunkten des Genres. Seine Gesellschaftsstudien sind differenziert, seine Protagonisten eben oft nicht comichaft-komisch.

Kein Zweifel: Die Bandbreite des illustrierten Romans ist groß und lässt sich nur bedingt durch Thema, Stil oder Formalitäten eingrenzen. Seine absatztechnischen Vorteile gegenüber dem Comic liegen auf der Hand: Die grafische Novelle lässt sich besser verkaufen und vermarkten. Was früher bloß als Comic galt, steht heute oft unter dem Etikett Graphic Novel im Regal. Dieser Boom hat jedoch auch Schattenseiten. Überzeugte etwa Eisner noch durch seinen charakterstarken Strich, zeigen viele Neuerscheinungen, was Stil, Bildsprache, Innovation und Fantasie betrifft, Schwächen. Die derzeitige Nachfrage hat zur Folge, dass viel Zweitklassiges den Markt überschwemmt. Eisner mahnte schon im Vorwort von „Ein Vertrag mit Gott": „Die Zukunft der Graphic Novels liegt in der Relevanz der Themen und in der Innovation der Darstellung." Das Genre hat sehr an Status gewonnen. Doch wahre zeichnerische und sprachliche Qualität bleibt die Ausnahme. ★

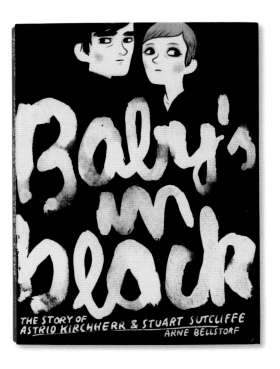

Arne Bellstorf zeichnet in „Baby's in Black" die kurze Liebesgeschichte von Stuart Sutcliffe und Astrid Kirchherr. Als Leser fühlt man sich gleich mitten im Gespräch unter Freunden. Denn Bellstorf setzt den Betrachter durch Nahaufnahmen und Bildausschnitte mitten ins Geschehen.

In "Baby's in Black", Arne Bellstorf illustrates the short love story of Stuart Sutcliffe and Astrid Kirchherr. Readers will immediately feel like they are chatting amongst friends. For Bellstorf puts the beholder right at the heart of the action with close-ups and image details.

characterized by a clear stroke in the style of the 1950s and 1960s, an analytical perspective and masterful lettering. Though Clowes himself might be critical of the label graphic novel his works number amongst the highlights of this genre. His studies of society are differentiated, his protagonists are very often not funny in the manner of comics.

Without a doubt – the scope of the graphic novel is large and cannot be narrowed down according to topic, style, or formalities. Its sales advantages vis-à-vis the comic are obvious: graphic novels are more easily sold. What was once considered a comic now stands on the shelf under the label graphic novel. However this boom has downsides. While a Will Eisner impresses us with the strength of character in his stroke, many new publications fall short as regards style, imagery, innovation and imagination. The current demand has led to the market being inundated with much second-class material. Already in his foreword to "A Contract With God" Eisner warns: "The future of the graphic novel lies in the relevance of the topics and the innovation of the depiction." The genre has gained a great deal of status but true illustrative and linguistic quality remains the exception. ★

carlsen.de
eichborn.de
reprodukt.com
sz-shop.sueddeutsche.de
waldegraf.ch

LITERATUR / REVIEWED TITLES

1 „David Boring", Daniel Clowes. Reprodukt, Berlin, 2010
   ISBN: 978-3-931377-75-5. 128 Seiten / pages, 20 €

2 „Wilson", Daniel Clowes. Eichborn, Frankfurt, 2010
   ISBN: 978-3-8218-6128-9. 77 Seiten / pages, 19,95 €

3 „Ein Vertrag mit Gott", Will Eisner. Süddeutsche Zeitung Edition,
   München, 2011. ISBN: 978-3-8661-5872-6. 508 Seiten / pages, 19,90 €

4 „Alpha ... directions", Jens Harder. Carlsen, Hamburg, 2010
   ISBN: 978-3-551-78980-8. 360 Seiten / pages, 49,90 €

5 „The Beats – Die Geschichte der Beat-Literatur", Harvey Pekar
   und Paul Buhle. Walde + Graf, Zürich, 2010. ISBN: 978-3-03774-014-9
   208 Seiten / pages, 22,95 €

6 „Baby's in Black", Arne Bellstorf. Reprodukt, Berlin, 2010
   ISBN: 978-3-941099-12-8. 216 Seiten / pages, 20 €

   „Genesis", Robert Crumb. Carlsen, Hamburg, 2009
   ISBN: 978-3-551-78637-1. 224 Seiten / pages, 29,90 €

CORPORATE DESIGN

BAURS CRESCENDO
THE SOUND OF TYPOGRAPHY

Text: Rahel Ueding
(redaktion@form.de)

★★

„ALLE WOLLEN IMMER EINEN MERCEDESSTERN, ABER DAS GEBÄUDE IST JA ALS SOLCHES SCHON EIN SIGNAL." RUEDI BAUR

★★

Ruedi Baur hat für die neue Elbphilharmonie in Hamburg ein Leitsystem entworfen – und das Corporate Design gleich dazu. Beides basiert auf drei übereinanderliegenden Schriften: Auf den ersten Blick scheint das fast unübersichtlich. Bis zum Praxistest dauert es wohl noch einige Jahre. Aber Baur hat uns schon mal erklärt, dass etwas Verwirrung auch durchaus nützlich sein kann.

Ruedi Baur has designed a signage system for the Elbphilharmonie. It is based on three typefaces, the one superimposed on top of the other. At first glance, it almost seems chaotic. However, the field test will not start till a few years have gone by. But Baur already told us why complexity can be good sometimes.

Ruedi Baur mag langwierige Projekte, sie entsprächen seinem Arbeitsstil, sagt er. Demnach müsste ihm das Projekt Elbphilharmonie in Hamburg ganz besonders liegen: Nach drei Jahren Bauzeit konnte diesen Mai gerade einmal das Richtfest gefeiert werden. Der Eröffnungstermin wurde allerdings – wie auch die Kostenschätzung – kürzlich zum wiederholten Mal korrigiert: auf den Herbst 2013. Ursprünglich dachte man an 2010. Ob die Architekten Jacques Herzog und Pierre de Meuron bereits ahnten, dass sich die Fertigstellung des Prestigeobjekts immer und immer wieder verzögern würde, als sie das Züricher Büro Intégral vor zwei Jahren beauftragten, die Signaletik zu entwickeln? Baurs Arbeitsweise kommt das Projekt jedenfalls entgegen. Der Designer ist Spezialist für komplexe Gebäude und verdichtete, teilweise auch umstrittene Lösungen dafür. Auf seiner Referenzliste stehen unter anderem das Centre Pompidou, der Flughafen Köln/Bonn und die Schweizerische Landesausstellung Expo.02.

Wie wird das Wegleitsystem eines Gebäudes aussehen, an das der Anspruch gestellt wird, zu so einem Wahrzeichen für Hamburg zu werden, wie es Jørn Utzons Operngebäude für Sydney ist? Baur verrät es an dieser Stelle – nicht. Zumindest nicht en détail. Er möchte

Ruedi Baurs Signaletik und Corporate Design für die Hamburger Elbphilharmonie stellen zahlreiche Bezüge zu Architektur, Musik und Hafen her. Über das Konzept soll man eigentlich gar nicht so viel erfahren – schließlich wird der Prestigebau wohl erst in zwei Jahren eingeweiht. Das Plakat für das Reeperbahnfestival gibt jedoch schon mal einen Ausblick.

Ruedi Baur's signage and corporate design for the Hamburg Elbphilharmonie make numerous references to architecture, music and the port. Actually, not that much is to be revealed about the concept – after all, it will likely be another two years before the prestige building is officially. But the billboard for the Reeperbahn festival provides a first insight.

★★

"EVERYONE ALWAYS WANTS A MERCEDES STAR, BUT THE BUILDING IS ALREADY A SIGN IN ITSELF." RUEDI BAUR

★★

Elbphilharmonie Programm Oktober 2011

Mittelachse Buchstabe

„In der Signaletik gibt es einen Kür- und einen Pflichtteil", sagt Ruedi Baur. „Wer letzteren, also das Engineering, nicht beherrscht, ist in dem Job fehl am Platz." Denn Maße zu beachten oder eine logische Nummerierung von Stuhlreihen zu erarbeiten sind notwendige Grundlagen für funktionierende Wegleitsysteme.

"There is a free part and a compulsory part in signage," says Ruedi Baur. "Anyone who has no command of the latter, in other words the engineering, should not be doing this job." After all, observing measurements or working out a logical seat row numbering system are absolutely fundamental to a function-ing signposting system.

Elbphilharmonie Programm Oktober 2011

Die DIN dominiert das Schriftbild. Auf der zweiten Ebene wird die New Esprit verwendet, durch die dritte wird das Konzept variabel: Für sie stehen 20 Schriften zur Auswahl, etwa die Edwardian Script ITC, die Egyptienne Roman und die Cooper Std Black.

The DIN standard dominates the font. On the second level, New Esprit is employed, the concept is varied throughout the third level with a choice of 20 typefaces, such as Edwardian Script ITC, Egyptian Roman and Cooper Std Black.

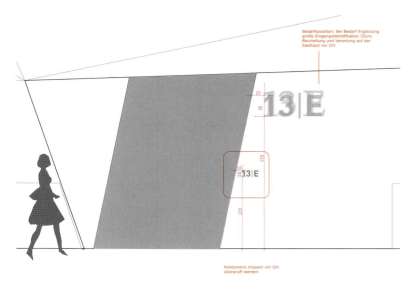

Laeiszhalle Elbphilharmonie Hamburg

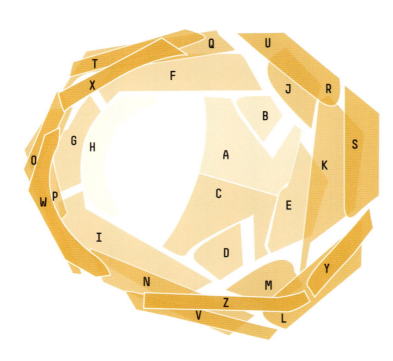

vermeiden, bereits vor der Eröffnung Kopisten auf den Plan zu rufen. Dennoch sind einige Elemente seiner Gestaltung schon im Einsatz.

Eines ist klar: ein klassisches Logo gibt es nicht, sondern ein in Teilen dynamisches Konzept. „Alle wollen immer einen Mercedesstern", sagt Baur gelangweilt. „Aber das Gebäude ist ja als solches schon ein Signal." Der Ansatz war, eine weitgehend typografische Lösung zu finden – ohne sie austauschbar erscheinen zu lassen. „Ich möchte bei jedem Projekt die Formen aus dem Kontext, aus der Problematik heraus entwickeln und nicht autoreferenziell sein. Ich habe deshalb versucht, alles andere, was ich bei Intégral bisher gemacht ha-be, zu vergessen. Unsere Signaletik in Hamburg sollte Bezug zum Ort und zum Thema haben." Jeweils drei Schriften legt Baur übereinander, die Ebenen transportieren unterschiedliche Inhalte, jede ist in einer anderen Graustufe gehalten, insgesamt 22 Schriftarten gehören zum Konzept. Auf der ersten Ebene wird stets die DIN verwendet, sie dient als Informationsträger. „Der Ursprung war eine Beschriftung, die wir im Hafen gefunden haben", erläutert Baur, „eine sehr harte, funktionale Schrift. Die haben wir mit der DIN aufgegriffen. Mit ihr wird das Ganze identifizierbar. Es ist egal, was dahinter passiert, weil die Schrift stark genug ist, sich durchzusetzen." Die beiden anderen Ebenen sollen die Vielschichtigkeit der Musik aufgreifen und eine Art visuellen Klangraum entstehen lassen. So wird auf der zweiten Ebene stets die ITC New Esprit von Jovica Veljovic eingesetzt: „Diese Schrift greift mit ihren sehr lebendigen Serifen Formen der Architektur des Neubaus auf und steht zudem im Bezug zur Dynamik in der Musik", erklärt Eva Plass von Intégral Zürich. Der inhaltliche Kontext ist die Musik: Begriffe wie „forte", „lunga" oder

„DER URSPRUNG WAR EINE BESCHRIFTUNG, DIE WIR IM HAFEN GEFUNDEN HABEN, EINE SEHR HARTE, FUNKTIONALE SCHRIFT. DIE HABEN WIR MIT DER DIN AUFGEGRIFFEN. MIT IHR WIRD DAS GANZE IDENTIFIZIERBAR." RUEDI BAUR

★★

„marcantissimo" sollen hier stehen, es existiert ein Pool von Wörtern unterschiedlicher Zeichenlänge, die stets jener der Wörter auf der Informationsebene entsprechen soll. Die dritte und letzte Ebene vollzieht dann auch visuell den Schulterschluss mit der Musik. Für die hier zugewiesenen Begriffe wie „allegro non troppo", „tutti" oder „piano" stehen 20 Schriften zur Verfügung, hier wird die Signaletik variabel. So soll die Wahl der Schriften unter anderem auch Ebenen und Orte im Gebäude kenntlich machen.

Es habe ihn erstaunt, erzählt der Designer, wie problemlos dieses komplexe Konzept akzeptiert worden sei, sowohl von den Architekten Herzog & de Meuron als auch von Christoph Lieben-Seutter, dem Generalintendanten des Hauses. Tatsächlich kann man sich über den Entwurf streiten: Die uneingeschränkte Lesbarkeit als eigentlich zentrale Eigenschaft von Leit- und Orientierungssystemen ist durch

Ruedi Baur likes long, drawn-out projects; they fit his style of working well, he says. This being the case, the Elbphilharmonie project in Hamburg must be right up his street. After a three-year construction phase, the topping-out ceremony did not take place until May. However, in light of a new cost estimate, the opening of the concert hall was recently put back once again – to the fall of 2013. The original completion date had been 2010. Could the architects Jacques Herzog and Pierre de Meuron have perhaps guessed that the completion of the prestigious building would repeatedly be delayed when they commissioned the Zurich-based studio Intégral two years ago to develop the signage? Ruedi Baur's working method fits the project bill. The designer specializes in complex buildings and equally complex, sometimes also controversial solutions for them. His references include the Centre Pompidou, Köln/Bonn Airport and the Swiss National Exhibition Expo.02.

What should we expect of a signage system for a building intended to be a landmark of Hamburg in the same way that Jørn Utzon's Opera House is of Sydney? Ruedi Baur is not prepared to let the cat out of the bag yet. At least not en détail. He wants to avoid bringing copy-cats on board before the building has even been inaugurated. That said, some elements of his design are already in use. One thing is clear: there is no classic logo, but an in part dynamic concept: "Everyone always wants a Mercedes star," says Baur. "But the building is already a sign in itself." He wanted to find a typographical solution without making it seem ordinary. "With every project, I like to develop the forms from the context, the basic problem, and not be self-referential. That is why I tried to forget everything else I have done so far at Integral. We wanted our signage system in Hamburg to make reference to the city and the project theme."

Baur positions three fonts one on top of the other. The levels communicate different content; each is in a different shade of gray. A total of 22 typefaces constitute the concept. The DIN standard is always used on the first level, serving to communicate information. "It came from lettering we found in the port," explains Baur, "a very hard, functional typeface. We used the idea with the DIN standard. It makes the whole thing identifiable. It doesn't matter what goes on behind it, because the font is strong enough to assert itself." The two other levels stand for the multilayered quality of the music and are intended to create a kind of visual sound space. ITC New Esprit by Jovica Veljovic is always used on the second level: "With its lively serifs, it references the architectural forms of the new building and also makes reference to the dynamism in the music," explains Eva Plass from Intégral in Zurich. The music informs the context: terms like "forte," "lunga," "marcantissimo" are to feature. There is a pool of words of different lengths that must always correspond to the lengths of the words on the information level. The third and last level completes the connection to the music in visual terms, too. There are 20 fonts for the designated terms for this level, including "allegro non troppo," "tutti" and "piano." Here the signage system is variable, and will be designed to provide information on the levels and places within the building, too.

The designer was amazed that this complex concept was so readily accepted, both by the architects Herzog & de Meuron and by Christoph Lieben-Seutter, the General Director of the Elbphilharmonie. In fact, there is a point of contention as regards the design, namely,

die Schichtung der Schriften nicht immer gegeben. Eine Signaletik dürfe nicht zu autoritär und funktional sein, sie müsse auch Freiräume geben und manchmal sogar Orte vorsehen, an denen man sich als Besucher verlieren könne, entgegnet Baur seinen Kritikern.

Auf Anraten von Herzog & de Meuron wurde Intégral seitens der Elbphilharmonie zusätzlich damit beauftragt, das Grundkonzept der Signaletik für das gesamte Corporate Design nutzbar zu machen. Da sich die Bauarbeiten mehr und mehr in die Länge ziehen, eine strategisch kluge Entscheidung. „Wir wurden gebeten, mit dem Erscheinungsbild zu beginnen, um schon im Vorfeld einen Esprit zu entwickeln", erzählt Bauer. Bereits jetzt werden etwa die Veranstaltungen der Reihe „Elbphilharmonie Konzerte" im neuen Design angekündigt. „Die Challenge bestand darin, eine Vorlage zu schaffen, die auch leicht von anderen umgesetzt werden konnte und natürlich auch, einen Wiedererkennungseffekt zu erzielen." Für jedes Jahr wird ein Key Visual definiert, das stilbildend für alle Drucksachen zu den Veranstaltungen ist. Im ersten Jahr wurde das Baustellen-Motiv verwendet – erneut, um einen konkreten Kontext zu schaffen. Für die Saison 2010 / 2011 werden doppelbelichtete Hafenbilder eingesetzt. Baur hat vor, diese Bildsprache immer mehr zu reduzieren. Nach der Eröffnung der Philharmonie seien neben der Typografie keine Bilder oder ähnlicher Schmuck mehr nötig, meint er. Bis dahin, und bis sich seine Signaletik in der Praxis beweisen kann und muss, ist allerdings nicht nur noch einiges Geld, sondern durchaus auch noch etwas Geduld nötig. Baur sieht dem gelassen entgegen. Seine bevorzugte Projektdauer beläuft sich auf fünf Jahre. ★

integral.ruedi-baur.eu
elbphilharmonie.de

that the layering of the fonts does not always guarantee the perfect legibility of the system, which is indeed the key quality of signage and orientation systems. Baur responds to his critics by saying that a signage system must not be too authoritarian and functional; it has to offer empty space, too, and sometimes even allow for places where you can lose yourself.

On the advice of Herzog & de Meuron, Intégral was also comissioned to adapt the basic signage system concept to its entire corporate design. This was an intelligent move in strategic terms, given that the completion date is repeatedly being postponed. "We were asked to start with the CI in order to generate a kind of esprit before the building is complete," says Baur. For example, the "Elbphilharmonie Concerts" series is already being announced in the new design. "The challenge was to create a model that others could easily use too, and, of course, also how to generate brand recognition." One key visual is defined for each year, which informs the style of all printed material on the events. In the first year, the motif used was of the construction site – again to create a definite context. Baur's plan is to continually reduce this visual language. After the opening of the Elbphilharmonie, he claims, images and similar decoration will no longer be necessary alongside the typography. However, until then, and until his signage system has proved itself in practice (and it must), not only is more money needed, but also more patience. Baur is rather laid back about it. His preferred project length is five years. ★

★ ★

"IT CAME FROM LETTERING WE FOUND IN THE PORT, A VERY HARD, FUNCTIONAL TYPEFACE. WE USED THE IDEA WITH THE DIN STANDARD. IT MAKES THE WHOLE THING IDENTIFIABLE." RUEDI BAUR

★ ★

24

WEB DESIGN

DESIGNER IM NETZ
WHAT THE WEB CAN DO FOR YOU

Text: Karianne Fogelberg
(redaktion@form.de)

Illustration: Andreas Töpfer
(andreas.toepfer@kookbooks.de)

Ich weiß etwas, was du nicht weißt: Das Web 2.0 macht uns zu Open-Source-Figuren, die ständig online sind.

I know what you don't know: Web 2.0 turns us into Open Source figures who are always online.

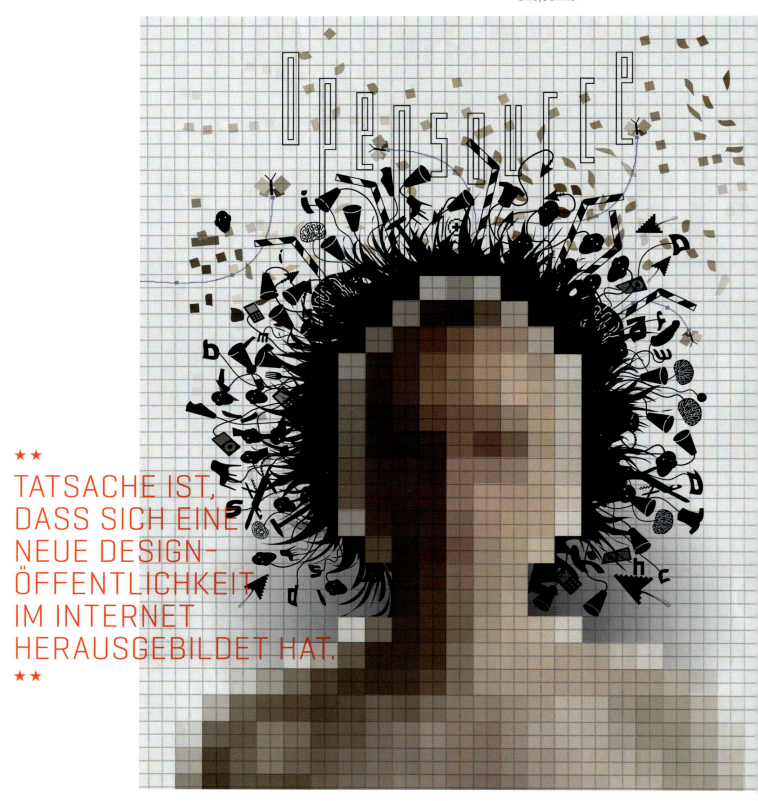

★★
TATSACHE IST, DASS SICH EINE NEUE DESIGN-ÖFFENTLICHKEIT IM INTERNET HERAUSGEBILDET HAT.
★★

Web 2.0, das Web zum Mitmachen, hat eine neue Design-Öffentlichkeit geschaffen. Foren und Blogs ermöglichen nicht nur den Meinungsaustausch und die Präsentation eigener Arbeiten, sondern auch neuartige Formen der kreativen Zusammenarbeit.

Web 2.0 ist in aller Munde. Während Unternehmen über gewinnbringenden Anwendungen brüten und Trendexperten Konferenzen zu dem Thema ausrufen, nutzen viele bereits die neuen Plattformen im Internet mit großer Selbstverständlichkeit. Dazu zählen auch Designer. Wer es etwa nicht zur diesjährigen Mailänder Möbelmesse geschafft hat, konnte sich auf zahlreichen Foren und Blogs über die dort präsentierten Entwürfe informieren. So vielseitig und bunt war das Mailand-Panorama im Internet noch nie. Allein an die 2000 Fotos sind auf www.flickr.com unter dem Suchbegriff „salone mobile 2007" hinterlegt, bei www.youtube.com werden 57 Filme dazu aufgerufen. Im Vergleich: Letztes Jahr waren es nicht einmal die Hälfte der Fotos und ein Viertel der Filme, 2005 gab es auf Youtube noch nichts. Online-Magazine wie www.designboom.com, dessen Mailand-Bericht fast schon ein Klassiker ist, und Blogs wie www.mocoloco.com oder www.core77.com taten ihr übriges, um einem weltweiten Design-Publikum die Highlights vorzustellen – teilweise in Echtzeit. „Das kann kein anderes Medium leisten", so Marcus Fairs, Gründer des im vergangenen November lancierten Blogs www.dezeen.com. Allein im April verzeichnete seine Website täglich durchschnittlich 7000 Besuche, insgesamt waren in den ersten vier Monaten des Jahres bereits 500 000 Besucher auf Dezeen. Seitdem ist Fairs' Blog im angesehenen Technorati-Ranking, das Weblogs nach Beliebtheit listet, von Platz 8002 rasant nach oben geklettert.

Warum sind diese Zahlen erwähnenswert? Tatsache ist, dass sich eine neue Design-Öffentlichkeit im Internet herausgebildet hat. Wachsende Zugriffszahlen und Postings belegen dies. Wo bislang herkömmliche Medien den Ton angaben, prägen heute Designer in Blogs und Foren die Diskussionen selbst. Dabei sind die Grenzen zwischen Online-Magazinen, Plattformen mit der Möglichkeit zum Posting und Blogs fließend. Die schon seit einigen Jahren in Online-Communities organisierten Schriftgestalter und Grafiker waren die Wegbereiter, Industrie-Designer holen jetzt auf. Diese jüngste Entwicklung birgt laut Stuart Constantine, Mitbegründer des Branchenforums Core77, enorme Chancen: „Früher musste man am richtigen Ort zur richtigen Zeit sein. Mit der täglich wachsenden Anzahl an Blogs hingegen entsteht eine nicht abreißende Nachfrage nach neuen Arbeiten. Gerade für junge Designer ist die Möglichkeit, ihre Entwürfe zu veröffentlichen und auf diesem Weg einen Hersteller zu finden, größer als je zuvor." So dauerte es nur zwei Tage, bis ein Leuchtenhersteller auf Core77 auf die LED-Kerzen von Richard Lawson aufmerksam wurde und den Designer kontaktierte.

Während die Macher von Core77 oder Designboom das Gros der Beiträge weiterhin nach redaktionellen Gesichtspunkten auswählen, wächst die Zahl der Plattformen, auf denen Designer ihre Entwürfe ausschließlich selbst online stellen können, kontinuierlich. Dazu zählt das Online-Magazin www.designspotter.com, das Gunnar Schmidt und Markus Gogolin vor zwei Jahren gegründet haben und das im ersten Quartal dieses Jahres erstmals über 150 000 Zugriffe verzeichnete. Ein ähnliches Angebot macht die aus Holland stammende Plattform www.productdesignforums.com jungen Industrie-Designern. Hier wird außerdem unterschieden zwischen Entwürfen in der Projektphase, Prototypen und Endprodukten, und die Zugriffszahlen sowie Kommentare werden für jedes einzelne Posting dokumentiert. Beide Websites leiden allerdings unter der dem Web 2.0 eigenen Beliebigkeit nutzergenerierter Inhalte und sind nur schlecht zu navigieren. Trotz dieser Mängel – zukunftsträchtig sind beide Konzepte allemal.

Wie erfolgreich man damit sein kann, seine Arbeiten selbst ins Netz zu stellen, hat Ora Ito schon vor Jahren vorgemacht. Der

Web 2.0, the do-it-yourself Web, has created a new design public sphere. Forums and blogs enable people to swap ideas, present their own work and also to forge novel ways of creative collaboration.

Web 2.0 is the topic of conversation. While companies brood over profit-making applications and trend experts call for conferences on the topic, for many people using the new platforms on the Internet is already a matter of course. They include designers. In numerous forums and blogs anybody who did not make it to this year's Milan furniture fair was able to find out about the designs on show there. The Milan panorama has never been this varied and colorful on the Internet before. Some 2,000 photos are available on www.flickr.com using the search engine "salone mobile 2007", and www.youtube.com has 57 films on the subject on offer. By way of comparison, last year the number of photos was not even half of that and that of films only a quarter, and in 2005 Youtube was just founded. Online magazines such as www.designboom.com and blogs such as www.mocoloco.com and www.core77.com did the rest to present the highlights to a worldwide design audience – partially in real time. As Marcus Fairs, the founder of www.dezeen.com says: "No other medium can achieve that". In April his website registered an average of 7,000 visits daily, and in the first four months of this year there were 500,000 visitors. Since then Fair's

THE FACT IS THAT A NEW DESIGN PUBLIC SPHERE HAS EMERGED ON THE INTERNET.

blog has swiftly risen from position 8002 in the Technorati ranking, which lists weblogs according to popularity.

Just why are these figures worth mentioning? The fact is that a new design public sphere has emerged on the Internet. Growing page impressions and postings are proof of this. Whereas previously traditional media set the tone, nowadays designers influence the discussions themselves in blogs and forums. And the boundaries between online magazines, platforms with an opportunity for posting and blogs are flowing. The font designers and graphic artists who for years now have been organized in online communities were the pioneers; industrial designers are now catching up. According to Stuart Constantine, co-founder of the sector forum Core77, this latest development offers enormous opportunities: "Previously you had to be in the right place at the right time. Now, with the number of weblogs growing daily there is a never-ending demand for new works. For young designers in particular there has never been more opportunity to publish their designs and find a manufacturer this way." It took only two days, for example, for a luminaire manufacturer to become aware of Richard Lawson's LED candles on www.core77.com and subsequently contact the designer.

Whereas the creators of Core77 and Designboom still select the majority of articles according to editorial criteria, the number of platforms on which designers put their designs online themselves is continually growing. One of these, for example, is the online magazine www.designspotter.com, which Gunnar Schmidt and Markus Gogolin founded two years ago and which in the first three months of this year registered over 150,000 hits for the first time. A platform from Holland, www.productdesignforums.com offers young industrial designers something similar. It also differentiates between designs at the project stage, prototypes and end products, and the hit rates

Der brasilianische Designer Nando Costa (rechts) schreibt nicht nur seinen eigenen Blog, er hat auch eine Plattform für die Design-Szene seines Landes aufgebaut. Links im Bild die Mailänder Redaktion des Online-Magazins Designboom: (v.l.n.r.) Chefredakteurin Birgit Lohmann, Massimo Mini, Anita Hackethal und Andy Butler.

Brazilian designer Nando Costa (right) not only writes his own blog but has also constructed a platform for the Brazilian design scene. On the r.: the editors of online magazine Designboom: (from l. to r.) Birgit Lohmann, Massimo Mini, Anita Hackethal and Andy Butler.

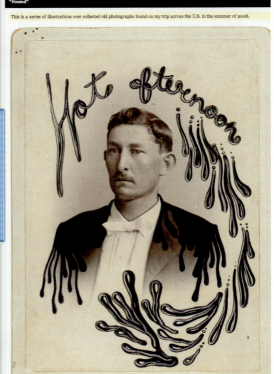

Verwirrende Vielfalt: Blogs wie Mocoloco, Designboom (linke Spalte) und der von Nando Costa (oben r.) werden ständig mit neuen Einträgen aufgefüllt. Die Qualität hängt davon ab, wer die Auswahl trifft – ein einzelner Blogger, eine Redaktion oder gar niemand. Immer mehr Designer nutzen auch populäre Web-2.0-Sites wie Youtube. Front zeigt dort einen Film über sein Changing Cupboard (r.).

Blogs such as Mocoloco, Designboom (left column) and that of Nando Costa (upper right) are constantly being filled with new entries. The quality depends on who makes the selection – an individual blogger, an editorial team or nobody. Swedish design group Front shows a film on its Changing Cupboard on Youtube (on the r.).

Auf seinem Blog www.dezeen.com widmet sich der frühere „Icon"-Herausgeber Marcus Fairs (links) vor allem den großen Namen des Möbel-Design. Obwohl erst seit einem halben Jahr online, gehört Dezeen schon jetzt zu den erfolgreichsten Design-Blogs überhaupt.

On his blog at www.dezeen.com former "Icon" publisher Marcus Fairs (on the left) mainly focuses on big-name furniture design. Although it has only been online for six months, Dezeen is already one of the most successful design blogs.

★★
SIE MÜSSEN SICH EINES PROGRESSIVEN ERSCHEINUNGSBILDS BEDIENEN UND SICH DURCH WIEDER-ERKENNBARKEIT AUS DER MENGE HERAUSHEBEN, FAST SCHON WIE POPSTARS ODER CELEBRITIES.
★★

★★
THEY HAVE TO USE A PROGRESSIVE IMAGE AND SET THEMSELVES APART FROM THE CROWD BY BEING RECOGNIZABLE, ALMOST LIKE POP STARS OR CELEBRITIES.
★★

WEB DESIGN

Eine neue Online-Community: Deutsche Blogger treffen sich auf der Typo in Berlin, dokumentiert auf www.slanted.de. Ganz rechts die Slanted-Redakteure Boris Kahl, Lars Harmsen und Flo Gaertner (v.l.n.r.).

A new online community: German bloggers met at the Typo in Berlin, as documented on www.slanted.de. On the far right Slanted editors Boris Kahl, Lars Harmsen and Flo Gaertner (from l. to r.).

and comments for each individual posting are documented. However, both websites suffer from the arbitrariness peculiar to Web 2.0 of user-generated contents and are difficult to navigate. Despite these faults the two concepts most certainly have future potential. Years ago Ora Ito demonstrated just how successful you can be by putting your works on the net yourself. In 1999 – in other words at a time when no one had yet heard of Web 2.0, the French designer came up with his own designs for products for established brands such as Louis Vuitton and Macintosh and published them on his website. The demand for the virtual collection was so enormous that it initially brought popularity and press reports and ultimately contracts from industry. Nowadays he would no longer receive so much attention. As Birgit Lohmann at Designboom says: "Back then there were just three voices on the Internet, whereas today there is so much that things get lost." Which is why it is all the more important to make use of the opportunities Web 2.0 offers. This is something that Robert Klanten, founder of Die Gestalten publishers has observed: "Through Myspace, Tagging and the numerous blogs identity has gained in importance. This presents new challenges for designers too. They have to use a progressive image and set themselves apart from the crowd by being recognizable, almost like pop stars or celebrities. That extends as far as disguise: There are designers who by means of their own blogs or Myspace pages are omnipresent in the net, but as designers are not exactly the most consistent with regard to output. I call this the hip-hop phenomenon: Whoever can shout 'I'm the greatest' the loudest is perceived to be so – it is a 'self-fulfilling prophecy'." The number of designers with their own blogs is indeed rising daily. One reason for this is the medium's new level of accessibility: "Technically speaking a blog with archive function is much simpler to set up than an HTML-programmed website with a decent data base", as Lars Harmsen says, co-publisher of the typography blog www.slanted.de. One designer who makes highly skilful use of the mechanism of the new Internet reality is Brazilian graphic designer Nando Costa. In addition to his own website www.nandocosta.com including diary link he has set up the www.brasilinspired.com blog, in his own words a "marketing tool for the Brazilian creative scene". Other designers, on the other hand, use the medium of film to illustrate their ideas. The Swedish design collective Front has a link for example to Youtube, where their projects are on view under the user name "frontfilm".

Web 2.0 also offers other forms of self-marketing. The font designer Heinrich Lischka recently auctioned off on Ebay the exclusive user rights for an as yet unpublished slender grotesque font: "The design had been lying around in one of my drawers for two years. I knew full well that I would never get the counter value of 8,000 euros on Ebay, but on the back of the auction I was the topic of conversation again in the font scene." He is certainly satisfied with the amount he got, 635 euros, and the attention he received in the typology forums www.fontblog.de and Slanted. During the auction, which lasted a week, his entry got a total of 1,024 visits. His auction also got

Der Fontblog von Jürgen Siebert (links) ist das wichtigste Forum der deutschen Typo- und Grafik-Szene. Unten: Das Urgestein unter den Design-Blogs, Core77, gibt es schon seit 1995. Aber erst seit einem Jahr verdienen die Macher damit wirklich Geld.

The Fontblog run by Jürgen Siebert (on the left) is the key forum for the German typo and graphic scene. Below: the first mover among the design blogs, Core77, has been up since 1995, but the minds behind it have first been making real money with it for a year now.

französische Designer entwarf 1999 – zu einem Zeitpunkt also, als Web 2.0 noch kein Begriff war – frei erfundene Produkte für etablierte Marken wie Louis Vuitton und Macintosh und veröffentlichte sie auf seiner Website. Die virtuelle Kollektion stieß auf so große Nachfrage, dass sie ihm zuerst Popularität und Presseberichte einbrachte und schließlich Aufträge aus der Industrie. Heute würde er wohl nicht mehr solche Beachtung finden. Birgit Lohmann von Designboom: „Damals gab es nur drei Stimmen im Internet, heute geht in dem großen Angebot vieles unter." Umso wichtiger ist es, die neuen Möglichkeiten des Web 2.0 für sich zu nutzen. Das beobachtet auch Robert Klanten, Gründer des Verlags Die Gestalten: „Durch Myspace, Tagging und die vielen Blogs hat das Thema Identität an Bedeutung gewonnen. Das stellt auch Designer vor neue Anforderungen. Sie müssen sich eines progressiven Erscheinungsbilds bedienen und sich durch Wiedererkennbarkeit aus der Menge herausheben, fast schon wie Popstars oder Celebrities. Das geht bis hin zum Mummenschanz: Da gibt es Gestalter, die mit ihren eigenen Blogs oder Myspace-Seiten im Netz omnipräsent sind, aber als Designer nicht gerade den konsistentesten Output haben. Ich nenne dies das Hip-Hop-Phänomen: Wer am lautesten ‚Ich bin der Größte' schreit, wird als solcher wahrgenommen – eine ‚self-fulfilling prophecy'." Die Zahl der Designer mit eigenen Blogs steigt tatsächlich täglich. Es gibt sogar Design-Studenten, die ihren eigenen Blog haben. Ein Grund dafür ist sicher die neue Zugänglichkeit des Mediums: „Technisch lässt sich ein Blog samt Archivfunktion viel

★★ KLASSIKER UND EXOTEN IM WEB 2.0
HOUSEHOLD STAPLES AND THE OUT OF THE ORDINARY

www.core77.com
Bereits 1995 von der gleichnamigen New Yorker Agentur lanciert, ist Core77 ein Klassiker unter den Industrie-Design-Foren im Internet. Seit einem Jahr arbeiten die Macher ausschließlich an der Website.

Already launched in 1995 by the New York agency of the same name, Core77 is one of the classic industrial design forums on the Internet. For the past year the makers have been working exclusively on the website.

www.dezeen.com
Die im November 2006 gegründete Plattform zählt bereits zu den meistbesuchten Design-Sites. Sie informiert über die großen Namen des Industrie-Design, für die Auswahl ist der frühere „Icon"-Herausgeber Marcus Fairs verantwortlich.

The platform established in 2006 is already one of the most-visited design sites. It primarily offers information on the big names in the design industry. The former "Icon" publisher, Marcus Fairs, is responsible for the selection.

www.designboom.com
Das Online-Magazin, in Mailand von einer dreiköpfigen Redaktion zusammengestellt, gibt es seit 1999. Der Blog führt allerdings eher ein Schattendasein.

The online magazine assembled in Milan by a three-member editorial team has been around since 1999. In comparison, the blog tends to be sidelined.

www.dezain.net
Der Meta-Blog im Design. Die tagesaktuelle Auswahl des Japaners Eizo Okada aus den relevantesten Design-Blogs weltweit ist immer einen Besuch wert. Mit in der Auswahl: Titelthemen von Magazinen und Studio-Neuigkeiten.

The meta-blog in design. It is always worth visiting Japanese Eito Okada's daily selection from the world's most relevant design blogs. His selection also includes the title themes of international magazines and news from studios.

www.fontblog.de
Die Pflichtlektüre der Typo-Szene. Der deutschsprachige Blog des Berliner Schriftenvertriebs Fontshop bringt tagesaktuell Neues aus der Grafikwelt. Die Leser machen regen Gebrauch von der Kommentarfunktion.

A must for the typo scene. The German-language blog of Berlin font business, Fontshop, presents up-to-date news from the graphic world. Readers are avid users of the comment function, are open to opinions and ready to dispute.

www.slanted.de
Bezeichnet sich als Typoblog, berichtet aber auch über Grafik und Design. Praktisch ist die automatische Sortierung nach Themen, auch nach meistkommentierten und zuletzt kommentierten Einträgen. Ein typische Blog-Funktion, die aber nicht alle Design-Blogs bieten.

Describes itself as a typo blog but also reports on graphics and design. Automatic sorting according to theme is a practical feature, but it is also sorted according to most commented-on and most recently commented-on entries. A typical blog feature that not all design blogs offer.

www.designmadeingermany.de
Deutschsprachiges Forum für Grafiker und Web-Designer. Die registrierten Nutzer tauschen sich hier über Druckereien, Software und Recht aus. Fragen werden in der Regel innerhalb weniger Stunden beantwortet.

German language forum for graphic artists and web designers. The registered users exchange information on printers, software and rights but also on search engines and online advertising. Questions are generally answered within a few hours.

www.designobserver.com
Kein Blog, sondern eine Website mit Magazin-Charakter zu Themen wie Grafik-Design und visuelle Kultur, behandelt von festen Autoren. Dazu zählen namhafte Größen wie Michael Bierut von Pentagram. Die Artikel sind anspruchsvoll und ausführlich, die Leser-Kommentare relevant.

Not a blog but a website with magazine character on themes such as graphic design and visual culture undertaken by regular authors. These include big names such as Michael Bierut from Pentagram. The articles are discerning and comprehensive. Reader comments are relevant.

www.thedesignencyclopedia.org
Die Design-Enzyklopädie basiert auf einer Version von Wikipedia. Hier sind die Leser die Autoren der Inhalte. Die New Yorker Herausgeber haben das Projekt 2005 ins Leben gerufen. Die Wunschliste der zu definierenden Einträge ist lang. Es gibt also noch viel zu tun.

The design encyclopedia is based on a version of Wikipedia where readers are the authors of the content. The New York publishers initiated the project in 2005. The wish-list of entries still to define is long, so lots to do.

www.magculture.com/blog
Die Adresse für die Zeitschriften- und Zeitungsliebhaber. Herausgegeben von Jeremy Leslie, Autor des gleichnamigen Buchs und Kreativdirektor beim Londoner Verlag für Kundenzeitschriften John Brown.

The address for magazine and newspaper lovers. Published by Jeremy Leslie, author of the book of the same name and creative director at London publishing company for customer magazines, John Brown.

www.acejet170.typepad.com/foundthings
Fundstücke aus der Welt der Schrift: In diesem Blog dokumentiert der englischen Grafiker Richard Weston seine Sammlung (typo)grafischer Kleinode. Neben Fotos und Beobachtungen gibt es eine Link-Liste.

Finds from the font world: In this blog English graphic artist, Richard Weston, documents a collection of typo(graphic) gems. In addition to photographs and observations there is a list of related links.

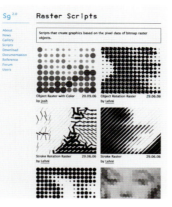

Teilen, Tauschen, Diskutieren – das sind die Prinzipien des Web 2.0. Der Schweizer Jürg Lehni (links) stellt auf www.scriptographer.com ein von ihm entwickeltes Plug-In für Adobe Illustrator zur freien Verfügung, mit dem man die Funktionsvorgaben der Software aufbrechen kann. Was daraus entsteht, ist ebenfalls auf seiner Website zu sehen. (links und unten).

Share, swap, discuss – the principles of Web 2.0. Swiss Jürg Lehni (on the left) makes the Plug-In he developed for Adobe Illustrator available for free on www.scriptographer.com – it enables you to break the software's functional specifications. The results are also shown on his website. (left and below).

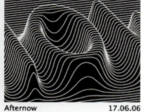

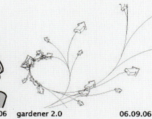

einfacher einrichten als eine HTML-programmierte Website mit einer vernünftigen Datenbank", sagt Lars Harmsen, Mitherausgeber des Typoblogs www.slanted.de. Ein Designer, der die Mechanismen der neuen Internet-Wirklichkeit mit großem Geschick bedient, ist der brasilianische Grafiker Nando Costa. Neben seiner eigenen Website www.nandocosta.com samt Tagebuch-Link hat er den Blog www.brasilinspired.com initiiert, laut eigener Aussage ein „Marketing-Werkzeug für die Kreativszene Brasiliens". Andere Gestalter wiederum, insbesondere jene, die mit neuartigen Prozessen arbeiten, verwenden das Medium Film zur Veranschaulichung ihrer Ideen. Das schwedische Design-Kollektiv Front verlinkt zum Beispiel auf Youtube, wo einzelne Projekte unter dem Benutzernamen „frontfilm" zu sehen sind.

Web 2.0 bietet aber noch andere Formen der Selbstvermarktung. Der Schriftgestalter Heinrich Lischka hat kürzlich das Exklusiv-Nutzungsrecht für eine noch unveröffentlichte schmale Grotesk-Schrift über Ebay versteigert: „Der Entwurf lag seit zwei Jahren bei mir in der Schublade. Mir war klar, dass ich bei Ebay niemals den geforderten Gegenwert von 8000 Euro erzielen würde, aber durch die Auktion war ich in der Schriftszene wieder in aller Munde." Mit dem erzielten Betrag von 635 Euro und der Aufmerksamkeit, die ihm in den Typoforen www.fontblog.de und Slanted zuteil wurde, ist er rundum zufrieden. Während der eine Woche lang laufenden Aktion verzeichnete sein Eintrag bei Ebay immerhin 1024 Besuche. Zugleich hat seine Auktion die Gemüter der Typo-Szene erhitzt. Auf Fontblog wurde etwa die Befürchtung geäußert, der Verkauf von Lizenzen für Design-Leistungen im Internet führe zum Honorardumping – wie es dem Dienstleistungsforum www.my-hammer.de bisweilen nachgesagt wird, wo bereits die Gestaltung von Logos und Visitenkarten ausgeschrieben wird. Lischka hält dagegen: „Solange Unternehmen nach exklusiven Lösungen suchen, die nur im Gespräch mit dem Designer entwickelt werden können, sind diese Befürchtungen unbegründet."

Auch der in Berlin lebende Produkt-Designer Ronen Kadushin sieht im partizipativen Internet mehr Chancen als Risiken – wobei es ihm nicht um den kommerziellen Vertrieb geht. Unter dem Begriff „Open Design" bietet er auf seiner Website Entwürfe zum freien Download an. Im Rahmen der Lizenzvereinbarungen der Website http://creativecommons.org kann jeder die Entwürfe auch individuell verändern. Pate stand die Open-Source-Bewegung, deren Erfolg auf dem Prinzip des freiwilligen Austauschs beruht. Kadushin: „Es gibt so viel ungenutztes kreatives Potential, viele Entwürfe werden nie hergestellt. Bei Open Design hängt die Umsetzung eines Entwurfs nicht mehr vom Hersteller ab, sondern liegt in den Händen des Gestalters." Die größte Resonanz hat der gebürtige Israeli mit seinem Konzept außerhalb der westlichen Industriestaaten, etwa in Brasilien. Er verzeichnet bis zu 100 Downloads im Monat, die meisten davon betreffen seinen bekanntesten Entwurf, die Obstschale Flat Knot, die er selber bei Berlinomat zum Ladenpreis von 120 Euro verkauft. Den Open-Source-Gedanken propagiert auch John Thackara, Gründer des weltweiten Design-Netzwerks Doors of Perception: „Diejenigen, die nur ihre eigenen Ideen schützen wollen, sind keine wertvollen Mitglieder für die Gemeinschaft. Wenn wir Ländern wie China und Indien den Anschluss an westliche Industrienationen ermöglichen wollen, darf Innovation nicht länger als privates Eigentum verstanden werden." Thackara geht es dabei nicht um den Ausverkauf von Design-Leistungen, sondern um die konsequente Anwendung des Web-2.0-Gedankens: Dort, wo Nutzer ihre Kenntnisse einbringen, entsteht Wertschöpfung. Der Schweizer Gestalter Jürg Lehni sieht das differenzierter: „Im Design geht es immer auch um Persönlichkeit und Individualität. Ein guter Designer würde seine Kniffe wohl kaum im Netz zur Verfügung stellen." Was experimentelle Projekte betrifft, gehört Lehni allerdings zu den Verfechtern von Open Source. Auf seiner Website www.scriptographer.com stellt er das von ihm unter dem Namen Scriptographer entwickelte Plug-In für Adobe Illustrator

those in the design worked up. On Fontblog someone expressed a fear that the sale of licenses for design work via the Internet would lead to fee dumping – such is said of the service forum www.my-hammer.de, where the design of logos and business cards is already tendered. Lischka counters the accusation: "As long as companies are on the lookout for exclusive solutions, which can only be created in discussion with the designer, these fears will be unfounded."

The designer Ronen Kadushin, who lives in Berlin, also sees more opportunities than risks in an Internet in which people can interact, though he is not concerned about commercial sales. Using the term "Open Design" he offers designs for free downloading on his website. Within the framework of the website's licensing agreements http://creativecommons.org anyone can make his own alterations to the designs. It was inspired by the Open Source movement, whose success is based on the principle of voluntary exchange. As he says: "There is so much unused creative potential, many designs are never produced. With Open Design, whether a design gets manufactured or not no longer

zum freien Download zur Verfügung. So will er andere Designer dazu anregen, die Funktionsvorgaben der Illustrator-Software aufzubrechen und zu erweitern. Lehnis Herangehensweise ist richtungsweisend: Er eignet sich die Möglichkeiten des Web 2.0 an, um innerhalb dieses Rahmens neue Anwendungen für Gleichgesinnte zu schaffen und sich darüber mit ihnen auszutauschen.

Was sich daraus in Zukunft entwickeln könnte, ist allerdings noch offen. Bisher nutzen erst wenige Gestalter die neuartigen Formen der kreativen Zusammenarbeit im Netz. Design-Blogs und -Foren und klassische Web-2.0-Plattformen wie Youtube und Flickr schaffen zwar eine neue Öffentlichkeit für Design-Themen. Das eigentliche Potential der neuen Vernetzung im Internet ist aber bei weitem noch nicht ausgeschöpft. ★

depends on the manufacturer but is in the hands of the designer." Kadushin has met with the greatest response to his concept outside western industrialized nations. He registers 100 downloads per month, most of them of his best-known design, a fruit bowl.

John Thackara, founder of the worldwide design network Doors of Perception also propagates the Open Source idea: "Those who are only interested in protecting their own ideas are not valuable members of the community. If we want to enable countries such as China to emulate western industrialized countries, innovation can no longer be seen as private property." Thackara is not interested in the sell-out of design achievements, but in the consistent application of the idea behind Web 2.0: Where users input their knowledge, value is added. Swiss graphic designer Jürg Lehni takes a more differentiated view: "In design, the focus is always on personality and individuality. A good designer would hardly put the tricks of his trade in the public domain." As regards experimental projects, Lehni nevertheless champions Open Source. On his website www.scriptographer.com he makes the Plug-in he developed for Adobe Illustrator under the name of Scriptographer available as a free download. In this way, he wishes to encourage other designers to break open the functional constraints of Illustrator software and expand it. Lehni's approach is trailblazing: He makes use of the opportunities afforded by Web 2.0 in order to create new applications for the like-minded there.

It is not yet clear what could evolve from this in the future. To date, few designers make use of the new forms of creative collaboration in the Net. Design blogs and forums as well as classic Web-2.0 platforms such as Youtube and Flickr may create a new public sphere for design issues. But the real potential of networking via the Web has by no means been tapped yet. ★

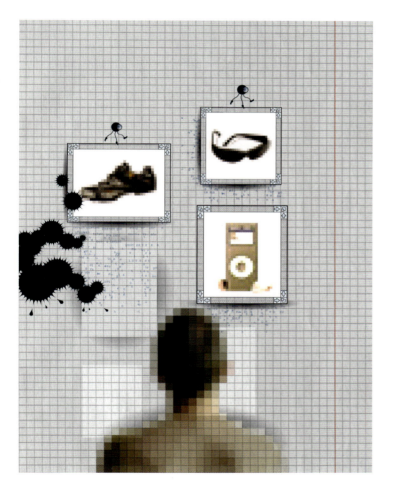

ABERHAM — ALLDESIGN
BAGGENDESIGN — BEAU BUREAU DESIGN — LOTHAR BÖHM
BOTSCHAFT PROF. GERTRUD NOLTE VISUELLE KOMMUNIKATION
UND BERATUNG — BRÖSSKE, MEYER & RUF GMBH
BÜRO GROTESK — CHRISTIAN WEISSER AGENTURGRUPPE
C&N DESIGN-AGENTUR GMBH
CREDO CONCEPT. COMMUNICATION — CYCLOS DESIGN
DISEGNO GBR — ELBEDESIGNCREW
IDENTIS — INDEPENDENT MEDIEN-DESIGN
JUNGEPARTNER — KISKA — KOREFE
MOSKITO KOMMUNIKATION UND DESIGN
NODESIGN — PURE COMMUNICATIONS
RINCÓN2 — BÜRO SIEBER
SIGN KOMMUNIKATION GMBH — STUDIO LAEIS
STUDIO 38 PURE COMMUNICATION GMBH
TRAWNY / QUASS VON DEYEN
VISUPHIL© DESIGN STUDIOS
BÜRO FÜR GESTALTUNG WANGLER & ABELE
REGELINDIS WESTPHAL GRAFIK-DESIGN
ZWÖLFTON DESIGN

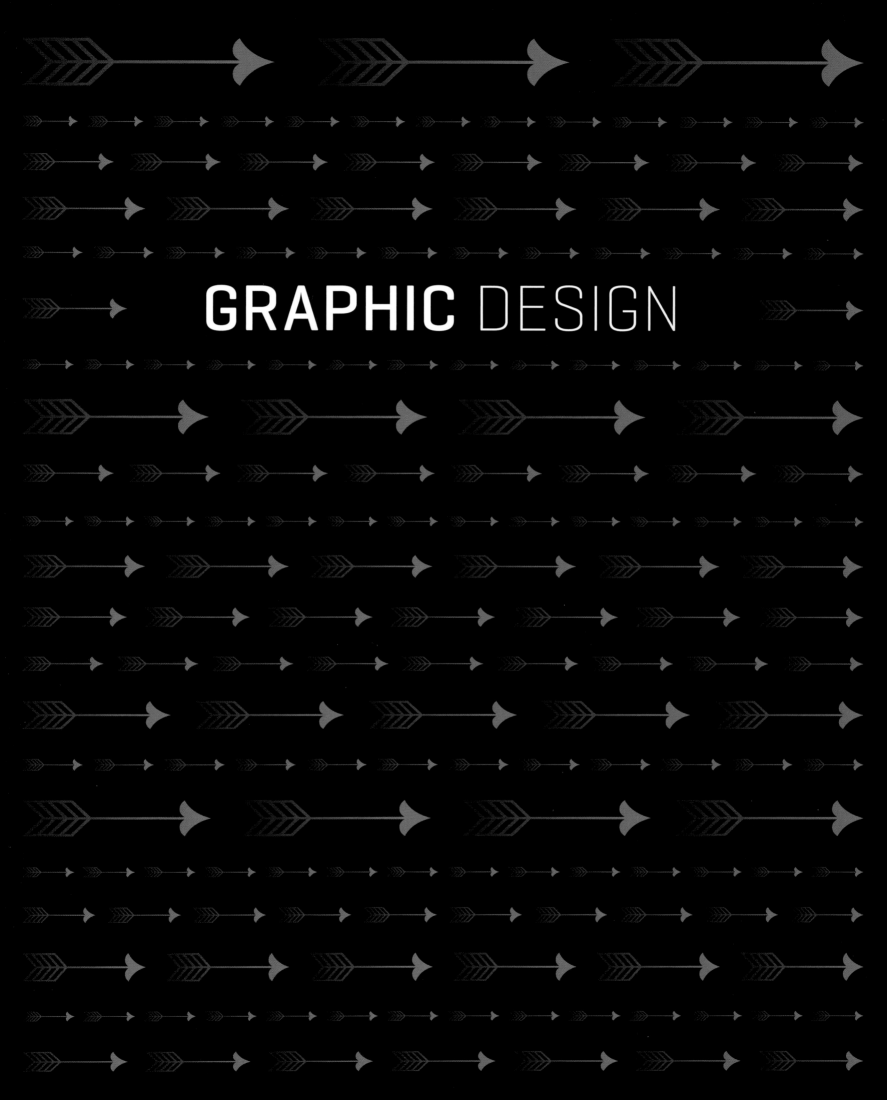

ABERHAM

FIRMENPHILOSOPHIE — CORPORATE PHILOSOPHY

ABERHAM bietet zielsichere Marken-Gestaltung und treffendes Kommunikations-Design für Unternehmen, Produkte, Verpackungen und Ereignisse in den unterschiedlichsten Märkten.

ABERHAM gestaltet bewusst lebendige Stil-Systeme, in denen die Kreation eigener Bildwelten und pointierter Text-Botschaften einen ebenso hohen Stellenwert einnimmt wie Logo-Design, Farbwelt und Typografie.

ABERHAM ist der persönliche, intensive Partner für die Konzeption von gut gedachten, stilprägenden Design-Lösungen, die Zukunft vermitteln.

ABERHAM provides perfectly targeted brand design as well as spot-on communications design for companies, products, packaging and events in a diverse range of markets.

ABERHAM deliberately designs style systems that appear alive, in which the creation of an original pictorial world and text, which is pointedly written, takes on an importance just as high as the logo design, color spectrum and typography.

ABERHAM is your personalized, intensive partner for the conception of well thought out, style-focused design solutions, which can convey the future.

TÄTIGKEITSFELDER — DISCIPLINES

Brand Evaluation, Brand Design, Brand Identity, Packaging Design, Corporate Design, Editorial Design, Naming & Claim

REFERENZEN — REFERENCES

Dr. Rimpler, Fripa, Konzerthaus Berlin, MERA Tiernahrung, Maredo

GESCHÄFTSFÜHRUNG — MANAGEMENT

Morris Aberham

GRÜNDUNGSDATUM — FOUNDATION

1980

MITARBEITER — EMPLOYEES

5

ANSCHRIFT — ADDRESS

Hansaallee 42
40547 Düsseldorf
Deutschland
T +49 (0) 211-5577510
F +49 (0) 211-5577520
info@aberham-design.de
www.aberham-design.de

> Der Relaunch einer Marke sollte immer eine »Renaissance« ihres genetischen Codes sein. Es gilt, diesen zu erkennen und mit Respekt und Mut in die Zukunft zu übersetzen.

Bisheriger Auftritt **Isabelle Lancray, Paris**

Bisherige Dachmarke **MERADOG**

Bisheriger Auftritt **SOLO**-Range (ALDI Nord)

ABERHAM
Intensive Design

Umfassender Relaunch des Gesamtauftritts der Premium-Kosmetikmarke **Isabelle Lancray, Paris**

Markanter Relaunch und Claim-Entwicklung für die Dachmarke der Premium-Hundenahrung **MERADOG**

Evolution aus einer Hand: Erneuter Relaunch des Auftrittes der **SOLO** Hygienepapier-Range (ALDI Nord)

ALLDESIGN

FIRMENPHILOSOPHIE — CORPORATE PHILOSOPHY
Kommunikation muss auffallen und die Zielgruppe erreichen.
Außergewöhnlich, eindrucksvoll, nachhaltig.
Auf fundierter Basis. Gut durchdachte Kommunikation hat die nötige Kraft für Ihren Erfolg.
Communication has to catch the eye and reach the target group.
Exceptional, impressive, lasting.
On a strong basis. Thoughtful communication has the necessary strength for your success.

TÄTIGKEITSFELDER — DISCIPLINES
Corporate & Brand Design
Brand Development
Web Development
Web Marketing
HR Marketing
Advertising and Media

REFERENZEN — REFERENCES
Größte und kleinste Unternehmen – www.alldesign.de/Kunden
The smallest and the largest companies – www.alldesign.de/kunden

GESCHÄFTSFÜHRUNG — MANAGEMENT
Andreas Lück

GRÜNDUNGSDATUM — FOUNDATION
1993

MITARBEITER — EMPLOYEES
14

ANSCHRIFT — ADDRESS
Alldesign
Inh. Andreas Lück
Schillerstraße 47
41061 Mönchengladbach
Deutschland
T +49 (0) 2161-29308-0
F +49 (0) 2161-29308-70
info@alldesign.de
www.alldesign.de

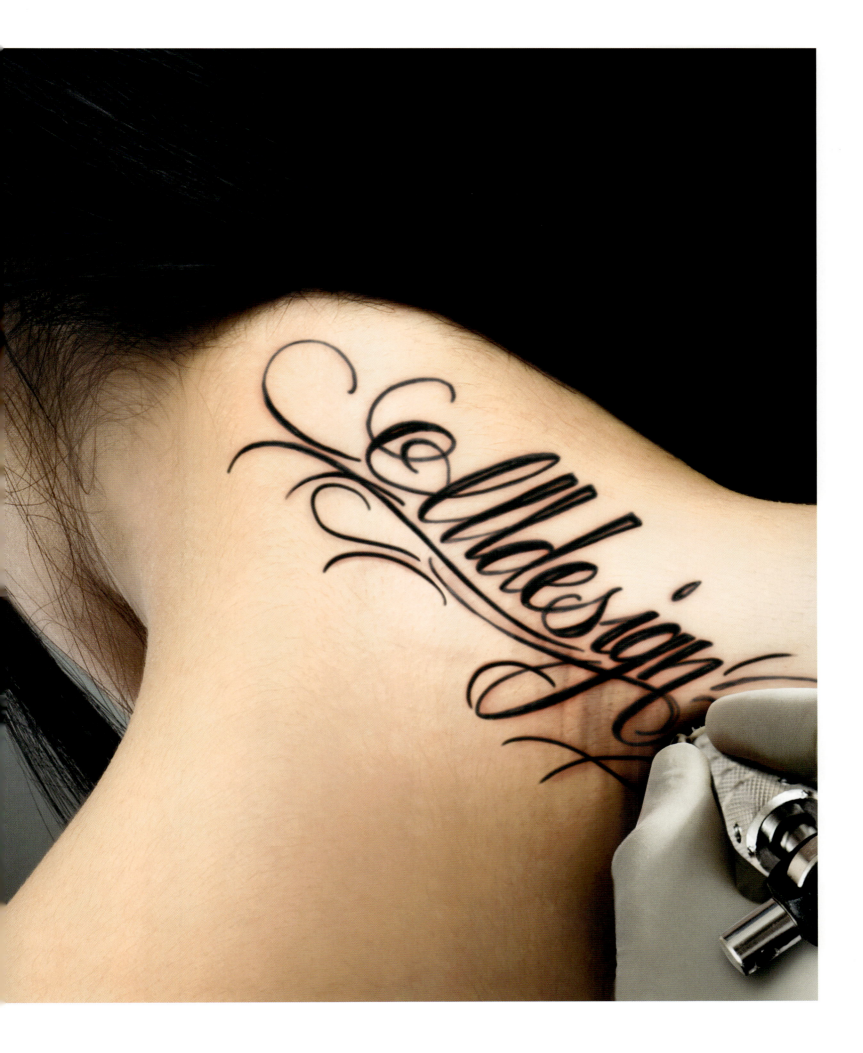

BAGGENDESIGN

FIRMENPHILOSOPHIE — CORPORATE PHILOSOPHY

Visuelle Kommunikation ist im besten Fall äußere Darstellung einer inneren Haltung. Gemäß diesem Leitsatz machen wir seit 2004 Marken sichtbar. In enger Zusammenarbeit mit führenden strategischen Markenberatern entwickeln und realisieren wir Aufgaben für unsere Kunden mit den Schwerpunkten Corporate Design und Unternehmenskommunikation. Hierbei legen wir darauf Wert, Qualität und Professionalität mit Effizienz und Flexibilität zu verbinden.

At its best, visual communication depicts an inner attitude to the outside world. Accordingly, since 2004, we have been working to make brands visible to the public. Working in close collaboration with leading strategic brand consultants, we develop and implement our clients' strategies, focusing on corporate design and corporate communications. In doing so, we offer a combination of quality and professionalism with efficiency and flexibility.

TÄTIGKEITSFELDER — DISCIPLINES

Corporate Design Entwicklung und Umsetzung, Unternehmenskommunikation, Visuelle Begleitung von Kunst- und Kulturveranstaltungen

Corporate design development and implementation, corporate communication and visual accompaniment for art and cultural events.

REFERENZEN — REFERENCES

aponeo, CBR, Ernsting's family, Eterna, g.e.b.b., HIL, NBRZ, OBI, quirin bank, Volkswagen Logistics, Vorwerk/Thermomix, WHU-Otto Beisheim School of Management et al.

GESCHÄFTSFÜHRUNG — MANAGEMENT

Stefan Baggen

GRÜNDUNGSDATUM — FOUNDATION

2004

MITARBEITER — EMPLOYEES

6

ANSCHRIFT — ADDRESS

Martinstrasse 47-55, Haus F
40223 Düsseldorf
Deutschland
T +49 211-61717627
F +49 211-61717621
info@baggendesign.de
www.baggendesign.de

B 42
GRAPHIC DESIGN

/// Hier gedeihen die neuesten Ideen: www.beau-bureau.de

BEAU BUREAU DESIGN

FIRMENPHILOSOPHIE — CORPORATE PHILOSOPHY
Kennen Sie den Unterschied zwischen Foreign Branding, Co-Branding, Site Branding und Debranding? beau bureau bringt Klarheit in Ihre Designstrategie und verbindet etablierte Methoden aus Innovationsprozessen wie Design Thinking mit Kreativität und Mut zum Experiment. Unsere Ideen führen zu hochwertigen und nachhaltigen Designlösungen, die aus der Masse herausstechen. beau bureau design ist eine Agentur für strategische Markenentwicklung mit Schwerpunkt Corporate Branding und Corporate Design.

Do you know the difference between foreign branding, co-branding, site branding and debranding? beau bureau offers to boost your design strategies. We combine creative and innovative techniques with established methods such as design thinking. New ideas lead to high quality and sustainable design that stands out from the crowd. beau bureau design specialises in strategic brand development with a focus on corporate branding and corporate design.

GRUNDSATZ — PRINCIPLE
gelbb macht glücklich!

TÄTIGKEITSFELDER — DISCIPLINES
Consulting & Design Strategy, Branding, Corporate Design, Exhibition Design, Editorial Design, Annual Reports, Books & Catalogues

REFERENZEN — REFERENCES
Fairtrade, Forest Stewardship Council (FSC), Goethe Institut, Stadtwerke Köln, Stedelijk Museum Roermond, Museum Schloss Rheydt, Kassenzahnärztliche Bundesvereinigung (KZBV), Knauber, Kölner Dommusik, Drogenhilfe Köln, Verlag M. DuMont Schauberg

GESCHÄFTSFÜHRUNG — MANAGEMENT
Katja M. Becker, M.A.

GRÜNDUNGSDATUM — FOUNDATION
2005

MITARBEITER — EMPLOYEES
5

AUSZEICHNUNGEN — AWARDS

ANSCHRIFT — ADDRESS
Händelstraße 26
50674 Köln / Cologne
Deutschland
T +49 (0) 221-16 86 706
F +49 (0) 221-16 86 707
form@beau-bureau.de
www.beau-bureau.de

beau bureau design

Identitäten
Geschäftspapiere
Publikationen
Ausstellungen
Webpräsenzen

LOTHAR BÖHM

FIRMENPHILOSOPHIE — CORPORATE PHILOSOPHY
"It takes great understanding of people to sucessfully create a brand."
Lothar Böhm

With offices in Hamburg, London and Warsaw, Lothar Böhm is one of the most experienced and prestigious packaging design agencies in Europe.

OUR APPROACH.
As a leading global agency Lothar Böhm guides global brands. We believe in long lasting relationships and understand our customers needs. Through exceptional creativity combined with high standards in design and implementation we are successfully increasing brand value. Being the entrepreneures for brands we are the experts in the field of packaging design. As an award winning company Lothar Böhm always aims for excellence.

TÄTIGKEITSFELDER — DISCIPLINES
Strategy
Consumer Insights / Market Audit & Analysis / Trend Monitoring
Packaging Design
Brand Design / Brand Architecture / Brand Navigation
3D Structural Design
Rapid Prototyping / Computer Generated Imagery / Technical Support
Execution
Final Artwork / Proof Printing Supervision / Quality Management

REFERENZEN — REFERENCES
Reckitt Benckiser, SCA, Johnson & Johnson, VARTA, Bongrain, Beiersdorf, BSN, Imperial Tobacco, Kraft Foods

GESCHÄFTSFÜHRUNG — MANAGEMENT
Lothar Böhm, CEO
Martina Kunert, Managing Partner
Christine Lischka, Managing Partner
Britt Reinhäckel, Managing Partner

GRÜNDUNGSDATUM — FOUNDATION
1972

MITARBEITER — EMPLOYEES
80

AUSZEICHNUNGEN — AWARDS

ANSCHRIFT — ADDRESS
Große Elbstrasse 281
22767 Hamburg
Deutschland
T +49 (0) 40 39 10 08 0
F +49 (0) 40 3910 08 44
Martina.Kunert@boehm-design.com
www.boehm-design.com

LIFESTYLE WHERE IT'S LEAST EXPECTED
Hygiene products for women need not be hidden anymore.
Produced for the UK market.

HAVE AN OOOOPS PROJECT?
we love creating femininity

LOTHAR BÖHM London

B 46
GRAPHIC DESIGN

BOTSCHAFT
PROF. GERTRUD NOLTE
VISUELLE KOMMUNIKATION
UND BERATUNG

FIRMENPHILOSOPHIE — CORPORATE PHILOSOPHY
Die BOTSCHAFTEN von PROF. GERTRUD NOLTE
Denken lehren, nicht Gedachtes.
Haltung und Stil befähigen zur Überzeugung.
Alles ist möglich. Außer. Gewöhnlich.
»Denken ist vorweggenommenes Handeln und kann damit
Handlungen unausgeführt lassen, denn wir sind auch verantwortlich
für das, was wir nicht tun und nicht tun sollten.«
Teach thinking, not thoughts.
Attitude and style provide the power to persuade.
Anything goes. Anything, but the ordinary.

TÄTIGKEITSFELDER — DISCIPLINES
info@botschaftnolte.de / beratung@botschaftnolte.de /
plakat@botschaftnolte.de / buch@botschaftnolte.de /
typographie@botschaftnolte.de / typeface@botschaftnolte.de /
text@botschaftnolte.de / corporate@botschaftnolte.de /
gestaltung@botschaftnolte.de / kultur@botschaftnolte.de /
botschaften@botschaftnolte.de

REFERENZEN — REFERENCES
BB: »An Gertrud Nolte ist das Quartett das Besondere.
Ausgezeichnet sowohl in Konzeption, logischem Denken
und Gestaltung als auch in Person und Mensch.
« KW: »Ihre Arbeiten gewinnen immer Neues, werden immer besser,
je öfter man hinschaut, und das möchte man!«
BB: "What distinguishes Getrud Nolte is her excellence
in strategy, logical thinking, and design, as well as her qualities
as a human being."
KW: "You discover new aspects every time you look at her work:
it gets better and better. And this is what you want."

GESCHÄFTSFÜHRUNG — MANAGEMENT
Prof. Gertrud Nolte

GRÜNDUNGSDATUM — FOUNDATION
1995

AUSZEICHNUNGEN — AWARDS

ANSCHRIFT — ADDRESS
Talstraße 24
40217 Düsseldorf
Deutschland
T +49 (0) 211-15 92 35-28
F +49 (0) 211-15 92 35-46
info@botschaftnolte.de
www.botschaftnolte.de

botschaft prof. gertrud nolte
visuelle kommunikation und beratung

UNTEN / BELOW:
*Manuelle kalligraphische Übung / art work;
calligraphy exercise*
WERK / WORK:
›Friedrich Hölderlin. An die Parzen‹

in botschaftstüten kommen keine Plattitüden,

die 'gemeine Tüte:
Hülle für jeglichen Inhalt
Transportmittel für jeglichen Inhalt,
   sowie die Gedanken des Herausgebes, den Autritt des
   Unternehmens, für den Träger selbst (Käufer/Nutzer)
Schutz
Vertuschung und Kaschierung von Inhalt, oder Delikatem
Bedienung für Voyeurismus
Sammler-Subjekt
Wegwerf-Objekt
Behälterwissenschaft
immer in Bewegung
ein Staffelstab

bewegen real und virtuell:

LINKS/LEFT:
WERK/WORK: *Schriftprobe als Faltplakat zur »Justus« von Volker Schnebel / Typeface advertisment for "Justus", edited by URW++; 2011*

RECHTS/RIGHT:
WERK/WORK: *Plakat »T^RAKT AT. Autorität durch Autorschaft« / poster "T^RAKT AT. Authority through Authorship", 2010*

zum VorTragen und MitTragen mit AusSicht auf InnenSicht

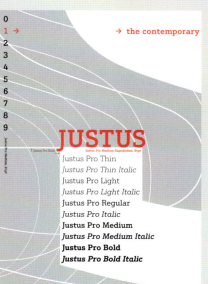

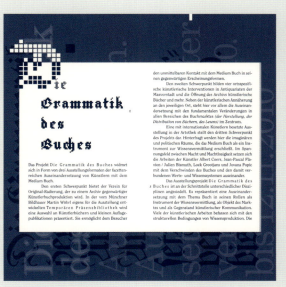

KUNDE/CLIENT
Verein für Originalradierung e.V. München /Munich
WERK/WORK:
Büchlein mit Buch im Buch für »Die Grammatik des Buches« / Folder for "The Grammar of Books", 2010

BRÖSSKE, MEYER & RUF GMBH

FIRMENPHILOSOPHIE — CORPORATE PHILOSOPHY
Markenqualität für Marken.

TÄTIGKEITSFELDER — DISCIPLINES
Design ist das visuelle Erscheinungsbild einer Strategie und somit untrennbar mit der Führung von Marken verknüpft. Brösske, Meyer & Ruf entwickelt Strategien zur Führung von Marken und setzt diese in Form von Designlösungen um:
– auf die Identität der Marke zugeschnitten
– substanziell und auf Langfristigkeit angelegt

Dabei umfassen die entwickelten Design-Lösungen alle klassischen Stufen des Marken- und Packungsdesigns:
– die grundlegende Ausrichtung
  von Marken über Neu-Entwicklungen
– die Pflege von Marken in Form von Facelifts,
  Relaunches und Line Extentions
– die zeitgemäße Aufladung von Marken
  über Promotion-Entwicklungen

Im Zuge einer ganzheitlichen Markenbetreuung entwickelt Brösske, Meyer & Ruf auch:
– Marken- und Produktnamen
– Formdesign
– POS-Präsentationen
– Sekundär-Verpackungen

REFERENZEN — REFERENCES
Brösske, Meyer & Ruf ist seit mehr als dreißig Jahren Partner namhafter nationaler und internationaler Unternehmen. Dazu zählt die langjährige Zusammenarbeit mit Bayer, Brandt, Dr. Oetker, Heinz, Henkel, Intersnack, Nestlé, Weight Watchers und vielen anderen Unternehmen in der Markenartikel-Industrie.

GESCHÄFTSFÜHRUNG — MANAGEMENT
Manfred Recklies, Christa Stein, Burkhard Böhm

GRÜNDUNGSDATUM — FOUNDATION
1978

MITARBEITER — EMPLOYEES
22

ANSCHRIFT — ADDRESS
Steinstraße 20
40212 Düsseldorf
Deutschland
T +49 (0) 211-1797 0
F +49 (0) 211-1797 111
hello@bmr-design.de
www.bmr-design.de

Brösske, Meyer & Ruf GmbH
Design-Agentur Düsseldorf

B 50
GRAPHIC DESIGN

BÜRO GROTESK

TÄTIGKEITSFELDER — DISCIPLINES
Corporate Identity, Corporate Design, Web Design, Exhibition Design, Editorial Design, Broschüren, Bücher, Magazine, Kataloge, Geschäftsberichte, Poster, Wertpapiere, Leitsysteme, Verpackung, …

REFERENZEN — REFERENCES
Anovia AG, Bernd M. Michael, Bertelsmann Stiftung, Deutschkontrolle, Düsseldorfer Schauspielhaus, Ehrenhof Düsseldorf, E.ON, Genusshandwerker, Ideo, Ingenieurkammer-Bau NRW, Kunsthalle Düsseldorf, Kunstverein Region Heinsberg, Ministerium für Bauen und Verkehr des Landes Nordrhein-Westfalen, MMacarons, NDF, Rheingold, …

GESCHÄFTSFÜHRUNG — MANAGEMENT
Helen Hacker

GRÜNDUNGSDATUM — FOUNDATION
1999

AUSZEICHNUNGEN — AWARDS
      Deutscher Plakat Grand Prix

ANSCHRIFT — ADDRESS
Wissmannstraße 15
40219 Düsseldorf
Deutschland
T + 49 (0) 211-1372796
gutentag@buero-grotesk.de
www.buero-grotesk.de

Foto © www.berndwichmann.de

CHRISTIAN WEISSER AGENTURGRUPPE

FIRMENPHILOSOPHIE — CORPORATE PHILOSOPHY
Unter diesem interdisziplinären Dach vereinen sich mit Brand Communication, Lifestyle Events und dem Designlabel diffus® unsere drei Agenturkompetenzfelder. Jedes für sich fokussiert und spezialisiert, zusammen effizient und übergreifend. Mit namhaften Kunden und außergewöhnlichen Referenzen sind wir seit 1999 zu dem geworden, was wir heute sind. Wir sind inhabergeführt und unabhängig. Wir denken und handeln wie ein Familienunternehmen, langfristig, nachhaltig und integriert. Das macht uns und unsere Kunden erfolgreich.

TÄTIGKEITSFELDER — DISCIPLINES
Design Consulting, Innovation Design, Corporate Design, Grafik Design, Editorial Design, Corporate Communication, Marketing POS Communication, Event Design, Exhibition Design, Graphic User Interface Design.

REFERENZEN — REFERENCES
Mercedes-Benz, Daimler, Landesmuseum Württemberg, Mercedes-Benz Museum, adidas, Grand Tirolia Golf & Ski Resort, Mack & Schühle, Rodenstock, Burkhardt Leitner constructiv, Hugo Boss, Deutsche Zöliakie Gesellschaft, Nederburg Wines, Bodegas Faustino, Blumen Großmarkt Stuttgart.

GESCHÄFTSFÜHRUNG — MANAGEMENT
Christian Weisser

GRÜNDUNGSDATUM — FOUNDATION
1999

MITARBEITER — EMPLOYEES
12

AUSZEICHNUNGEN — AWARDS

ANSCHRIFT — ADDRESS
Christian Weisser Brand Communication GmbH
Marienstraße 37
70178 Stuttgart
Deutschland
T +49 (0) 711 99 33 91 30
F +49 (0) 711 99 33 91 33
info@christianweisser.de
www.christianweisser.de

C&N DESIGN-AGENTUR GMBH

FIRMENPHILOSOPHIE — CORPORATE PHILOSOPHY
Eine gute Verpackung ist mehr als ein Karton. Sie ist der beste Verkäufer. Schon deshalb muss man sie gut pflegen. Denn wer ein tolles Produkt hat, sollte es auch entsprechend präsentieren. Wir haben das Glück für Kunden zu arbeiten, die das genauso sehen und sehr viel Wert auf gutes Design legen. Vielleicht haben wir deshalb so viel Spaß an unserer Arbeit und so zufriedene Kunden. Wenn wir auch für Sie und Ihre Marke etwas tun können, rufen Sie uns an.

Good packaging is more than a cardboard box. It is the best salesman. For that reason alone it has to be taken good care of. If you have any amazing product you should also present it the right way. We are in the fortunate position to work for customers who think the same way and who attach great importance to good design. Maybe this is the reason why we enjoy our work so much and have so satisfied customers. Just call us, if we can do something for you and your brand.

TÄTIGKEITSFELDER — DISCIPLINES
Packungsdesign, Corporate Design, Corporate Identity, Verkaufsförderung, Handelswerbung
Packaging Design, Corporate Design, Corporate Identity, Sales Promotion, Trade Advertising

REFERENZEN — REFERENCES
Ferrero, z.B. Ferrero Küsschen, Raffaello, Kinder Schokolade / Bama / Kiwi / Kiwi Select / Tana / Meltonian / Baluna / Käserei Champignon, z.B. Rougette, Cambozola, St. Mang

GESCHÄFTSFÜHRUNG — MANAGEMENT
Isolde Casper
Kurt Nussbächer

GRÜNDUNGSDATUM — FOUNDATION
1994

MITARBEITER — EMPLOYEES
12

ANSCHRIFT — ADDRESS
Wiesenau 27–29
60323 Frankfurt am Main
Deutschland
T +49 (0) 69-17 00 85-0
F +49 (0) 69-17 00 85-20
info@c-u-n.de
www.c-u-n.de

Schöne Verpackungen sind eben doch wichtig.
Obviously beautiful packaging is important.

GRAPHIC DESIGN

CREDO CONCEPT. COMMUNICATION

FIRMENPHILOSOPHIE — CORPORATE PHILOSOPHY
Wir arbeiten an der Schnittstelle zwischen Corporate Design und Klassischer Werbung. Als designorientierte Werbeagentur bieten wir integrierte Kommunikation als Full-Service-Paket für den Mittelstand an. Je nach Aufgabenstellung vernetzen wir uns mit passenden Spezialisten aus unserer breitgefächerten Netzwerkstruktur. Wenn Sie mehr wissen möchten: www.credo-concept.com

TÄTIGKEITSFELDER — DISCIPLINES
Corporate Design, Corporate Communication, Names & Claims, Kommunikationskonzepte, Werbung, Media, Messe- und Webdesign

REFERENZEN — REFERENCES
2basics IT-Consulting GmbH, Beutlhauser Baumaschinen GmbH (Mercedes Benz Nutzfahrzeuge, Liebherr, Linde Material Handling, Stihl), BMW Auto-Leebmann GmbH, CenTouris (Centrum für Tourismus), einStein Natursteinhandel GmbH, Europa Therme Bad Füssing, eyedentity Brillenvertrieb GmbH & Co. KG, HGP audioelektronik, Hotels (Haus Berlin, Haus Hamburg, Haus Salzburg), IFIS (Informationssysteme), KAPS GmbH (optik.foto.atelier), LOFT Lebensräume, MAP GmbH (Mode), ODEVIS AG (Automationssysteme), Passauer Tanztage, Passau Tourismus e.V., Perner Glocken GmbH & Co. KG, ScharfrichterHaus, Karin Scholz LederKunst, Serkem GmbH (SAP Channel Partner), Silvia Richter Modedesign, Stadtwerke Passau GmbH, Statik Breinbauer (Ingenieurbüro), Unikat Schmuckgalerie, Universität Passau, vonBogen Brillendesign GmbH

GESCHÄFTSFÜHRUNG — MANAGEMENT
Stefan Dahinten, Dipl.-Kfm. Univ.

KONTAKTPERSONEN — CONTACT
Stefan Dahinten, Beratung, Konzeption, Text; Nadine Geißler, Grafik-Design; Ludwig Gutsmiedl, Dipl.-Grafikdesigner; Markus Muckenschnabl, Dipl.-Grafikdesigner; Teresa Neuhauser, Grafik- & Webdesign; Silke Steinle, Dipl.-Grafikdesignerin

GRÜNDUNGSDATUM — FOUNDATION
1998

MITARBEITER — EMPLOYEES
8

AUSZEICHNUNGEN — AWARDS
BDG:Logowettbewerb: HGP audioelektronik, ScharfrichterHaus, eyedentity
Deutscher Tourismuspreis: Bad Füssing

ANSCHRIFT — ADDRESS
Bischof-Wolfger-Straße 30
94032 Passau
Deutschland
T +49 (0)8 51 9 52 02 34
F +49 (0)8 51 9 52 02 35
ISDN +49 (0)8 51 9 52 02 36
info@credo-concept.com
www.credo-concept.com

credo concept.
communication

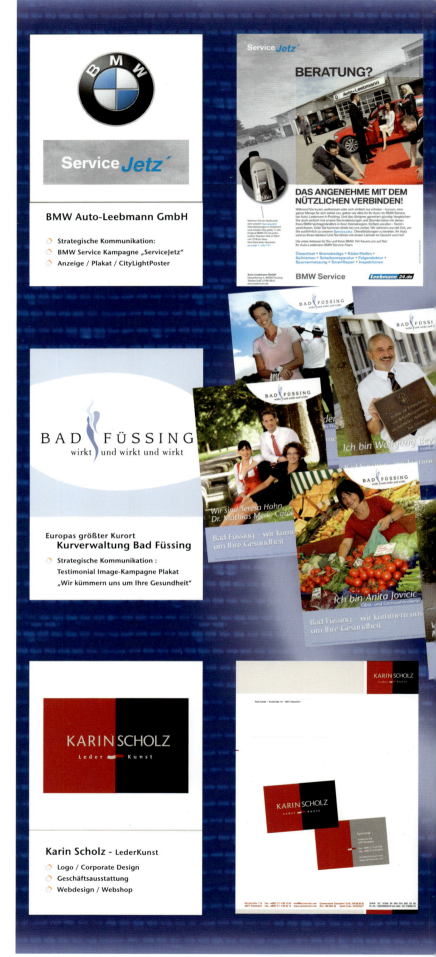

CYCLOS DESIGN

FIRMENPHILOSOPHIE — CORPORATE PHILOSOPHY

Marken brauchen Leidenschaft. cyclos design hat sich auf die Entwicklung einzigartiger Markenkonzepte spezialisiert. Mit strategischem Gespür für die Wechselbeziehung der verschiedenen Kommunikationskanäle – egal ob online oder offline – entwickeln wir einzigartige Design- und Kommunikationskonzepte für die Markenwelt unserer Kunden. Daher wird jedes Medium nicht isoliert betrachtet, sondern immer als Element in einem komplexen Gefüge integrierter Kommunikation. Das ist die Basis für nachhaltige Markenauftritte.

TÄTIGKEITSFELDER — DISCIPLINES

Corporate Identity und Corporate Design	40 %
Branding, Packaging	20 %
Internet, Multimedia, Social Media und Mobile	20 %
Ausstellungs- und Messedesign	20 %

REFERENZEN — REFERENCES

Wohnambiente und Lifestyle, Konsum- und Luxusgüter, Schmuck und Kosmetik, Babyausstattung // Lebensmittel, Getränke und Spirituosen // Finanz- und Versicherungsdienstleister // Industrie und Handel, Bauwirtschaft, Einzelhandel // Gartenmöbel, Garten- und Landschaftsbau, Biochemie und Erden // Technologie, Consumer-Electronics, IT-Dienstleister // Papier- und Druckindustrie // Health Care, diakonische Einrichtungen, Stiftungen // Kultur- und Stadtmarketing

GESCHÄFTSFÜHRUNG — MANAGEMENT

Jutta Schnieders, Frank Seepe

GRÜNDUNGSDATUM — FOUNDATION

1995

MITARBEITER — EMPLOYEES

34

AUSZEICHNUNGEN — AWARDS

4 x red dot award: communication design 2011 // Deutsche Post Mailing-Wettbewerb: 3. erfolgreichstes Mailing Deutschlands // Internationale Kalenderschau: Preis der Jury in Silber sowie Award of Excellence // Japan Calendar Award: Special Prize

ANSCHRIFT — ADDRESS

Hafenweg 24
48155 Münster
Deutschland
F +49 251. 915 998 - 0
T +49 251. 915 998 -10
info@cyclos-design.de
www.cyclos-design.de

KAMPAGNENKONZEPT Dometic WAECO

MARKENENTWICKLUNG Gärtner von Eden

MARKENENTWICKLUNG UND KATALOGKONZEPT blomus

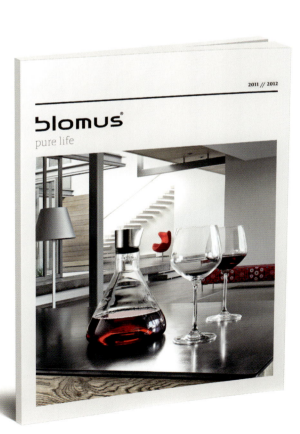

DISEGNO GBR

FIRMENPHILOSOPHIE — CORPORATE PHILOSOPHY
Wir verstehen Gestaltung als Suche und Prozess, bemühen uns in enger individueller Zusammenarbeit mit den Auftraggebern, gute, ungewöhnliche und der Aufgabe angemessene Lösungen zu finden.
We understand design as a search and process, work diligently in close individual cooperation with our clients to find excellent, unusual solutions that meet the respective brief.

TÄTIGKEITSFELDER — DISCIPLINES
Corporate design, Culture and institutions, Publishing, Corporate communication, Product communication, Web design

GESCHÄFTSFÜHRUNG — MANAGEMENT
Merten Durth und Annemarie Tegethoff-Sommerfeld

GRÜNDUNGSDATUM — FOUNDATION
1994

MITARBEITER — EMPLOYEES
Uneingeschränkt belastbares Team lieber freier Verbündeter.
A team of freelance allies capable of withstanding any amount of pressure.

ANSCHRIFT — ADDRESS
Seydlitzstrasse 9
42281 Wuppertal
Deutschland
T +49 (0) 202-86435
F +49 (0) 202-2802074
hallo@disenjo.de
www.disenjo.de

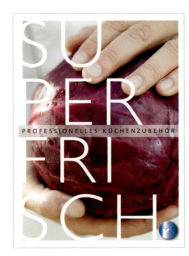
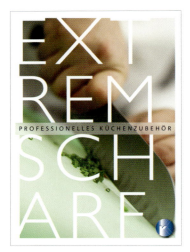
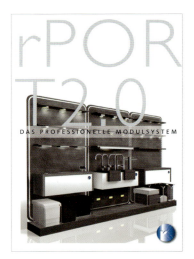

DISEGNO | visuelle kommunikation

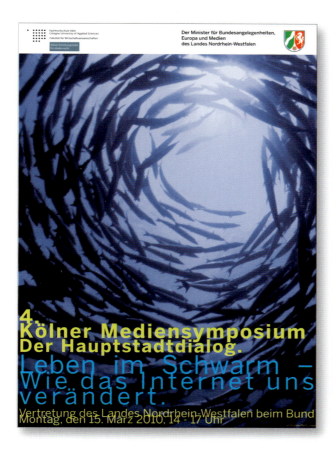
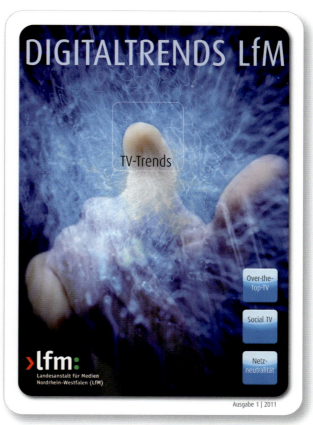

ELBEDESIGNCREW

FIRMENPHILOSOPHIE — CORPORATE PHILOSOPHY
creating brand character
Unsere Heimat ist die Elbe als Sinnbild der unerschöpflichen Ideenquelle. Unser Thema ist das Design voller Kreativität, Fantasie und Innovationskraft. Unsere Stärke ist die Crew mit ihrem nach vorne gerichteten Crew-Spirit. Wir schaffen es, über das Packaging-Design das Besondere aus der Marke herauszuholen, ihr Eigenständigkeit und Charakter zu verleihen. elbedesigncrew bietet alle Disziplinen von der initialen Strategie und Ideenentwicklung bis hin zur Produktion. Dies machen wir seit mehr als 22 Jahren und verfügen über ein sehr großes Erfahrungsspektrum.

Our home is the Elbe River as emblematic of the inexhaustible wellspring of ideas. Our subject is design full of creativity, imagination and innovative power. Our strength is the crew with its forward-looking team spirit. By means of the packaging design, we are able to work out the special essence of a brand, and lend it uniqueness and character. elbedesigncrew offers all disciplines starting with the initial strategic planning and idea development, and ranging all the way to production. We have been doing this for more than 22 years and have a very wide range of experience at our disposal.

TÄTIGKEITSFELDER — DISCIPLINES
brand & packaging design, form design, naming, promotion / pos, production

REFERENZEN — REFERENCES
Alete, Bayer Vital, Carlsberg Deutschland, cosnova, Ehrmann, fit, Gaba, Hermes Arzneimittel, Hochland, J.J.Darboven, König Brauerei, Maggi, Nestlé, Purina, Ritex, Thomy, Weleda

GESCHÄFTSFÜHRUNG — MANAGEMENT
Jens Heise

GRÜNDUNGSDATUM — FOUNDATION
1989

MITARBEITER — EMPLOYEES
30

ANSCHRIFT — ADDRESS
Bernhard-Nocht-Straße 99
20359 Hamburg
Deutschland
T +49 (0) 40-899690-0
F +49 (0) 40-899690-44
j.heise@elbedesigncrew.de
www.elbedesigncrew.de

>>
DIE AUGEN ESSEN NICHT NUR MIT.
SIE BESTIMMEN, WAS SCHMECKT.

Nudeln sind einfach leckerer, wenn man sie Pasta nennt. Ein Gericht schmeckt besser, wenn man es liebevoll arrangiert und dekoriert. Genauso verführt uns eine appetitlich designte Packung schneller zum Kauf. Wir verstehen uns darauf, die Geschmacksknospen visuell wach zu kitzeln – und zum Probieren zu verführen.

IDENTIS

FIRMENPHILOSOPHIE — CORPORATE PHILOSOPHY
Wir drücken unsere Philosophie durch unseren Namen aus: identis. Das Expertenteam der Agentur macht Identität sichtbar und erlebbar. Ob es sich um die Identität von Marken, Unternehmen, Institutionen, Events oder Ideen handelt, in jedem Fall werden Einzelbotschaften gebündelt – durch ein einheitliches Gesicht und eine durchgängige Kommunikationshaltung. Damit schaffen wir eine konsistente Wahrnehmung und schließlich eine erhöhte Wirkung.

TÄTIGKEITSFELDER — DISCIPLINES
Corporate Design, Corporate Branding, Corporate Architecture, Unternehmenskommunikation, Produktkommunikation, Exhibition Design, Messe Design, Informationssysteme

REFERENZEN — REFERENCES
bulthaup, DaimlerChrysler AG, EDF Électricité de France, Électricité de Strasbourg, EnBW Energie Baden-Württemberg AG, Europa-Park, Gazprom, Nord Stream AG, Novartis, Staufenstiftung, Yello Strom, Volkswagen Financial Services AG, Volkswagen Zentrum Freiburg

GESCHÄFTSFÜHRUNG — MANAGEMENT
Joseph Pölzelbauer

GRÜNDUNGSDATUM — FOUNDATION
1978

MITARBEITER — EMPLOYEES
10

AUSZEICHNUNGEN — AWARDS

ANSCHRIFT — ADDRESS
Bötzinger Straße 36
79111 Freiburg
Deutschland
T +49 (0) 7 61 40 13 79-0
F +49 (0) 7 61 4 20 30
info@identis.de
www.identis.de

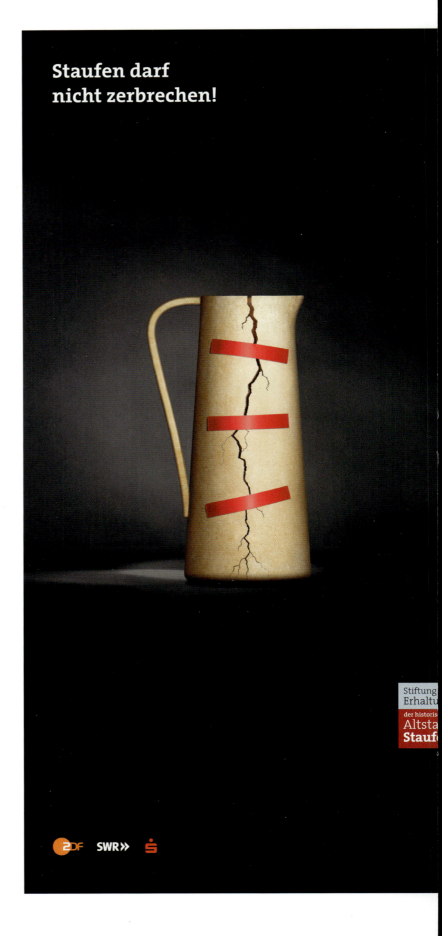

Für die Staufenstiftung entwickelte identis eine visuelle Sprache, die alle Aktivitäten zugunsten der bedrohten Staufener Altstadt bündelt. Die Bedrohung durch Hebungsrisse wird dramatisiert durch das Motiv des Risses und der roten Tapes, die versuchen, den Riss zusammenzuhalten.

INDEPENDENT MEDIEN-DESIGN

FIRMENPHILOSOPHIE — CORPORATE PHILOSOPHY
›Surprise me‹ ist der Titel des internationalen Standardwerks von Horst Moser zum Thema Editorial-Design. ›Surprise me‹ ist auch das Prinzip, nach dem das Büro in München und Zürich (Primafila) konzipiert und gestaltet. Visuelle und inhaltliche Überraschung nicht als oberflächlicher Effekt, sondern als Kommunikations-Strategie in überfüllten Märkten.

»Surprise me« is the title of the international standard work on editorial design by Horst Moser. »Surprise me« is also the principle according to which the offices in Munich and Zurich (Primafila) conceive and design. Visual and contentual surprises not as superficial effects but as communication strategies in overcrowded markets.

TÄTIGKEITSFELDER — DISCIPLINES
Editorial Design (Magazines, Books), Corporate Publishing, Corporate Design, Corporate Heritage, Branding, Annual Reports, Exhibition Design, Webdesign

REFERENZEN — REFERENCES
Allianz AG, Bystronic Laser AG, Clariant, Compaq, Credit Suisse, Deutscher Caritasverband, Gräfe und Unzer Verlag, Hewlett Packard, Leica Camera AG, MLP AG, Siemens AG
Verlage: Baedeker, Bertelsmann, Bruckmann, Burda, Callwey, Carl Hanser, C.H. Beck, Computerwoche, MAIRDUMONT, DVA, Fischer, Gräfe und Unzer, Gruner+Jahr, Hallwag, Handelsblatt, IDG, Langenscheidt, Merian, Polyglott, Prestel, Ringier, Süddeutscher, Tagesanzeiger, Taschen, Teubner, Urban und Vogel, Weltwoche

GESCHÄFTSFÜHRUNG — MANAGEMENT
Ilse Moser

GRÜNDUNGSDATUM — FOUNDATION
1994

MITARBEITER — EMPLOYEES
20

AUSZEICHNUNGEN — AWARDS

ANSCHRIFT — ADDRESS
Widenmayerstraße 16
80538 München
Deutschland
T +49 (0) 89-29 00 15-0
F +49 (0) 89-29 00 15-15
info@independent-medien-design.de
www.independent-medien-design.de

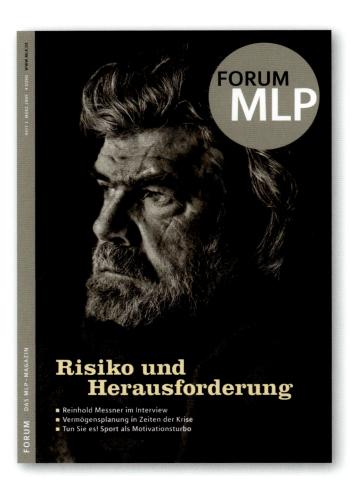

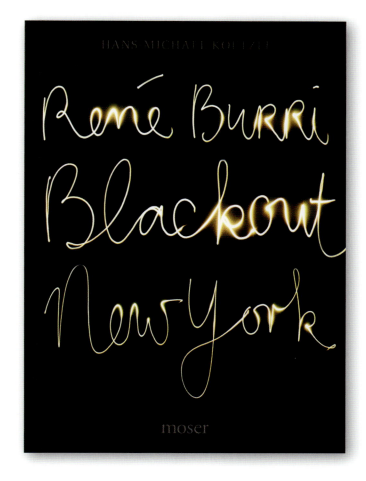

JUNGEPARTNER

FIRMENPHILOSOPHIE — CORPORATE PHILOSOPHY

Mit Gespür für die Sehgewohnheiten verschiedener Zielgruppen, Sinn für Typografie und Ästhetik und hohem technischem Know-how gestalten wir an die tausend Zeitschriften- und Katalogseiten pro Jahr – jede anders und individuell abgestimmt auf das Konzept der jeweiligen Publikation. Schließlich soll jede neue Ausgabe die Leser überraschen und neugierig auf eine Fortsetzung machen. Unser Leistungsspektrum umfasst die konzeptionelle Planung, Unterstützung der Text- und Bildredaktion, gestalterische und technische Umsetzung inklusive permanentem Relaunch sowie die Produktionsbegleitung bis hin zur Online-Ausgabe für iPad & Co.

With a sense of the various target groups' viewing patterns, a sense of typography and aesthetics and a high technical know-how, every year we design around thousand magazine- and catalog pages – each one is different and individually created to the concept of the particular publication. After all, we want each new issue to surprise the readers and make them curious for a continuation. Our business activities include conceptual planning, support with text and photography, creative and technical output - with permanent relaunch. We offer you production assistance to the point of online-output for iPad & Co.

TÄTIGKEITSFELDER — DISCIPLINES

Corporate Design, Editorial Design, Kampagnen, WebDesign, Anzeigen Außenwerbung, Broschüren, Coverdesign, Displays, Fahrzeugbeschriftung, Flyer, Geschäftsberichte, Illustrationen, Infografiken, Kalender, Kataloge, Magazine, Orientierungssysteme, Plakate, Präsentationen, Pressemappen, Schilder, Stempel, Verpackungen, Visitenkarten, Werbemittel, Zeitschriften

GESCHÄFTSFÜHRUNG — MANAGEMENT
Andreas A. Junge

GRÜNDUNGSDATUM — FOUNDATION
1991

MITARBEITER — EMPLOYEES
10

ANSCHRIFT — ADDRESS
Wullener Feld 60
58454 Witten
Deutschland
T +49 (0) 2302-9140910
F +49 (0) 2302-9140911
info@jungepartner.eu
www.jungepartner.eu

jungepartner
beraten und gestalten

Wir lieben die guten Seiten. Sie auch?

70
GRAPHIC DESIGN

KISKA

FIRMENPHILOSOPHIE — CORPORATE PHILOSOPHY
Nur was begehrt ist verkauft sich und ermöglicht neue Investitionen. Bei KISKA ist Designing Desire Alltag. Wir entwickeln einzigartige Kommunikationskonzepte und Designs, welche Marken stärken und Lösungen in klare Botschaften verpacken. In einem einzigen Augenblick erzählen wir die unverwechselbare Geschichte einer Marke.

Mit unserem Integrated Design Development (I.D.D.) Ansatz kreieren wir Design-Lösungen, die die richtigen Botschaften den richtigen Zielgruppen überbringen, konsistent und über alle markenrelevanten Medien. Dabei verbinden wir grundsätzliche markt- und markenstrategische Erkenntnisse mit unseren eigenen Überlegungen, bevor wir eine abgestimmte und zielgerichtete Maßnahme entwickeln. Wir widmen uns mit I.D.D. den wichtigsten Elementen einer Marke: dem Produkt, seiner Umgebung und der Kommunikation.

TÄTIGKEITSFELDER — DISCIPLINES
Brand Consultancy, Research, Analysis, Marketing Services, Visual Product Language, Design Development, Styling, Innovation, Corporate Design, Advertising, Product Graphics, Digital Design.

REFERENZEN — REFERENCES
adidas, AKG, Atomic, Audi, Bajaj, Braun, Bosch Siemens, Gasteiner, HILTI, Husaberg, Kästle, Kettler, KTM, Moeller, Palfinger, Rika, Siteco, Stiegl, Wiberg

GESCHÄFTSFÜHRUNG — MANAGEMENT
Gerald Kiska (AUT), Gründer und CEO
Steve Masterson (UK), COO
Marcus Waldmann (GER), Partner Product Design
Paul Friedl (AUT), Partner Communication Design
Sebastien Stassin (BEL), Partner Transportation Design

GRÜNDUNGSDATUM — FOUNDATION
1990

MITARBEITER — EMPLOYEES
100+, 15 verschiedene Nationen

AUSZEICHNUNGEN — AWARDS

ANSCHRIFT — ADDRESS
St. Leonharder-Straße 4
5081 Anif-Salzburg
Austria
T +43 (0)6246 73488 - 0
F +43 (0)6246 73488 - 1044
office@kiska.com
www.kiska.com

+designing desire

Was macht ein Bergkristall in der Haute Cuisine?

+ Eine bessere Figur als vorher. Ausgehend von unserem neu kreierten Flaschendesign, haben wir für GASTEINER ein anspruchsvolles und in der Gastronomie differenzierendes Corporate Design erstellt. Vor allem der Ursprung des Wassers in den Tauern wird kristallklar über den gesamten Markenauftritt hinweg kommuniziert.

Corporate Design

Wie schnell ist Orange?

Im Gelände unschlagbar, aber wie sieht's auf der Straße aus? Um dieses Segment zu erobern, haben wir gemeinsam mit KTM einen Brandingprozess rund um neue Produktsegmente und deren Corporate Wording aufgesetzt. Damit bringen wir den orangefarbenen Motorradhersteller auf die Überholspur.

Brand Consultancy

Um wieviel Grad dreht sich ein Rasierapparat?

Genau um 180. Denn am Ende eines spannenden Marktforschungsprozesses mit Tiefeninterviews in den USA und der EU stand fest, dass unser Kunde BRAUN bei der Entwicklung eines revolutionären Rasierers an den Marktbedürfnissen vorbei produziert hätte. Mit unseren strategischen Überlegungen brachten wir die Entwickler und Designer auf den richtigen Weg und begleiteten das Produkt bis zur Marktreife.

Research

Wieviel Energie verträgt ein Anstoß?

Mehr als erwartet. adidas sucht nach neuen Wegen im Materialeinsatz und Materialmix für mehr Funktionalität neuer Produkte. Wir kennen neueste Technologien aus Forschung und Entwicklung und viele kreative Köpfe aus unterschiedlichen Branchen. Beides bringen wir zusammen und heraus kommen neue, innovative Projekte.

Innovation

Kann Styling klangvoll sein?

Aber unbedingt! Die Visual Product Language für den Hersteller von hochwertigen Kopfhörern ist entscheidend für dessen Akzeptanz und Positionierung im Markt. Für AKG haben wir nicht nur ein sehr edles, reduziertes Farbkonzept und Styling kreiert, sondern wir geben auch die Richtung für zukünftige Designkonzepte vor.

Styling

kiska.

KOREFE

FIRMENPHILOSOPHIE — CORPORATE PHILOSOPHY

KOREFE ist die integrierte Design- und Innovationsagentur von Kolle Rebbe.
Arbeitsschwerpunkte sind Corporate Identity, Corporate Design, Packaging sowie Produktinnovationen. Das Team, bestehend aus Designern, Strategen und Konzeptionern, bietet das gesamte Spektrum des Innovationsprozesses – von der Marktanalyse bis zu Naming und Design. KOREFE – Kolle Rebbe Form und Entwicklung – zählt zu den höchst ausgezeichneten Design-Agenturen Deutschlands.

KOREFE is the integrated design and innovations agency of Kolle Rebbe.
Main tasks areas are: Corporate Design, Corporate Publishing, Packaging and Product Development. The team consists of designers, strategists and conceptual designers. KOREFE provides the whole spectrum of the innovations process – from market analysis to naming and design. KOREFE – Kolle Rebbe Form und Entwicklung – counts as one of Germany's most highly awarded design agencies.

TÄTIGKEITSFELDER — DISCIPLINES

Corporate Identity, Corporate Design, Corporate Publishing, Communication Design, Markeninnovationen, Produktentwicklung, Packaging Design

REFERENZEN — REFERENCES

ADC of China, Bionade, Borkebjs, EnBW, The Deli Garage, Deka Investmentfonds, Göttinger Literaturherbst, Google, Hansgrohe, Inlingua, OTTO, Slow Fast Food, STOP THE WATER WHILE USING ME!, Warsteiner, YouTube

GESCHÄFTSFÜHRUNG — MANAGEMENT

Stefan Kolle

GRÜNDUNGSDATUM — FOUNDATION

2006

MITARBEITER — EMPLOYEES

10

AUSZEICHNUNGEN — AWARDS

ANSCHRIFT — ADDRESS

Dienerreihe 2
20457 Hamburg
Deutschland
T +49 (0) 40-325423 0
F +49 (0) 40-325423 23
info@korefe.de
www.korefe.de

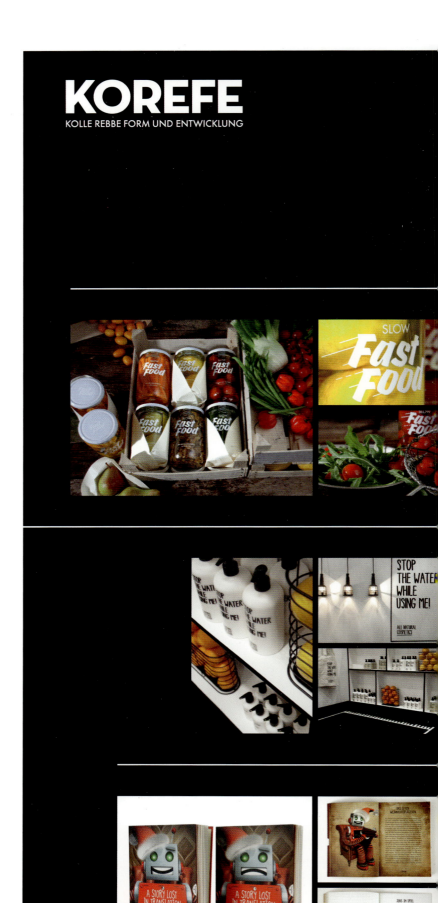

THE DELI GARAGE
ESSLACK

LOW FAST FOOD

THE DELI GARAGE
BACKSTEINE

STOP THE WATER WHILE USING ME!
ALL NATURAL COSMETICS

NLINGUA
A STORY LOST IN
TRANSLATION

BORKEBJS
DIE RÜCKKEHR DER MONSTER

MOSKITO KOMMUNIKATION UND DESIGN

FIRMENPHILOSOPHIE — CORPORATE PHILOSOPHY

Mit gezielten Stichen ein Maximum an Wirkung erzielen – für unverwechselbare Erscheinungsbilder und Unternehmensidentitäten. moskito erschafft Marken und führt sie erfolgreich: vom Design über die Inszenierung bis zur crossmedialen Strategie. Zudem sind wir stark in Themenmanagement und Corporate Publishing und damit erste Wahl auch für komplexe Aufgaben. „Wer schaffen will, muss fröhlich sein." Das leben wir tagtäglich in unserer Arbeit für kleinere, mittlere und große Unternehmen (fast) aller Branchen.

We use well-aimed strategies to create maximum impact – for unmistakable visual images and corporate identities. moskito creates and successfully manages brands: from design via careful orchestration to cross-media strategy. In addition, we are experts in issue management and corporate publishing – making us first choice for such complex tasks. "Who wants to leave a mark on the world, should be happy." We put this philosophy into practice for small, medium-sized and large corporations in (almost) every sector.

TÄTIGKEITSFELDER — DISCIPLINES

CI- und CD-Entwicklungen, Markenbildung und -führung, Crossmediale Kommunikationsstrategien, Social Media Marketing, Corporate Publishing und Direct Marketing

Corporate identity and corporate design development, brand building and brand management, cross-media communication strategy, social media marketing, corporate publishing and direct marketing.

REFERENZEN — REFERENCES

Auszug aus unserer Kundenliste / Extract from our client list:
City Airport Bremen; BEGO-Gruppe, Bremen; Creative Inneneinrichter, Darmstadt; Daimler AG, Stuttgart; EWE AG, Oldenburg; Klimahaus Bremerhaven; Roche Diagnostics Deutschland, Mannheim; swb AG, Bremen

GESCHÄFTSFÜHRUNG — MANAGEMENT

Sabine Szabó
Eckard Christiani
Axel Stamm

GRÜNDUNGSDATUM — FOUNDATION

1992

MITARBEITER — EMPLOYEES

32

AUSZEICHNUNGEN — AWARDS

ANSCHRIFT — ADDRESS

Hoerneckestraße 25–31, Schuppen 2
28217 Bremen
Deutschland
T +49 (0)421 33558-701
F +49 (0)421 33558-729
agentur@moskito.de
www.moskito.de

NODESIGN

FIRMENPHILOSOPHIE — CORPORATE PHILOSOPHY

nodesign ist ein 1995 gegründetes, derzeit vierköpfiges Designbüro, das schwerpunktmäßig für Kunden aus dem Kultursegment arbeitet. Ob Markenentwicklung oder Kampagnen, eine einfache Postkarte oder ein 1500-seitiger Katalog, schnelle Landing-Page oder hochkomplexes Online-Projekt – wir machen unsere Arbeit leidenschaftlich und souverän. Wir entwickeln ehrliche, gegen den Strom schwimmende Kommunikation und Gestaltung, die die Essenz der Identität unserer Klienten einfängt. Wir sind neugierig, wir diskutieren gerne, wir erfinden gerne, wir gehen gerne neue Wege – und gestalten dabei mit viel Spaß die Zukunft unserer Partner.

nodesign is a design agency founded in 1995. Currently manned by a team of four, the agency focuses on clients from the cultural segment. Whether brand development or campaigns, simple postcard or 1500-page catalogue, quick landing page or highly-complex online project: we pursue our work with passion and aplomb. We create honest communication and design that bucks the trend and captures the essence of our clients' identity. We are curious, we like to discuss matters, we like to invent, and we enjoy taking new paths – and in doing so we have fun moulding the future of our partners.

TÄTIGKEITSFELDER — DISCIPLINES

Design Strategy, Corporate Design, Brand Consulting, Editorial Design, Books & Catalogues-, Posters-, Webdesign, Content Management Systems, Photography

REFERENZEN — REFERENCES

2011: NRW Kultursekretariat (w), Börsenverein des Deutschen Buchhandels (p), mediacampus frankfurt (p), Auktionshaus Kaupp (p), Bielefelder Philharmoniker (p/w), Theater Bielefeld (p), Suchthilfe Direkt Essen (p/w), Ingenhoven Architekten (p), Institut für Kredit- und Finanzwirtschaft (p/w), Bündnis 90/Die Grünen Berlin

GESCHÄFTSFÜHRUNG — MANAGEMENT

HD Schellnack

GRÜNDUNGSDATUM — FOUNDATION

1995

MITARBEITER — EMPLOYEES

5

AUSZEICHNUNGEN — AWARDS

ANSCHRIFT — ADDRESS

Mintropstraße 61
45239 Essen
Deutschland
T +49 0201766569
F +49 02017509009
design@nodesign.com

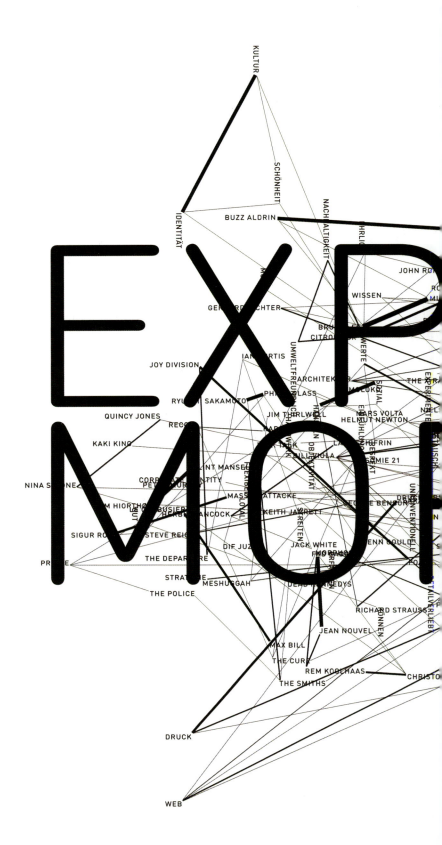

PURE COMMUNICATIONS

FIRMENPHILOSOPHIE — CORPORATE PHILOSOPHY
Pure Communications betrachtet Produkte und Dienstleistungen in ihrem Umfeld und in ihrer Unternehmenskultur. Wir konzipieren, realisieren und betreuen auf dieser Basis Corporate Designs, Printmedien- und Kommunikationsprojekte sowie Signaletikanwendungen. Unverwechselbar und formstark. Weiter sind wir stark in der künstlerischen Illustration. Kunden in der ganzen Schweiz überzeugen wir durch Kontinuität, Konsequenz und Verantwortungsbewusstsein.

TÄTIGKEITSFELDER — DISCIPLINES
Konzeption, Realisation und Betreuung von Design-, Illustrations- und Werbeprojekten, Signaletik, Art Direction

REFERENZEN — REFERENCES
Amt für Berufsbildung Graubünden, Amt für Volksschule und Sport Graubünden. Aua Extrema Expo.02, EWZ Elektrizitätswerk Zürich, Flims Laax Falera Tourismus, Frauenkulturarchiv Graubünden, ibW Höhere Fachschule Südostschweiz, intershop Holding AG, Kantonsspital Graubünden, Philipp Wieting – Werknetz Architektur, Stiftung Science et Cité Bern, VBZ Verkehrsbetriebe Zürich und viele viele mehr…

GESCHÄFTSFÜHRUNG — MANAGEMENT
Anna-Rita Stoffel

GRÜNDUNGSDATUM — FOUNDATION
1992

ANSCHRIFT — ADDRESS
Sägenstrasse 4
7007 Chur
Schweiz
T +41 (0)81 252 24 20

Seebahnstrasse 85
8003 Zürich
Schweiz
T +41 (0)44 450 47 00

info@purecommunications.ch
www.purecommunications.ch

Pure Communications. Agentur für Grafik, Werbung und Medien.
Anna-Rita Stoffel. Grafikerin SGD, CAS Art Direction, Executive Master in Design Culture.

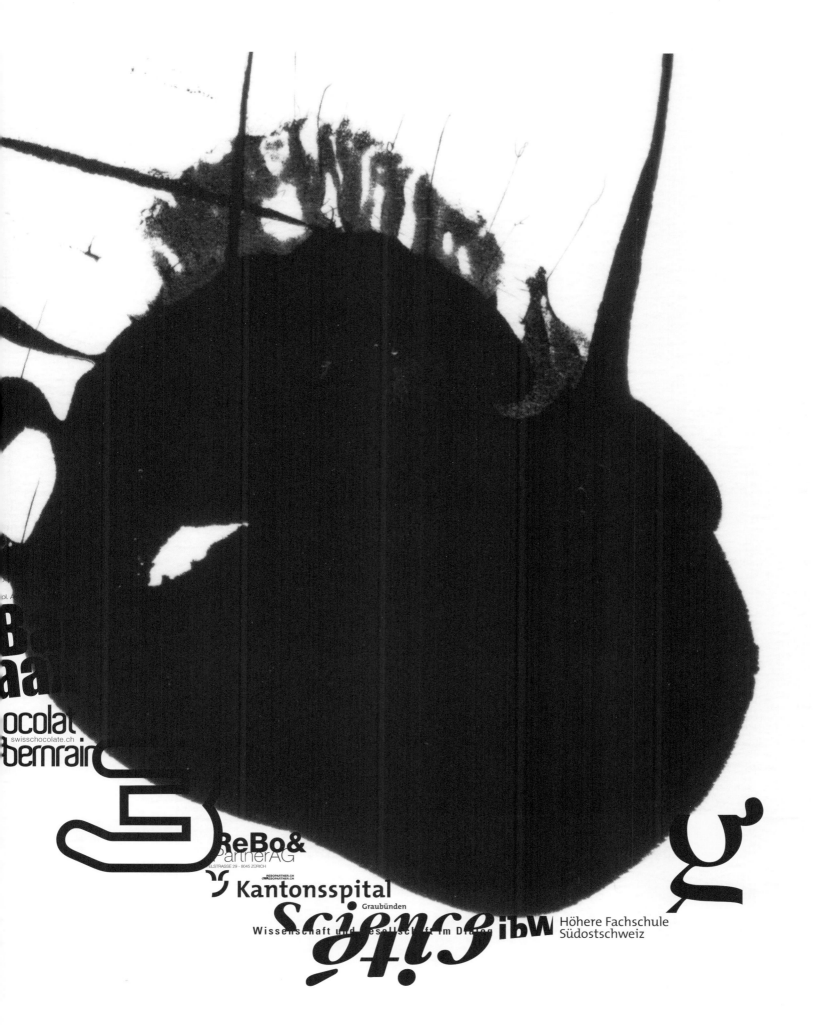

RINCÓN2

FIRMENPHILOSOPHIE — CORPORATE PHILOSOPHY
Kommunikation soll Nutzen versprechen und Nutzen begründen. Das tut sie nur, wenn sie in verschiedensten Medien für Aufmerksamkeit sorgt, zur Auseinandersetzung anregt und zur Aktion motiviert. Wirksame Kommunikation ist stimulativ, überzeugend und erinnerungsstark.
  Communication is meant to promise and deliver a benefit. In fulfilling this aim, it crucially relies on a whole host of different media to attract attention, inspire debate and motivate people to become active. Effective communication is stimulating, convincing and lingers on in people's minds.

TÄTIGKEITSFELDER — DISCIPLINES
Corporate Design, Produktkommunikation, Unternehmenskommunikation, Interior-Konzepte, Werbung, Webdesign, Webredaktion, CMS-Realisierung auf Basis des eigenen webVanilla® Systems

REFERENZEN — REFERENCES
Sportarena
Wanderzeit
Geuder
Zinser Mode
iPartment
PAN Klinik
Homes & More
NOVENTIZ
Spedition H. Freund

GESCHÄFTSFÜHRUNG — MANAGEMENT
Matthias Rincón

GRÜNDUNGSDATUM — FOUNDATION
1996

MITARBEITER — EMPLOYEES
10

AUSZEICHNUNGEN — AWARDS
  Nominiert für Designpreis Deutschland 2012
Auszeichnung der „Initiative Mittelstand 2008" für das agentureigene Content Management Sytem webVanilla®
Silber / European Design Award 2010

ANSCHRIFT — ADDRESS
Gilbachstraße 29a
50672 Köln
Deutschland
T +49 (0) 221 - 921 636 0
F +49 (0) 221 - 921 636 10
info@rincon.de
www.rincon.de

PARTNER — PARTNERS
rmh2 new media GmbH, www.rmh.de
thinc2 Kommunikation

01

   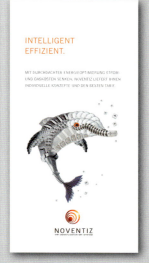

02

01 RESTAURANT CHEF
Erscheinungsbild für das erste New York-style Steakrestaurant in Köln. Das umfassende Corporate Design und Textkonzept wurde 2010 beim European Design Award in der Kategorie Brand Implementation mit Silber prämiert und ist für den Deutschen Designpreis 2012 nominiert.

02 NOVENTIZ
Kommunikationskonzept für den systemunabhängigen Ent- und Versorgungsdienstleister NOVENTIZ. Materialien wie Verpackungsabfälle, Altgeräte oder Bauschutt werden zu Tieren collagiert, deren Kerneigenschaft die Botschaft des jeweiligen Fachbereichs transportiert.

03 MODE ZINSER
Entwicklung, Redaktion und Fotoproduktion des halbjährlich erscheinenden Magazins :season von Mode Zinser in Tübingen.

03

S 82
GRAPHIC DESIGN

BÜRO SIEBER

FIRMENPHILOSOPHIE — CORPORATE PHILOSOPHY
Als strategisch ausgerichtetes Kommunikationsbüro betreuen wir unsere Auftraggeber in allen Disziplinen der Kommunikation. Wir realisieren Lösungen, die Bestand haben. Durch unsere Arbeit machen wir die Stärken und Kompetenzen unserer Auftraggeber sichtbar. Print, digitale Medien, Messeauftritte, Pressearbeit und viele weitere Bereiche greifen ineinander, Synergien entstehen.
As a strategically oriented communications office, we attend to our clients in all communication disciplines. We bring about long-lasting solutions. Through our work we visualise the strengths and skills of our clients. Print, digital media, trade show appearance, public relations and lots of other terms intertwine; synergies are created.

TÄTIGKEITSFELDER — DISCIPLINES
Kommunikationsgestaltung, Web Design, Editorial Design, Messe- und Ausstellungsgestaltung, Öffentlichkeitsarbeit.
Communication design, Web design, Editorial design, Individual tradeshow booths, Public relations.

REFERENZEN — REFERENCES
Bundesverband Lederwaren und Kunststofferzeugnisse e.V., Dometic Seitz GmbH/Electrolux-Gruppe, Edelmetallverband Schwäbisch Gmünd, Glaser-Innung Ostalb, GSB International, Hauptverband der Deutschen Schuhindustrie e.V., Hesta GmbH & Co.KG, HolzAluForum e.V., Inver GmbH, Philharmonie Schwäbisch Gmünd e.V., Schenk Werkzeug- & Maschinenbau GmbH & Co, Stadt Schwäbisch Gmünd, Verband der Fenster- und Fassadenhersteller e.V., Vistan Brillen GmbH, Ziegler GmbH & Co.KG und viele mehr / and many more

GESCHÄFTSFÜHRUNG — MANAGEMENT
Rudolf Sieber

GRÜNDUNGSDATUM — FOUNDATION
1981

MITARBEITER — EMPLOYEES
4

ANSCHRIFT — ADDRESS
Parlerstraße 34
73525 Schwäbisch Gmünd
Deutschland
T +49 (0) 7171-30040
F +49 (0) 7171-30052
info@buero-sieber.de
www.buero-sieber.de

buero-sieber.de
DESIGN & KOMMUNIKATION

Ganzseitige Anzeigen, Kataloge, Plakate, Informationsschriften u.v.m. in allen wichtigen europäischen Sprachen für **INVER**. Inver produziert Wasser- und Pulverlacke für die Industrie und die Architektur. Neben dem Stammhaus in Bologna betreibt INVER Niederlassungen und Verkaufsbüros in allen Ländern Europas.

Corporate Design, Kataloge, Displays, Plakate u.v.m. für **ROY ROBSON**-Eyewear.

Corporate Design, Anzeigen, Broschüren, redaktionelle Informationsschriften, Internet-Auftritt, Pressearbeit, Messestände für die **Gansler-Gruppe**. Die Gansler-Gruppe ist ein Verbund von vier süddeutschen Firmen im Bereich des Maschinen- und Vorrichtungsbaus (Schenk, Ziegler, KMF, Hesta).

Corporate Design, Anzeigen, Plakate, Broschüren, redaktionelle Informationsschriften, Pressearbeit u.v.m. für die GSB International.
Die GSB International (mit Mitgliedern aus mehr als 20 Nationen) erstellt Güte- und Prüfbestimmungen zur Beschichtung von Bauteilen
aus Aluminium und Stahl und sichert so den internationalen Qualitätsstandard.

Corporate Design, Kataloge, Displays, Plakate, Optiker-Onlineshop (international),
Endkunden-Website, Kinospot, Pressearbeit, Messestände u.v.m. für Vistan.
Vistan produziert und vertreibt Korrektionsfassungen und Sonnenbrillen weltweit.
Vistan belegte in der letzten „markt intern"-Umfrage Platz 2 in Deutschland.

Corporate Design, Erstellung der Gestaltungsrichtlinien für Online-Medien und Druckerzeugnisse
für den Bundesverband der Deutschen Schuhindustrie e.V. und für den Bundesverband Lederwaren und Kunststofferzeugnisse e.V.

Corporate Design, Anzeigen, Plakate, Broschüren, redaktionelle Informationsschriften,
Internet-Auftritt, Pressearbeit für das HolzAluForum. Ziel des HolzAluForums
ist die Steigerung des Bekanntheitsgrades der HolzAlu-Fenstersysteme,
die Stärkung und Unterstützung der Verarbeiter sowie die Steigerung der
Marktanteile von HolzAlu-Produkten.

Plakate, Flyer, Programmhefte, CD-Booklets, Internet-Auftritt u.v.m. für die Philharmonie Schwäbisch Gmünd.
Ein semiprofessionelles Orchester, das aus dem Kulturleben des Ostalbkreises nicht mehr wegzudenken ist.

Plakate, Einladungen u.v.m. zu den Einzelausstellungen der Galerie im Prediger Schwäbisch Gmünd.

Konzeption von Messeständen und Aufbaukoordination:
Asta Pirkkahalissa (FIN) / Caravan Salon Düsseldorf / CMT Stuttgart / CRIO Dortmund /
Eisenwarenmesse Köln / Euroguss Nürnberg / Fensterbau-Frontale Stuttgart / GIFA Düsseldorf /
IAA Hannover / K-Messe Düsseldorf / Mondo Natura Parma / Motek Stuttgart / R+T Stuttgart /
Salon de Vehicules Paris / Silmo Paris / Spielwarenmesse Nürnberg u.v.a.

S
84
GRAPHIC DESIGN

SIGN KOMMUNIKATION GMBH

FIRMENPHILOSOPHIE — CORPORATE PHILOSOPHY
Sign wurde 1972 in Frankfurt am Main gegründet. Schon in den Siebzigern gehörte die Gestaltung von Magazinen zum Leistungsspektrum. Die Gestaltung von Corporate Literature, von Kaufzeitschriften, Kunden- und Mitarbeitermagazinen bis zu gesamten Büchern ist auch heute nach einem Generationswechsel noch einer unserer Schwerpunkte. Wir bieten Grafik Design und Konzeption. Reine Gestaltungsprojekte, vom Layout bis zur Übergabe einer druckfähigen Datei. Oder wir initiieren Projekte, die ein Konzept und eine komplette Redaktion beinhalten. So oder so bemühen wir uns, aus jeder Aufgabe das Beste zu machen. Und werden auch immer wieder dafür ausgezeichnet.

Sign was founded in 1972 in Frankfurt am Main. Even in the seventies editorial design was one of our main business activities. The design of corporate literature, of various magazines and complete books is still our focal point. The second generation of Sign is about print design in all of its applications. We do classic graphic design from first layout to print production. And we initiate projects including a concept idea and a complete editorial team. Whatever the challenge, we try to give it our best. And have received several awards over the years.

TÄTIGKEITSFELDER — DISCIPLINES
Corporate Design, Design Strategy, Editorial Design, Kultur und Institution, Produktkommunikation, Unternehmenskommunikation, Verlagswesen

REFERENZEN — REFERENCES
Audi Urban Future Award, Deutsches Architekturmuseum, e15, Hear the World Initiative, Merck, Merten, Messe Frankfurt, Orben Wasseraufbereitung, Palomba Serafini Associati, Psychologie Heute, serien.lighting, Schneider Electric, Stylepark, Trademark Publishing, Verlag Hermann Schmidt Mainz, Wilkhahn, Zucchetti

GESCHÄFTSFÜHRUNG — MANAGEMENT
Antonia Henschel

GRÜNDUNGSDATUM — FOUNDATION
1972

MITARBEITER — EMPLOYEES
10

AUSZEICHNUNGEN — AWARDS

ANSCHRIFT — ADDRESS
Oskar-von-Miller-Str. 14
60314 Frankfurt am Main
Deutschland
T +49 (0) 69-944 324 0
F +49 (0) 69-944 324 50
info@sign.de
www.sign.de

STUDIO LAEIS

FIRMENPHILOSOPHIE — CORPORATE PHILOSOPHY

Studio Laeis hat die kreative Energie für Botschaften, die ankommen. Seit 1972 verhelfen wir unseren Kunden durch qualitativ hochwertige Design- und Werbekonzepte zu einem zielgruppengenauen Auftritt – und damit zu einem echten Wettbewerbsvorteil.

Studio Laeis has the creative energy for messages that hit the mark. Since 1972, our high-quality design and advertising concepts have been helping our clients to reach exactly the right target groups – and thus to achieve a real cutting edge over the competition.

TÄTIGKEITSFELDER — DISCIPLINES

Strategie und Beratung, Corporate Design, Konzeption, Design und Text für produkt- und unternehmensbezogene Werbekampagnen, Printmedien, Internetauftritte, Ausstellungen und visuelle Leitsysteme.

Strategy and consultancy, Corporate Design, conception, design and copy for product and company-related advertising campaigns, print media, websites, exhibitions and visual guidance systems.

REFERENZEN — REFERENCES

AXA Art Versicherung AG, Braunschweigisches Landesmuseum, Bundesverwaltungsamt, Deutscher Bundestag, Deutsche Fondstreuhand GmbH, GEZ Gebühreneinzugszentrale, HTB Schiffsfonds GmbH & Co. KG, HTB Immobilienfonds GmbH & Co. KG, KLINK & KRÜGER Klassische Motorboote & Automobile, Kölnisches Stadtmuseum, LANGEN Metallbau, Museumsstiftung Post und Telekommunikation, Pfeifer & Langen KG Zuckerfabrik, P. J. DAHLHAUSEN & Co. GmbH, Römisch Germanisches Museum, VITA Zahnfabrik H. Rauter GmbH & Co. KG

GESCHÄFTSFÜHRUNG — MANAGEMENT
Carsten Brandt

GRÜNDUNGSDATUM — FOUNDATION
1972

MITARBEITER — EMPLOYEES
13

AUSZEICHNUNGEN — AWARDS

ANSCHRIFT — ADDRESS
Lindenallee 43
50968 Köln
Deutschland
T +49 (0) 2 21 88 87 87-0
F +49 (0) 2 21 88 87 87-8
info@laeis.com
www.laeis.com

Ad-Game

Entwicklung eines Jump-and-Run-Games fuer das Dentalunternehmen VITA. Im Fokus des futuristischen Abenteuers: Die fortschrittliche Produktwelt des Weltmarktfuehrers fuer Zahntechnik.

STUDIO 38

FIRMENPHILOSOPHIE — CORPORATE PHILOSOPHY
Wann ist Design gutes Design? Wir denken, dass Gestaltung überzeugt, wenn sie von einer starken Idee getragen ist, die den Betrachter emotional berührt. Der Spaß an ästhetisch durchdachter, intelligenter und überraschender Kommunikation verbindet alle unsere Projekte. Und weil die Idee im Ergebnis nur dann stark wirkt, wenn auch das Detail perfekt ist, konzentrieren wir uns nach der Inspiration genauso auf effiziente, sorgfältige Projektsteuerung und Produktion.
Für uns: Moments of pleasure and treasure.

TÄTIGKEITSFELDER — DISCIPLINES
Brand Strategy & Consulting
Retail Marketing & Visual Merchandising
Branded Events & Architecture
Interactive Concepts & Campaigns
Production & Services

REFERENZEN — REFERENCES
ann taylor, banana republic, biotronik, bmw, brodowin, comma, commerzbank private banking, daimler chrysler, esteé lauder, fraunhofer institute, galeries lafayette, görtz, honda, hugo boss, keith haring foundation, lever fabergé, levi strauss, lindemann, man, messe berlin, miele, mini, neoplan, nike, panasonic, puma, rena lange, samsung, shoecom, siemens mobile, s.oliver, spm, street one, timberland, universal film

GESCHÄFTSFÜHRUNG — MANAGEMENT
Yannah Bandilla, Kathrin Janke-Bendow, Reinhard Knobelspies

GRÜNDUNGSDATUM — FOUNDATION
1996

MITARBEITER — EMPLOYEES
15

ANSCHRIFT — ADDRESS
Rosenthaler Straße 38
10178 Berlin
Deutschland
T +49 (0) 30-2851870
F +49 (0) 30-28518718
contact@studio38.de
www.studio38.de

STUDIO 38
pure communication™ gmbh

Puma / Visual Concepts

Levis / VM und POS Concepts

Panasonic / Photokina

TRAWNY / QUASS VON DEYEN

FIRMENPHILOSOPHIE — CORPORATE PHILOSOPHY

Trawny / Quass von Deyen ist eine Designagentur. Von der strategischen Beratung bis zur visuellen Umsetzung begleiten wir unsere Auftraggeber durch eine zunehmend komplexere Welt von Medienkanälen.
Wir kommunizieren visuell. Unternehmen sehen wir im Spannungsfeld von Branding und Informationsdesign. Jede Information muss ihre Adressaten in adäquater Weise erreichen – jede Information muss die Identität des Absenders in sich tragen. Das auf sensible Weise zu erreichen, verlangt Erfahrung und Kompetenz, die wir unseren Auftraggebern mit Leidenschaft zur Verfügung stellen. Dabei arbeiten wir gleichermaßen auf Papier, Bildschirmen oder im Raum.

TÄTIGKEITSFELDER — DISCIPLINES

Corporate Identity, Corporate Communication, Online media, Interface and Application Design

REFERENZEN — REFERENCES

Generali Deutschland Holding AG, Sal. Oppenheim jr. & Cie., Holzmann Medien, Canada Life Assurance Europe Limited, BNP Paribas Real Estate GmbH, Gruner + Jahr Wirtschaftspresse, Wolters Kluwer Deutschland GmbH, MCI Management Center Innsbruck, Stadtwerke Köln Konzern, IHK Köln, LWV Hessen, VKU Verband kommunaler Unternehmen, oeco capital Lebensversicherung AG, vitos GmbH, Klöckner AG, KHS GmbH, Stadt Münster, Edeka Zentrale AG & Co. KG

GESCHÄFTSFÜHRUNG — MANAGEMENT

Heinz-Willhelm Trawny, Rüdiger Quass von Deyen

GRÜNDUNGSDATUM — FOUNDATION

1989

MITARBEITER — EMPLOYEES

14

ANSCHRIFT — ADDRESS

Hohenstaufenring 42
50674 Köln
Deutschland
T +49 (0) 221 921621 0
F +49 (0) 221 921621 21
mail@kdkoeln.de
www.kdkoeln.de

INTERFACE AND APPLICATION DESIGN

EDITORIAL DESIGN

INVESTOR RELATIONS DESIGN

CORPORATE COMMUNICATION DESIGN

VISUPHIL© DESIGN STUDIOS

FIRMENPHILOSOPIE — CORPORATE PHILOSOPIE
Design ist Bestandteil jeder strategischen Markenführung. visuphil® entwickelt visuelle Kommunikation für Unternehmen und Marken und unterstützt sie dabei, ihre eigene Ausdrucksweise zu finden. Unser Ergebnis sind individuelle Design-Lösungen, die wie eine eigene visuelle Sprache wirken und sich mit jeder neuen Anwendung weiterentwickeln. Auch in der Sprache der Gestaltung entscheidet oft der richtige Ton über Erfolg oder Misserfolg. Ihn zu treffen und sich gewählt auszudrücken, ist unser Ziel.

Design is part of all strategic brand management. visuphil® develops visual communications for enterprises and brands, while also supporting them in finding their own expressive style. We produce customized design solutions that catch the eye for their own unique visual language and are advanced with every new application. In the language of design, too, it is often the right tone which is the key factor for success. Our aim is to make certain the company's tone is right, and to develop appropriate means of expressing it.

TÄTIGKEITSFELDER — DISCIPLINES
Corporate Design, Corporate Communication, Annual Reports

REFERENZEN — REFERENCES
Bosch Thermotechnik, Dewey & LeBoeuf, Essanelle Hair Group, Flick Gocke Schaumburg, Mevis Medical Solutions, Hetjens Museum, itelligence, Paion, Roth & Rau, Salans, Schott Solar

GESCHÄFTSFÜHRUNG — MANAGEMENT
Lars Monshausen

GRÜNDUNGSDATUM — FOUNDATION
2002

MITARBEITER — EMPLOYEES
4

ANSCHRIFT — ADDRESS
Konkordiastraße 20
40219 Düsseldorf
Deutschland
T +49 (0) 211-3036007
F +49 (0) 211-3036221
look@visuphil.com
visuphil.com

visuphil®

W 94
GRAPHIC DESIGN

BÜRO FÜR GESTALTUNG WANGLER & ABELE

FIRMENPHILOSOPHIE — CORPORATE PHILOSOPHY
Unsere Aufgabe ist die Visuelle Kommunikation. Wir gestalten Erscheinungsbilder und konzipieren Gestaltungsrichtlinien. Wir planen Orientierungssysteme und erarbeiten Gestaltungskonzepte für den öffentlichen Raum, für Architektur und Ausstellungen. Wir machen Strukturen sichtbar, hinterfragen, stellen Zusammenhänge dar, reduzieren auf Wesentliches, entwickeln neue Sichtweisen, vermitteln Inhalte verständlich, lesbar, frisch und kreativ.

Our task is visual communication. We transfer the image you would like to project into a visual public profile, drawing up concepts for related design guidelines. We plan signage systems, develop design concepts for public spaces, for buildings and exhibitions. We visualize structures, question, establish links, reduce to the basics, develop new approaches and convey the contents clearly, legibly, creatively and with a fresh approach.

TÄTIGKEITSFELDER — DISCIPLINES
Corporate Design, Design Guidelines, Publications, Webdesign, Signage, Exhibition Design

REFERENZEN — REFERENCES
Flughafen München, Landeshauptstadt München, BMW Welt, Olympiastadion Berlin, Parlamentsbauten Berlin, Deutscher Bundestag, Medizinische Hochschule Hannover, Universitätsklinikum Erlangen, Leibniz Universität Hannover, Messe München, Koelnmesse, Hamburg Messe, Pinakothek der Moderne, Stiftung Moritzburg Kunstmuseum des Landes Sachsen-Anhalt

GESCHÄFTSFÜHRUNG — MANAGEMENT
Ursula Wangler, Frank Abele

GRÜNDUNGSDATUM — FOUNDATION
1983 / 2000

MITARBEITER — EMPLOYEES
12

AUSZEICHNUNGEN — AWARDS

ANSCHRIFT — ADDRESS
Hohenzollernstraße 89
80796 München
Deutschland
T +49 (0) 89-273 702 60
F +49 (0) 89-273 702 80
info@bfgest.de
www.bfgest.de

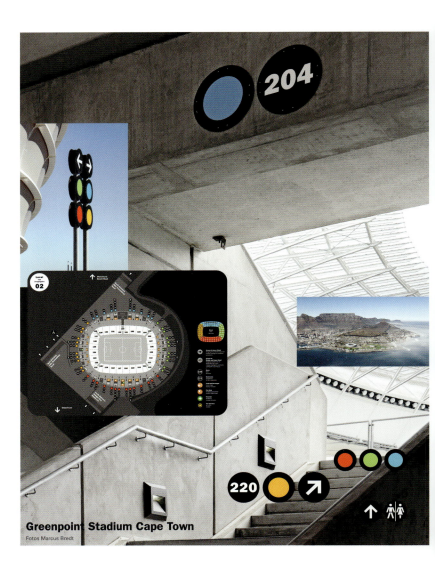

Greenpoint Stadium Cape Town
Fotos Marcus Bredt

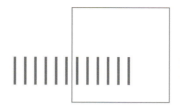

NS-Dokumentationszentrum
München

Lern- und Erinnerungsort zur
Geschichte des Nationalsozialismus

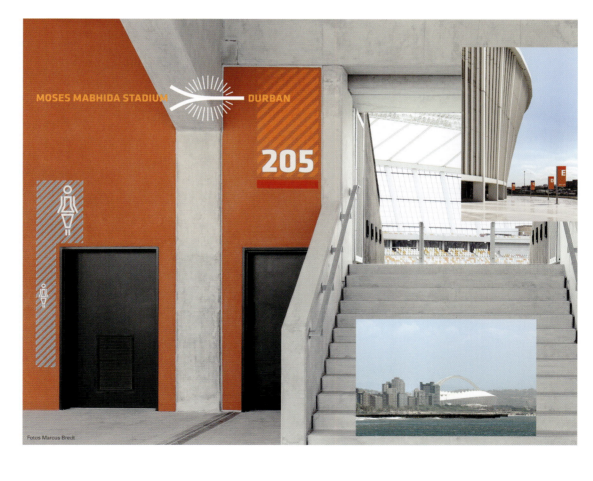

FRIEDRICH-ALEXANDER
UNIVERSITÄT
ERLANGEN-NÜRNBERG

REGELINDIS WESTPHAL GRAFIK-DESIGN

FIRMENPHILOSOPHIE — CORPORATE PHILOSOPHY

Gute Gestaltung heißt Dienstleistung. Es gilt komplexe Inhalte zielgruppenorientiert so zu organisieren und zu gestalten, dass Inhalt und Form in Einklang gebracht und damit eine perfekte gestalterische Lösung gefunden wird. Jedes Projekt hat den Anspruch auf ein Höchstmaß an konzeptionellem, grafischem und herstellerischem Fachwissen, präziser Terminüberwachung und professioneller Koordination.

Good design is a service. The trick is to organize and arrange complex contents with an eye to the target audience in such a way that content and form harmonize, producing the perfect design solution. Every project deserves the highest degree of conceptual, graphic and production expertise, the strict maintenance of deadlines and professional coordination.

TÄTIGKEITSFELDER — DISCIPLINES

Konzeption, Gestaltung und Herstellungskoordination von Medien für alle Bereiche der visuellen Kommunikation

Conception, design and production coordination for media in all fields of visual communication

REFERENZEN — REFERENCES

Auszug aus der Kundenliste / Extract from our client list:
Auswärtiges Amt, BFF Bund Freischaffender Fotodesigner, Cornelsen Verlag, Deutscher Bundestag, Der Bundesbeauftragte für die Unterlagen des Staatssicherheitsdienstes der ehemaligen DDR, Frölich&Kaufmann, Lelesken Verlag, Pyramide Verlag

GESCHÄFTSFÜHRUNG — MANAGEMENT

Regelindis Westphal

GRÜNDUNGSDATUM — FOUNDATION

1980

MITARBEITER — EMPLOYEES

4

AUSZEICHNUNGEN — AWARDS

ANSCHRIFT — ADDRESS

Willdenowstr. 5
13353 Berlin
Deutschland
T +49 (030) 4624006
F +49 (030) 4622728
mail@westphalgrafikdesign.de
www.westphalgrafikdesign.de

Eisbox / Corporate design
Adriaan Held – Kulinarische Maßarbeit / Corporate design

Die Rechte der Frauen / Ausstellungskonzept in Zusammenarbeit mit dem Deutschen Bundestag / Ausstellungsgestaltung und Typografie
For the Rights of Women / Exhibition concept in cooperation with the German Bundestag / Exhibition Design and Typography

Gestaltung von Bildbänden, Ausstellungskatalogen, Fachbüchern und Sprachlehrwerken
Illustrated book, exhibition catalogue, specialist book and language textbook design

ZWÖLFTON DESIGN

FIRMENPHILOSOPHIE — CORPORATE PHILOSOPHY
Zwölfton Design entwickelt anspruchsvolle Kommunikationslösungen für Unternehmen, Marken und Institutionen in digitalen und Printmedien. Wir praktizieren Kommunikationsdesign interdisziplinär. Das bedeutet konzeptionell: Analyse und Exploration wirtschaftlicher, wissenschaftlicher, gesellschaftlicher, technischer und ästhetischer Infrastrukturen. In der Entwicklung: Balance von Effizienz, Eleganz, intellektueller Phantasie und Mut zum Eigensinn.
 Zwölfton Design devises sophisticated communications solutions for companies, brands and institutions in the digital and print media. We see and practice communications design from an interdisciplinary viewpoint. What this means in terms of concept is the analysis and exploration of economic, scientific, social, technical and aesthetic infrastructures. And in terms of development: a balance of efficiency, elegance, intellectual imagination and the courage of our convictions.

TÄTIGKEITSFELDER — DISCIPLINES
Corporate Design, Corporate Naming & Wording, Brand Design, Printmedien-Design, Informationsarchitekturen und -design, Webdesign- und -applications

REFERENZEN — REFERENCES
U.a. Aimetis, Bertelsmann Group, come closer / sustainable design, Corinphila Auktionen AG, d.i.i. / Deutsche Invest Immobilien, Hessisches Sozialministerium, Hessisches Umweltministerium, Hessische Technologiestiftung, J.P.Morgan, Kieback & Peter, Messe Frankfurt, Neue Sentimental Film

GESCHÄFTSFÜHRUNG — MANAGEMENT
Uve Gierth

GRÜNDUNGSDATUM — FOUNDATION
2004

MITARBEITER — EMPLOYEES
5

AUSZEICHNUNGEN — AWARDS

ANSCHRIFT — ADDRESS
Sonnenberger Str. 21
65193 Wiesbaden
Deutschland
T +49 (0) 611-1885353
F +49 (0) 611-1885353
projekt@zwoelfton.de
www.zwoelfton.com

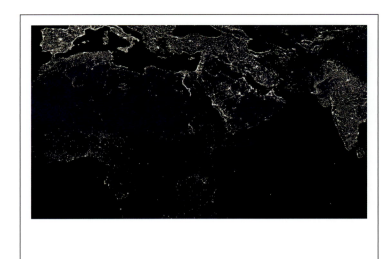
www.zwoelfton.com

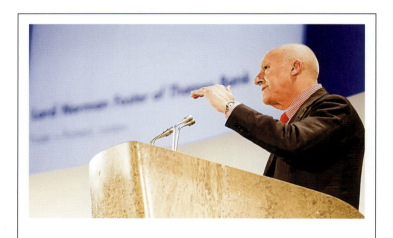
www.audiluma.de

www.kunsthochschule-mainz.de

In the making:
www.neuesentimentalfilm.com

www.opera-civil.de

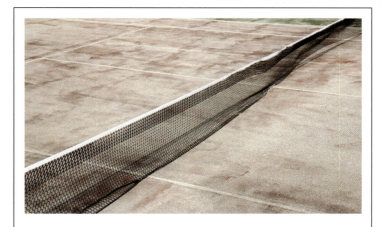

www.come-closer.net

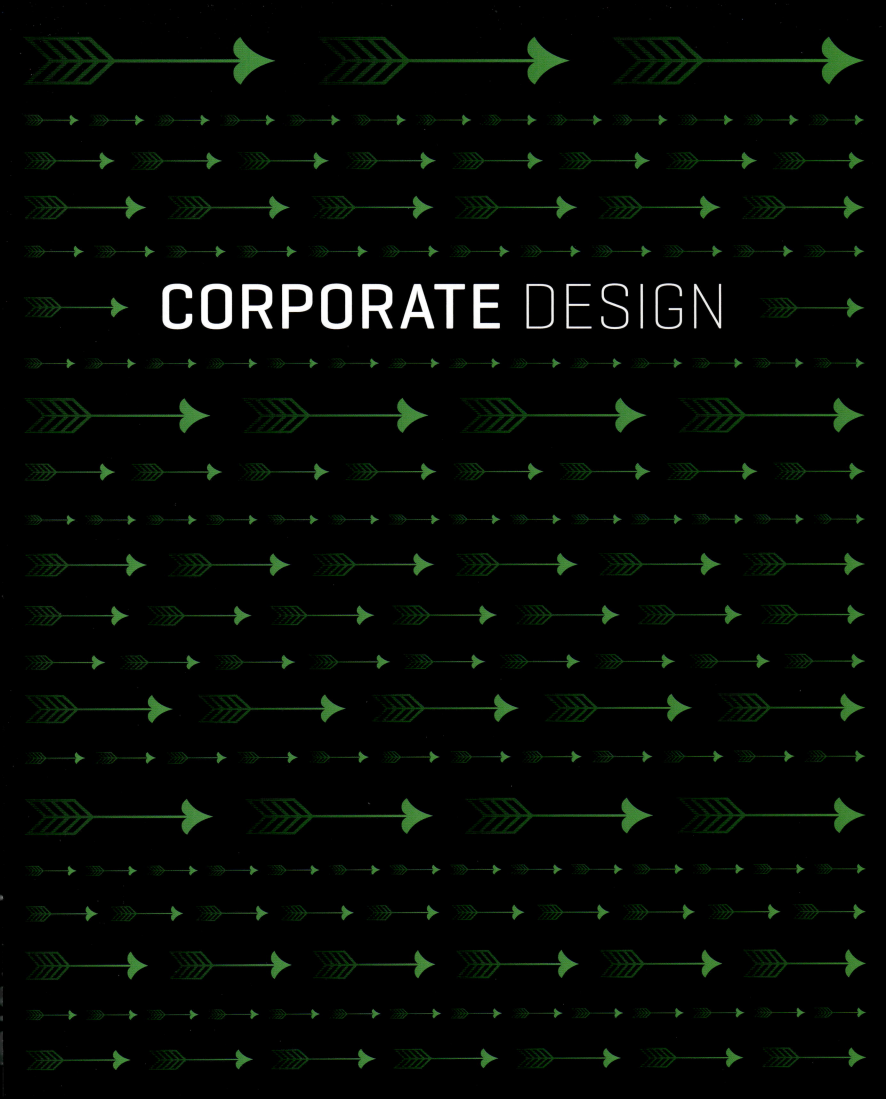
CORPORATE DESIGN

BRANDTOUCH

FIRMENPHILOSOPHIE — CORPORATE PHILOSOPHY

brandtouch creates brand value!
brandtouch verbindet Branding und Design mit der Expertise einer klassischen Kommunikationsagentur und schafft ganzheitliche Markenerlebnisse. Wir erschließen neue Wege, von innovativen Strategien bis zum einzigartigen Markenerlebnis. Im Raum, im sozialen Kontext, im Design, über alle sensorisch relevanten Dimensionen, über alle touchpoints. Die Beziehung von Konsument und Marke verstehen wir als sich ständig erneuerndes Eco-System, das um eine Markenkernidee kreist. brandtouch ist inhabergeführt, verfügt durch seinen Gründer Günter Sendlmeier über ein internationales Netzwerk und ist mit Partneragenturen in Wien, Madrid und New York verbunden.

brandtouch brings together branding and design with the expertise of a classical communication agency and accomplishes holistic brand experiences. Our standard is to open up new ways - from innovative strategies to unique brand experiences. We understand the relationship between consumer and brand as an eco-system continuously reinventing itself around the brand core idea. brandtouch is owner-operated and internationally networked through the vita of its founder Günter Sendlmeier and linked with partner agencies in Vienna, Madrid and New York.

TÄTIGKEITSFELDER — DISCIPLINES

Brand-, Design-, Communication-Strategy, Corporate Design, Packaging Design, Industrial Design, Brand Architecture, Naming, Webdesign, Advertising, Workshops

REFERENZEN — REFERENCES

Auvida, Bacardi, Beck's, Berlinale, Bet3000, Blume2000, Cotton made in Africa, Chiesi, DVAG, Dymo, Frankonia, Fürst Bismarck, Heel, Herzogtum Lauenburg, L'Oréal, Nestlé, Opel Nutzfahrzeuge, Osram, Otto Group, yalook, Philip Morris, Telefunken, TESA, Zentis and others.

GESCHÄFTSFÜHRUNG — MANAGEMENT

Günter Sendlmeier

GRÜNDUNGSDATUM — FOUNDATION

2011

AUSZEICHNUNGEN — AWARDS

ANSCHRIFT — ADDRESS

Holstenwall 7
20355 Hamburg
Deutschland
T +49 (0) 40-350 1930 0
F +49 (0) 40-350 1930 29
contact@brandtouch.com
www.brandtouch.com

Deutsche Vermögensberatung

Bacardi Deutschland — Martini Prosecco

Opel Nutzfahrzeuge

OTTO Group — yalook.com

BURKARDT | HOTZ

FIRMENPHILOSOPHIE — CORPORATE PHILOSOPHY
Mit klarem Blick, sicherem Gefühl und routinierter Hand: durchdachte Konzepte und strukturierte Inhalte, sensibel und pointiert in Form gebracht, zuverlässig und detailbewusst ausgeführt.
With a keen perception, a reliable feeling and an experienced hand: thought-out conception and well structured contents put in the right form with sensibility and pithiness, executed with reliability and awareness for detail.

TÄTIGKEITSFELDER — DISCIPLINES
Editorial Design
Corporate Design
Bücher
Plakate

REFERENZEN — REFERENCES
Bilfinger Berger
Braun
Deutsche Börse Group
Deutscher Fachverlag
Lamy
Stadt Frankfurt am Main

GESCHÄFTSFÜHRUNG — MANAGEMENT
Christoph Burkardt
Albrecht Hotz

GRÜNDUNGSDATUM — FOUNDATION
1991

ANSCHRIFT — ADDRESS
Luisenstraße 83
63067 Offenbach am Main,
Deutschland
T +49 (0) 69-881424
F +49 (0) 69-881423
mail@burkardt-hotz.de
www.burkardt-hotz.de

Mitgliederzeitschrift: AGD Quartal
Allianz deutscher Designer (AGD)

Relaunch: form – Zeitschrift für Gestaltung
Verlag Form

Editorial Design

Corporate Design, Wettbewerb
Landesregierung Hessen

Wort- und Dachmarkenentwicklung: agrarzeitung
Deutscher Fachverlag

Corporate Design

Internationales Jahrbuch Kommunikations-Design
Verlag Form

Der Frankfurt Sound – Eine Stadt und ihre Jazzgeschichte(n)
Stadt Frankfurt am Main

Bücher

Ausstellungsplakat: Fotografien aus der Sammlung F.C. Gundlach
Museum für Angewandte Kunst Frankfurt

Veranstaltungsplakat: Schultheatertage Frankfurt
Künstlerhaus Mousonturm

Plakate

B 106
CORPORATE DESIGN

BÜRO BENSELER

FIRMENPHILOSOPHIE — CORPORATE PHILOSOPHY
Systematische Analyse, Konzeption, modulare Umsetzung, ganzheitliche Beratung.

TÄTIGKEITSFELDER — DISCIPLINES
Corporate Identity, Corporate Design, Finanzkommunikation (Geschäftsberichte, Quartalsberichte, IR-Präsentationen), Corporate Social Responsibility (CSR-Berichte), Interne Kommunikation (Mitarbeiterzeitschriften etc.), Leit- und Orientierungssysteme, Farbberatung

REFERENZEN — REFERENCES
Krones, Kurtz Ersa, WashTec, Hüthig Jehle Rehm, Maurer Söhne und viele andere

GESCHÄFTSFÜHRUNG — MANAGEMENT
Thomas Benseler

GRÜNDUNGSDATUM — FOUNDATION
1985

MITARBEITER — EMPLOYEES
4

ANSCHRIFT — ADDRESS
Eckener Straße 10
86415 Mering
Deutschland
T +49 (0) 8233-4388
F +49 (0) 8233-1599
buero.benseler@t-online.de

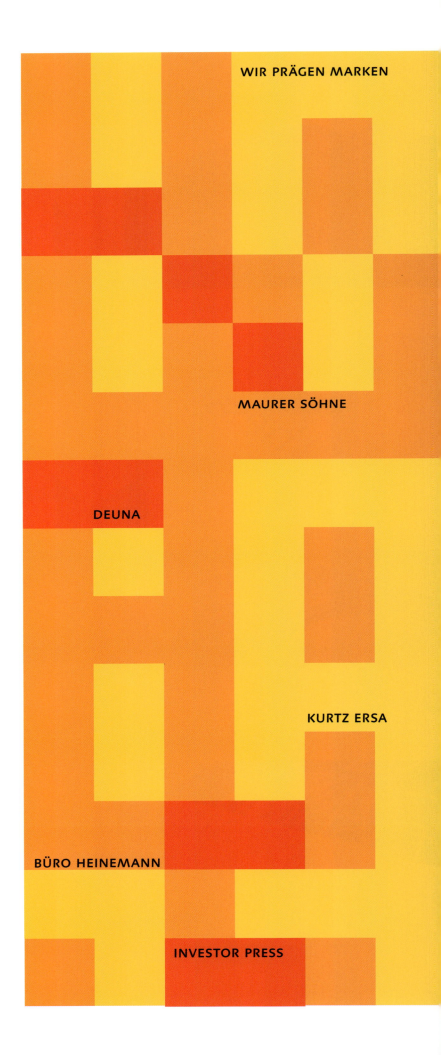

D 108
CORPORATE DESIGN

DESIGNSHIP

FIRMENPHILOSOPHIE — CORPORATE PHILOSOPHY
Unser Erfolg basiert auf der Entwicklung von Konzepten nach der designship Methode. Anforderungsspezifisch entstehen zu Beginn des Entwicklungsprozesses *technische* sowie *formale Designkonzepte*. Vorteil der Parallelentwicklung: Technische, strukturelle und ökonomische Optimierung entsteht losgelöst von emotionalen und formalen Überlegungen. Formale, emotionale, die Sinne ansprechende Lösungen entstehen ohne technische Zwänge. Die anschließende Symbiose von *technischem* und *formalem Designkonzept* schafft vielseitige Innovation und Emotion. Nationale wie internationale Design Awards und patentierbare, technische Lösungen für unsere Kunden bestätigen diesen Weg.

Our success is based to a great extent on the development of design concepts according to the designship method. Specific to the demand, at the beginning of the development process *technical* and *formal design concepts* result. Advantage of parallel development: technical, structural and economic optimisation results, detached from emotional and formal considerations. Formal, emotional solutions corresponding to meaning result without technical constraints. The subsequent symbiosis of *technical* and *formal design concept* creates varied innovation and emotion. National as well as international Design Awards and patentable, technical solutions for our customers confirm this path.

TÄTIGKEITSFELDER — DISCIPLINES
Design Strategy, Corporate Design_Consumer_ Product_ Machine_ Furniture_ Interface Design_Prototyping

REFERENZEN — REFERENCES
AL-KO, Basel Istanbul, Betek, Drossbach, Elektra Talfingen, Elero, ESTA, EWM Welding, GEZE, Harro Höfliger, Interstuhl, Iwka, Kallfass, Klöber, Köra-Packmat, PESTER Packaging, Schuler, Sedus, Teamtechnik, T-Systems, Uhlmann Pac-Systeme, Wilkhahn, WMF, Zeiss

GESCHÄFTSFÜHRUNG — MANAGEMENT
Thomas Starczewski

GRÜNDUNGSDATUM — FOUNDATION
1986

MITARBEITER — EMPLOYEES
4

AUSZEICHNUNGEN — AWARDS

ANSCHRIFT — ADDRESS
Heimstraße 29
89073 Ulm
Deutschland
T +49 (0) 731-28046
www.designship.de

1

2

3

4

5

6 7

8

1— Volume8. Interstuhl
2— Meet chair. Sedus
3— Bedienoberfläche. Teamtechnik
4— KfZ Informationssystem. T-Systems
5— Folienpacker. Kallfass
6— Anhängerkupplung. AL-KO
7— Rangiersystem. AL-KO
8— Vertikalpresse. Schuler

IFP

FIRMENPHILOSOPHIE — CORPORATE PHILOSOPHY
Customers´ best purchasing decisions are those we take for them.
—development and creation of brand design and packaging communication for more than 50 years
—experience in various sectors of industry focussing on FMCG
—customers are national and international market leaders
—presence of designs in more than 35 countries
—long-term customer relationships

TÄTIGKEITSFELDER — DISCIPLINES
Project and process management, insight-based design strategy, packaging and assortment design, brand and corporate design, shape design, naming, trade and PoS communications, final artwork, design logistics and implementation.

REFERENZEN — REFERENCES
Beiersdorf, Collonil, Kühne, Lactalis, Melitta, Molinari, Solicut, tesa, et al.

GESCHÄFTSFÜHRUNG — MANAGEMENT
Matthias Ribbe (Managing Director)
Thomas Schäfertöns (Creative Managing Director)

GRÜNDUNGSDATUM — FOUNDATION
1957

MITARBEITER — EMPLOYEES
15

AUSZEICHNUNGEN — AWARDS

ANSCHRIFT — ADDRESS
Poststraße 14-16
20354 Hamburg
Deutschland
T +49 (0) 40-3003 92-10
F +49 (0) 40-3003 92-99
info@ifp-design.de
www.ifp-design.de

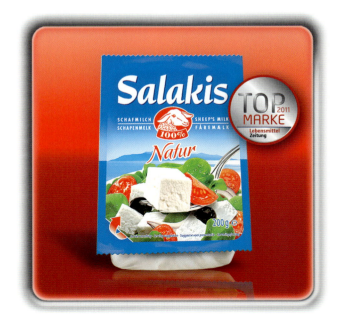

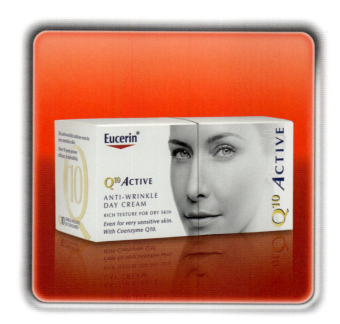

INTERBRAND

FIRMENPHILOSOPHIE — CORPORATE PHILOSOPHY
Interbrand, 1974 gegründet, hat als eine der ersten Markenberatungen überhaupt, die Bedeutung von Marken als unternehmerischen Vermögenswert erkannt und ist meinungsführend auf dem Gebiet des wertorientierten Markenmanagements. Mit insgesamt 37 Büros in 27 Ländern zählt Interbrand heute zu den führenden Markenberatungsunternehmen weltweit. Mit analytischer Präzision und kreativen Ideen macht Interbrand Marken zu einem wirkungsvollen Instrument unternehmerischen Handelns und schafft Wert für die Kunden. Interbrand veröffentlicht jährlich die allgemein anerkannte Studie „Best Global Brands". Weitere Informationen über Interbrand auf www.interbrand.com.

Founded in 1974, Interbrand is recognized for being at the forefront of the dialogue on brands as business assets. Today, Interbrand is amongst the largest brand consultancies and has grown to include 37 offices in 27 countries. The combination of rigorous strategy and analytics with world-class design creativity help its clients to create and manage brand value in all market dynamics. It is widely respected for its annual study, The Best Global Brands, and creating a broader platform for the discussion on brands in the Webby-award winning website brandchannel.com. For more on Interbrand, visit www.interbrand.com.

TÄTIGKEITSFELDER — DISCIPLINES
Analytics, Brand Engagement, Brand Strategy, Brand Valuation, Corporate Design, Digital, Digital Brand Management, Naming, Packaging Design, Retail Design, Verbal Identity

REFERENZEN — REFERENCES
ABB, Actelion, Bank Vontobel, Beiersdorf, BMW Group mit den Marken BMW, MINI und Rolls-Royce, Credit Suisse, Deutsche Telekom, Deutscher Sparkassen- und Giroverband, DMK Deutsches Milchkontor, graubünden, HUGO BOSS, JTI, Landesbank Baden-Württemberg, Lucerne Festival, Mercedes AMG, OMV, Procter & Gamble, Philips, Roche, SAP, Schindler, Siemens, Unilever, Usiminas, Wrigley u. a.

GESCHÄFTSFÜHRUNG — MANAGEMENT
Cassidy Morgan, Chief Executive Officer
Dr. Jürgen Häusler, Chairman
Andreas Rotzler, Chief Creative Officer
Richard Veit, Managing Director Hamburg
Nina Oswald, Managing Director Köln
Christoph Marti, Managing Director Moskau
Michel Gabriel, Managing Director Zürich

GRÜNDUNGSDATUM — FOUNDATION
1974

AUSZEICHNUNGEN — AWARDS

ANSCHRIFT — ADDRESS
Kirchenweg 5
8008 Zürich, Schweiz
T +41 44-388 78 78
F +41 44- 388 77 90
cee.contact@interbrand.com
www.interbrand.com

Office Hamburg:
T +49 (0)40 355 366 0
Office Köln:
T +49 (0)221 95 172 0
Office Moskau:
T +7 495 787 4600

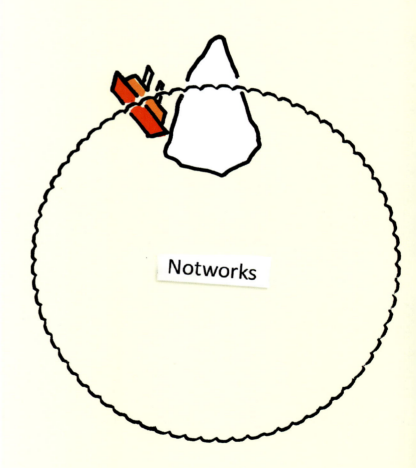

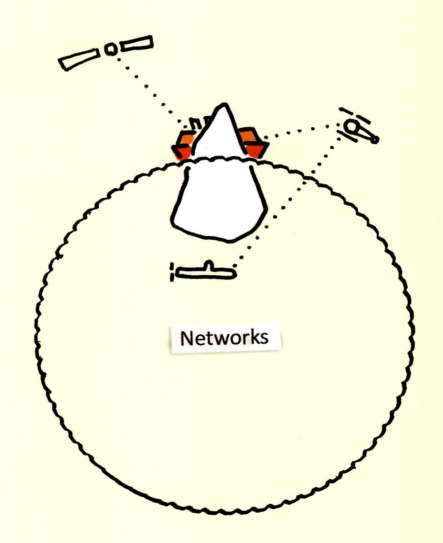

KW43 BRANDDESIGN

FIRMENPHILOSOPHIE — CORPORATE PHILOSOPHY
KW43 ist Design Value. KW43 ist der Corporate Identity und Corporate Design Spezialist der GREY Group, der nachweisbar wertvolleres Design bietet. Die Agentur kombiniert hohe gestalterische Kreativität und strategische Kompetenz zu Designlösungen, die beweisbar funktionieren und so Werte für Kunden schaffen. Design, das nicht erkennbar die gewünschte Wirkung erzeugt, ist wertlos.
Seit 1998 steht KW43 für Launch, Relaunch und die Führung von Marken. Für exzellente Designlösungen wurde die Agentur vielfach ausgezeichnet.

KW43 is Design Value. KW43 – a division of the GREY Group – is the expert in Corporate Identity and Corporate Design who knows how to create more valuable design – verifiably. The agency combines high grade creativity and strategic competence with design solutions that work and create value for customers – measurably. Design, which does not generate the intended and desired impact and value is worthless.
Since 1998, KW43 stands for launch, relaunch and management of brands. The agency has received several awards for excellent design solutions.

GESCHÄFTSFÜHRUNG — MANAGEMENT
Michael Rewald, Prof. Rüdiger Goetz

GRÜNDUNGSDATUM — FOUNDATION
1998

MITARBEITER — EMPLOYEES
25

AUSZEICHNUNGEN — AWARDS

KONTAKT — CONTACT
Platz der Ideen 1
40476 Düsseldorf
Deutschland
T +49 211 557783-0
F +49 211 557783-33
info@kw43.de
www.kw43.de

116
CORPORATE DESIGN

TÄTIGKEITSFELDER — DISCIPLINES
Strategic Brand Consultancy, Corporate Identity, Corporate Design, Employer Branding, Naming, Literature, Packaging, Promotion Material, Annual Reports / IR Communications, B2B & B2C Communications, Product Design

REFERENZEN — REFERENCES
A. Lange & Söhne, Bayer, Bogner, Deichmann, DocMorris, E.ON, Eterna, Fitness First, George Gina & Lucy, Intersnack Group, Karstadt, Merck, Mitsubishi Electric, Orthomol, Porsche Design, QVC, RTI Sports, Schlecker, Strenesse, ThyssenKrupp, Toshiba, Wentronic

Relaunch Clicktronic
Relaunch Schlecker
Launch Phorm Comfort Science

enjoy cycling & ride with comfort

schle

phorm
comfort science

MEYER-HAYOZ DESIGN ENGINEERING GROUP

FIRMENPHILOSOPHIE — CORPORATE PHILOSOPHY
Die Meyer-Hayoz Design Engineering Group zählt heute zu den international führenden Designunternehmen mit umfassenden Dienstleistungen für High-Tech-Entwicklungen, Medizinaltechnik und anspruchsvolle Konsumgüter. Das Unternehmen berät Start-up-, Klein- und mittelständische Unternehmen sowie Weltmarktführer in den Bereichen Innovationsentwicklung, Design Research, Usability Engineering sowie Brand-Strategy.

The Meyer-Hayoz Design Engineering Group ist one of the leading international design enterprises of today, with comprehensive design services for high-tech developments, medical technology and demanding consumer goods. The company advises start-up, small and medium firms as well as world brand leaders in innovation development, design reserach, usability engineering and brand strategy.

TÄTIGKEITSFELDER — DISCIPLINES
Design Strategy, Industrial Design, User Interface Design, Temporary Architecture, Communication Design

REFERENZEN — REFERENCES
ABB, Benninger, B. Braun Avitum, Ferag, Gallus Group, Groz-Beckert, Kirsten Soldering, Kistler Instrumente, Körber Schleifring Gruppe, MKR, Polytype, Rieter Textile Systems, Securiton, Siemens, Spühl, SVG Medizinsysteme, VITA Zahnfabrik u.a.

GESCHÄFTSFÜHRUNG — MANAGEMENT
Wolfgang K. Meyer-Hayoz

GRÜNDUNGSDATUM — FOUNDATION
1985 (CH) / 1989 (D)

AUSZEICHNUNGEN — AWARDS

ANSCHRIFT — ADDRESS
Zollernstrasse 26
78462 Konstanz
Deutschland
T +49 (0) 7531-90 93 0
F +49 (0) 7531-90 93 90
info.de@meyer-hayoz.com

Jägerstrasse 2
8406 Winterthur
Schweiz
T +41 (0) 52-209 01 01
F +41 (0) 52-209 01 09
info.ch@meyer-hayoz.com
www.meyer-hayoz.com

Kirsten Soldering

VITA · vPad excel
VITA Zahnfabrik H

VITAVM® · VITA Zahnfabrik H. Rauter GmbH & Co. KG

Premion Line by SVG · Corporate Design

MEYER-HAYOZ
DESIGN ENGINEERING

Design Strategy
Industrial Design
User Interface Design
Temporary Architecture
Communication Design

BLOHM
EWAG
JUNG
MÄGERLE
MIKROSA
SCHAUDT
STUDER
WALTER

Körber Schleifring Gruppe · Corporate Design

Design Strategy
Industrial Design
r Interface Design
Temporary Architecture
mmunication Design

www.swissicons.ch

GmbH & Co. KG

Parker Siemens Alliance · Exhibition-Study

parker siemens alliance

MOYSIG
RETAIL DESIGN GMBH

FIRMENPHILOSOPHIE — CORPORATE PHILOSOPHY

Die moysig retail design GmbH entwirft und realisiert weltweit Flagshipstores, Shop-in-Shop-Systeme und Showrooms sowie Modehäuser und Multilabelflächen. Neben unserem Schwerpunkt Fashion sind wir mittlerweile auch in den Bereichen Food, Kosmetik, Automobil und Multimedia aktiv. Nach über 10.000 Projekten in über 50 Ländern auf 5 Kontinenten gibt es bei uns keine Standardlösungen. Jeder Store und jeder Showroom ist für uns wie eine Premiere. Denn unserer Meinung nach ist gutes Retail Design mit einer gelungenen Theaterinszenierung vergleichbar: Ihre Marke ist der Star – und wir als Designer und Planer geben ihr die Bühne, auf der sie ihr Publikum begeistern kann.

Wir schaffen interaktionsfähige Räume, in denen Marken für Menschen erlebbar werden. Räume, die alle Sinne ansprechen, die zum Verweilen und Ausprobieren einladen; dafür arbeiten wir eng mit Ihnen zusammen. Mit viel Neugier und Leidenschaft.

Und wir können noch mehr! Wir kreieren sowohl den Raum, in dem sich Ihre Marke voll entfalten kann als auch das grafische und visuelle Kommunikationskonzept, welches die Markenbotschaft konsequent unterstützt. Unser Anspruch ist es, an Ihrem POS ein Umfeld zu schaffen, in dem sich der Kunde intensiv mit Ihrer Marke beschäftigt.

Dabei realisieren wir Ihr Projekt für Sie mit stetem Blick auf optimale Qualität, Termineinhaltung und Kostenkontrolle. Selbstverständlich gehen wir mit Ihnen auch ungewöhnliche Wege, wenn es die Aufgabe verlangt. Weltweit.

TÄTIGKEITSFELDER — DISCIPLINES

Retail Design, Rollout Planning, Projekt Management, Dachmarken Konzepte, Brand Communication

REFERENZEN — REFERENCES

Tamaris . Loewe . L'Occitane . Ludwig Beck . Puma . more & more . Leo's . Laurèl . Bugatti . Nobilia . shoecom . Nordsee . Ahlers AG . IFF . Airfield . Claire's . Pampolina . Feyenoord . Eterna . Bianca . Rituals . Tottenham Hotspurs . VFB Stuttgart . Roy Robson . Gelco . Emilio Adani . S.Oliver . Doris Hartwich . Engbers . Pikeur Eskadron . Wiesmann . Benvenuto .

GESCHÄFTSFÜHRUNG — MANAGEMENT

Dirk Moysig CEO, Stefanie Elsner, Nicole Lepper, Jörg Walter

GRÜNDUNGSDATUM — FOUNDATION

1996

MITARBEITER — EMPLOYEES

48

AUSZEICHNUNGEN — AWARDS

Janus 2008 de l'Industrie

ANSCHRIFT — ADDRESS

Vilsendorfer Straße 62
32051 Herford
Deutschland
T +49 5221. 99 446.10
F +49 5221. 99 446.11
info@moysig.de
www.moysig.de

London & Bern

Natürliche Materialien und regionaler Bezug kennzeichnen die zwei neuen Stores von Roy Robson. Ökologische Aspekte wurden zum Bestandteil des Designs. Two new Roy Robson stores are characterised by natural materials and regional references. Ecological concerns were also incorporated in the design.

Roy Robson

Location *London & Bern*

What *Stores*

Size *London 110 sqm, Bern 170 sqm*

Same standard system but with a stunningly different impact: stores in Berne and London are distinct in themselves. The Chesterfield and flock wall covering in London exude British sophistication, a cowhide and natural wood surfaces in Berne are a reflection of Switzerland's abundant natural treasures. The mosaic wall has been designed exclusively for Roy Robson and is a real eye-catcher.

Gleiches Standardsystem, aber ganz andere Wirkung: Sowohl London als auch der Berner Store haben einen unverwechselbaren Charakter. In London verleihen Ausstattungselemente wie Chesterfield-Sofa und bordeauxfarbene Tapete einen Hauch von kultivierter, britischer Behaglichkeit. In Bern herrscht mit Kuhfell und unbehandeltem Holz eine eher natürlichere Atmosphäre. Die Mosaikwand ist ein echter Blickfang und wurde exklusiv für Roy Robson entworfen.

MOYSIG
RETAIL DESIGN GMBH

FIRMENPHILOSOPHIE — CORPORATE PHILOSOPHY

moysig retail design GmbH designs and realizes worldwide flagship stores, shop-in-shop systems, showrooms, fashion stores and multi-label areas. As well as our focus on fashion, we are now also active in the fields of food, cosmetics, cars and multimedia.

However, despite being involved in over 10,000 projects in more than 50 countries on five continents we never offer standard solutions. For us, every store and every showroom feels like our first. The reason: as we see it, a store is comparable to a successful theater set. Your brand is the star -- and we, as designers and planners, offer it the kind of platform where it can delight its audience.

We create the kind of rooms where interaction is possible, enabling people to experience brands. The kind of rooms that appeal to all the senses, that invite people to linger and to try things on; and we work closely with you to achieve this. With great curiosity and passion.

And that's not all! We create not only the kind of rooms where your brand can unfold its personality completely, but also the kind of graphics and visual communications concept that consistently underscore your brand's message. What we aim to do is create the kind of environment at your POS where your customers can become completely engrossed in your brand. And we implement your project for you with a permanent regard for optimum quality, adherence to deadlines and cost control. And of course we choose unusual paths with you if the brief so demands. Worldwide.

TÄTIGKEITSFELDER — DISCIPLINES

Retail design, rollout planning, project management, umbrella brand concepts, brand communication

REFERENZEN — REFERENCES

Tamaris . Loewe . L´Occitane . Ludwig Beck . Puma . more & more . Leo's . Laurèl . Bugatti . Nobilia . shoecom . Nordsee . Ahlers AG . IFF . Airfield . Claire's . Pampolina . Feyenoord . Eterna . Bianca . Rituals . Tottenham Hotspurs . VFB Stuttgart . Roy Robson . Gelco . Emilio Adani . S.Oliver . Doris Hartwich . Engbers . Pikeur Eskadron . Wiesmann . Benvenuto .

GESCHÄFTSFÜHRUNG — MANAGEMENT

Dirk Moysig CEO, Stefanie Elsner, Nicole Lepper, Jörg Walter

GRÜNDUNGSDATUM — FOUNDATION

1996

MITARBEITER — EMPLOYEES

48

AUSZEICHNUNGEN — AWARDS

Janus 2008 de l'Industrie

ANSCHRIFT — ADDRESS

Vilsendorfer Strasse 62
32051 Herford
Deutschland
T +49 5221. 99 446.10
F +49 5221. 99 446.11
info@moysig.de
www.moysig.de

Living Kitchen

Gradlinig, offen und einladend. So präsentiert sich der Küchenhersteller Nobilia auf über 800 m2. Straight-line, open and inviting. This is how kitchen manufacturer Nobilia is presenting itself on more than 800 square metres.

→ *Eyecatcher ist die rote Bar am Eingang des Messestandes; hier können erste Kontakte geknüpft werden.* The red bar at the entrance of the booth is a real eyecatcher - perfect to establish first contacts.

Nobilia

Location *Köln/Cologne*

What *Fair*

Size *800 sqm*

Der Messestand von Nobilia war einer der größten auf der Living Kitchen in Köln. Präsentiert wurde das gesamte Spektrum von modern-trendigen bis zu klassisch-zeitlosen Einbauküchen. Dennoch sieht man dem Stand seine Größe nicht an. Statt geschlossener Wände wählten wir Lamellen, so dass man bereits von außen Einblicke in die Ausstellung bekommt. Unterstützt wird die offene und einladende Atmosphäre durch das zurückgenommene Farbkonzept, bei dem die Hausfarbe Weiß dominiert. Akzente in Rot bieten Orientierung und machen es leicht, sich zurechtzufinden.

The Nobilia booth was one of the biggest at Living Kitchen in Cologne. The whole range was presented there, reaching from modern and trendy built-kitchens up to classical and timeless ones. Nevertheless, it is not possible to estimate the size of the booth. Instead of closed walls we chose slat blinds in order to enable the visitor to view parts of the exposition already from outside. The open and inviting ambiance is supported by the discsreet colour concept, whereas the house colour white is predominating. Red accents enable you to find your way easily.

M 124
CORPORATE DESIGN

MUTHMARKEN

FIRMENPHILOSOPHIE — CORPORATE PHILOSOPHY

Mut zu starken Marken.
muthmarken ist eine Agentur für Branding, Design und Communication in Frankfurt am Main. Wir betreuen unsere Kunden ganzheitlich bei der Entwicklung und Pflege ihrer Marken – von der Markenstrategie, der Corporate Identity, der Namensentwicklung bis hin zur Umsetzung in Logo, Corporate Design und der Entwicklung von interner und externer Kommunikation. Dabei konzentrieren wir uns immer auf die Profilierung starker Marken, die besonders intensive Beziehungen zu ihren Kunden entwickeln. Beziehungsmarken sind besonders wertvoll, stark und erfolgreich im Wettbewerb. Aber es erfordert Mut, Mühe und Leidenschaft, solche Marken zu entwickeln und zu pflegen. muthmarken hilft Ihnen dabei. muthmarken ist aus dem Werbe- und Brandingbereich der ehemaligen Agentur Citigate Demuth entstanden.

Committed to strong brands.
muthmarken is a branding, design and communication agency based in Frankfurt/Main. We offer our clients all-round support in the development and maintenance of their brands – from brand strategy, corporate identity, and naming to the conception of the logo, corporate design and the development of internal and external communication. We always focus on the development of strong brands that build particularly intensive relations with their customers. Relationship brands are especially valuable, strong and successful on the market. But courage, effort and passion are required to develop and maintain them. And that is where muthmarken can help you.

muthmarken entwickelt Erscheinungsbilder, die sich durchsetzen – setzt aber auch Marken in Szene, wie zum Beispiel die Steigenberger Grandhotels.

muthmarken develops corporate design and brings brands to life, e.g. Steigenberger Grandhotels.

TÄTIGKEITSFELDER — DISCIPLINES

Branding, Namensentwicklung, Corporate Design, Corporate Identity, Markenarchitektur, Unternehmens- und Produktkommunikation, Geschäftsberichte, Messe- und Ausstellungsdesign, Webdesign.

Branding, naming, corporate design, corporate identity, brand architecture, corporate and product communication, annual reports, trade fair and exhibition design, Web design.

REFERENZEN — REFERENCES

AE&E // AirPlus International // Altana // Axaron // Bayerischer Rundfunk // BeitenBurkhardt // Bethmann Bank // BHF-BANK // Boehringer Ingelheim // Concord // Deutsche Guggenheim // DiBa // Fresenius Kabi // Freunde der Goethe-Universität // Hannoversche Leben // Hessischer Rundfunk // Hitachi Zosen Inova // Impress // ISC St. Gallen // ista // Legal & General // Lupus Alpha // Mediclin // Merck Finck & Co. // Philipps-Universität Marburg // Proactiv // Schott // Sensakus // Song Chuan // Speedel // SRH // St. Katharinen Hospiz // Steigenberger Hotel Group // Talanx // Zeiss

GESCHÄFTSFÜHRUNG — MANAGEMENT

Tina Brettschneider, Cornelius Muth

GRÜNDUNGSDATUM — FOUNDATION

2009

ANSCHRIFT — ADDRESS

Bockenheimer Landstr. 31
60325 Frankfurt am Main
Deutschland
T +49 (0) 69 17 00 71 72
F +49 (0) 69 17 00 71 33
info@muthmarken.de
www.muthmarken.de

PETER SCHMIDT GROUP

FIRMENPHILOSOPHIE — CORPORATE PHILOSOPHY
Strategische Kompetenz und ausgeprägte Leidenschaft für Design verbinden sich zu gestalterisch herausragenden und kundenspezifischen Lösungen. Der hohe Anspruch, den die Peter Schmidt Group dabei an ihre Leistungen stellt, wird durch rund hundert nationale und internationale Awards und Auszeichnungen seit der Gründung 1972 belegt.
Unparalleled strategic competence and a passion for distinct design come together to create differentiated designs and customised solutions for Peter Schmidt Group's clients. Our high standards are highlighted by the approx. 100 national and international awards that we have received since our founding in 1972.

TÄTIGKEITSFELDER — DISCIPLINES
Brand Strategy, Corporate Design, Packaging Design, Interactive Design, Corporate Architecture, Corporate Sound, Naming, Implementation

REFERENZEN — REFERENCES
BayWa, Bertelsmann, Danone, Deutsche Börse, Dr. Babor, DZ BANK, FashionDirect, Feldschlösschen, Görtz, Goethe-Institut, Haniel, Henkel, HUGO BOSS, Imperial Tobacco, ITC, Juchheim, KAO Brands, KION, Lufthansa, Media-Saturn, Nezu Museum, Postbank, REWE Group, Stiftung Preußischer Kulturbesitz, The Linde Group, Viessmann, W.L. Gore, Weleda

GESCHÄFTSFÜHRUNG — MANAGEMENT
Dr. Alex Buck, Senior Partner & Chairman
Gregor Ade, Managing Partner
Armin Angerer, Managing Partner

GRÜNDUNGSDATUM — FOUNDATION
1972

MITARBEITER — EMPLOYEES
180

AUSZEICHNUNGEN — AWARDS

ANSCHRIFT — ADDRESS
ABC-Straße 47
20354 Hamburg
Deutschland
T +49 (0) 40-441804-0
F +49 (0) 40-441804-70
info@peter-schmidt-group.de
www.peter-schmidt-group.de

WEITERE STANDORTE
Düsseldorf, Frankfurt am Main, München, Tokio, Zürich

PETER SCHMIDT GROUP

PETER SCHMIDT GROUP

180 PEOPLE WITH PASSION FOR GOOD DESIGN.
IDEAS OF CONSTANCY.

128
CORPORATE DESIGN

POLYFORM

FIRMENPHILOSOPHIE — CORPORATE PHILOSOPHY
Polyform entwickelt Erscheinungsbilder. Gemeinsam mit dem Kunden entstehen Konzepte, die einfühlsam auf den Charakter eines Unternehmens oder einer Institution eingehen und so zu durchdachten individuellen Lösungen führen. Ein Schwerpunkt des Büros ist die Erweiterung des Corporate Design in räumliche Erscheinungsbilder. Durch eine klare Kommunikationsstrategie und die überzeugende Umsetzung visueller Sprache an der Schnittstelle zur gebauten Architektur schaffen wir Identität im Raum. Es gehört zu unserer Arbeitsweise, die Projekte über alle Leistungsphasen zu betreuen.
At polyform we create visual identities. In close collaboration with the client, we develop concepts that sensitively answer the specific needs of a company or an institution. Our goal is to arrive at sophisticated individual solutions. The extension of corporate design into three dimensional space is a main focus of the office. A clear communication strategy and convincing implementation of the visual language into the environment create a strong spatial identity.

TÄTIGKEITSFELDER — DISCIPLINES
Corporate Design, Räumliche Erscheinungsbilder, Leitsysteme, Ausstellungsgestaltung, Digitale Informationssysteme

REFERENZEN — REFERENCES
Museumsinsel Berlin, Jüdisches Museum Berlin, Augustinermuseum Freiburg, Deutsches Schiffahrtsmuseum Bremerhaven, Buddenbrookhaus Lübeck, Staatsbibliothek zu Berlin, Hochschule für Wirtschaft und Technik Berlin, Potsdam Institut für Klimafolgenforschung, Paritätischer Wohlfahrtsverband Berlin, provitro GmbH

GESCHÄFTSFÜHRUNG — MANAGEMENT
Dietmar Götzelmann, Joachim Schumann, Karl Stark

GRÜNDUNGSDATUM — FOUNDATION
1999

MITARBEITER — EMPLOYEES
10

AUSZEICHNUNGEN — AWARDS

ANSCHRIFT — ADDRESS
Brunnenstraße 196
10119 Berlin
Deutschland
T +49 (0) 30 2804979-0
F +49 (0) 30 2804979-9
info@polyform-net.de
www.polyform-net.de

1

Deutsches Schiffahrtsmuseum › Geschäftspapiere

Deutsches Schiffahrtsmuseum › CD Handbuch

provitro › Produktkataloge

2 3 4 5

LOGOS
1 Deutsches Schiffahrtsmuseum – eine von drei Wellen-Variationen
2 Spastikerhilfe Berlin
3 Sinneswandel – Gesellschaft zur Förderung hörgeschädigter Menschen
4 provitro – molekularpathologisches Dienstleistungsunternehmen
5 Empire Riverside Hotel, Hamburg
6 Museen der Stadt Freiburg, Wettbewerbsbeitrag
7 Museen der Stadt Dresden
8 Ausstellung »Gesichter der Renaissance« 2011 in Berlin

6 7 8

Museumsinsel Berlin > Leitsystem Neues Museum > Leitschild innen

Deutsches Schiffahrtsmuseum > Leitschwarm

Museumsinsel Berlin > Leitsystem > Orientierungs- und Plakatstele

PROFORMA

FIRMENPHILOSOPHIE — CORPORATE PHILOSOPHY
Gutes Corporate Design erfordert die Idee für das Wesentliche und erfolgreiches Teamwork. Deshalb beginnt bei uns gutes Design im intensiven Dialog. Mit unseren Kunden und untereinander. Wir hören zu und denken mit. Wir versetzen uns in unsere Kunden und brennen für die gute Idee. So finden wir den Kern, das Herzstück. Das, was ein Unternehmen ausmacht. Daraus wird gutes Corporate Design. Wir analysieren, entwickeln individuelle Strategien und ganzheitliche Konzepte. Immer mit dem Blick auf eine schlüssige Kommunikationslösung. Immer mit Herz. Denn das Ergebnis soll nicht nur funktionieren. Es soll berühren.

TÄTIGKEITSFELDER — DISCIPLINES
Beratung: Analyse, Positionierung, Kommunikationsstrategie, Naming
Kreation: Corporate Design, Logoentwicklung, Broschüren, Webdesign
Umsetzung: Programmierung, Content Management Systeme, Druckbetreuung

REFERENZEN — REFERENCES
Medizin (Auswahl):
Institut für Laboratoriumsmedizin Berlin, CompuGROUP, Renta med, TMF e.V., VHITG, vita-x AG, QVH Qualitätsverbund, Kassenärztliche Vereinigung Rheinland-Pfalz, Laboratoriumsmedizin Dortmund, metanomics Health GmbH und viele mehr.

Institutionen/NGO/Non-Profit (Auswahl):
Bundesamt für Sicherheit in der Informationstechnik, BMBF, BMU, BMVBS, Bundesverband Solarwirtschaft, Stiftung zur Aufarbeitung der SED-Diktatur und viele mehr.

GESCHÄFTSFÜHRUNG — MANAGEMENT
Clemens Rosenow

GRÜNDUNGSDATUM — FOUNDATION
1994

MITARBEITER — EMPLOYEES
8

ANSCHRIFT — ADDRESS
Bülowstraße 66
10783 Berlin
Deutschland
T +49 (0) 30-780976-0
F +49 (0) 30-780976-77
proforma@proforma.de
www.proforma.de

KOMMUNIKATION
FÜR GESUNDHEIT

PROFORMA

GESUNDHEITSZENTRUM
Corporate Identity

VITASPORT
Der Mensch im Mittelpunkt

LABORGRUPPE
Formulare und Broschüren

SCHWANGERSCHAFTSVORSORGE

Gesetzliche Vorsorge und private Zusatzleistungen

ZAHNARZTPRAXIS
Corporate Design

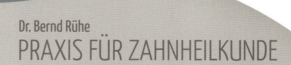

Dr. Bernd Rühe
PRAXIS FÜR ZAHNHEILKUNDE

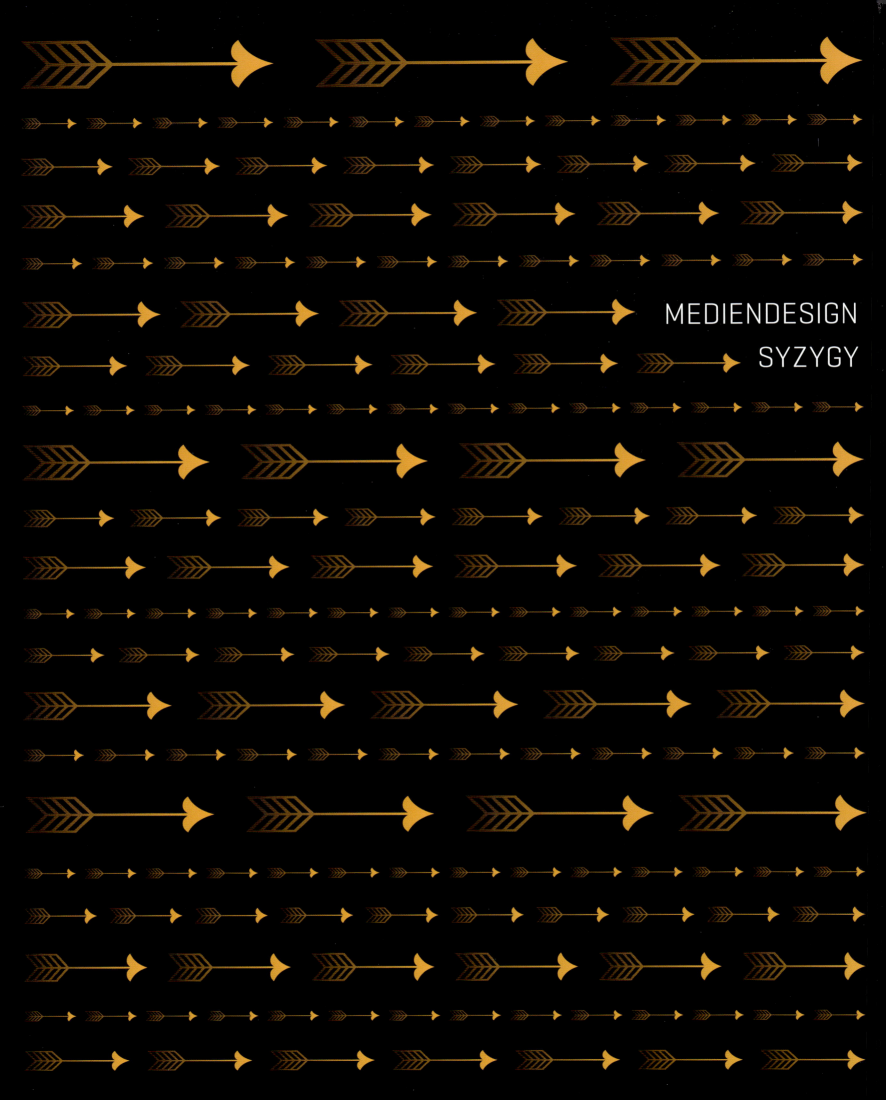

MEDIENDESIGN
SYZYGY

MEDIENDESIGN

FIRMENPHILOSOPHIE — CORPORATE PHILOSOPHY
mediendesign konzipiert, entwickelt und gestaltet interaktive Medien für Unternehmen. Interface-Design, Software-Entwicklung und Online-Marketing sind unsere Kernkompetenzen. Dabei arbeiten Designer und Techniker Hand in Hand, um Produkte zu erstellen, die dem Benutzer gerecht werden. Über 15 Jahre Erfahrung helfen Ihnen, Ihre Geschäftsabläufe zu verbessern und Ihre Kommunikationsziele einfacher und schneller zu erreichen. Wir arbeiten branchenübergreifend für Dienstleister, Hersteller und den Handel.

mediendesign creates and develops interactive media. We are specialized in user interface design, software development and online marketing. Designers and engineers work closely together to accomplish results with great user experience. Please let us know what we can do for you.

TÄTIGKEITSFELDER — DISCIPLINES
User Interface Design, Usability Engineering, Software Development, Internet Applications, Webdesign, Online Marketing, Corporate Design

REFERENZEN — REFERENCES
Beiersdorf, Danone - Nutricia, Euroassekuranz, GfK, Lions-Club LCNAD, Lufthansa - Albatros Versicherungsdienste, stayfriends, STRABAG Facility Management, Teambank

GESCHÄFTSFÜHRUNG — MANAGEMENT
Jörg Meier

GRÜNDUNGSDATUM — FOUNDATION
1994

MITARBEITER — EMPLOYEES
20

ANSCHRIFT — ADDRESS
Bartholomäusstraße 26
90489 Nürnberg
Deutschland
T +49 911 39 36 0-0
info@mediendesign.de
www.mediendesign.de

medien | design

Jörg Meier

Telefon +49 911 39 36 0-0
E-Mail meier@mediendesign.de

Für viele nur drei Farben. Für uns ein ganzes Spektrum:
Interface-Design, Software-Entwicklung und Online-Marketing.

www.mediendesign.de/rgb

S

136 MULTIMEDIA DESIGN

SYZYGY

FIRMENPHILOSOPHIE — CORPORATE PHILOSOPHY
Die Teams von SYZYGY in Bad Homburg und London gestalten und realisieren digitale Erlebniswelten, die Menschen berühren und Prozesse vereinfachen. Wir erzählen Geschichten, umwerben und verführen Nutzer, überraschen und begeistern sie. Wir inszenieren Marken und bedienen dabei die genau richtigen Kanäle, um die jeweilige Zielgruppe bestmöglich zu erreichen. Ganz gleich ob Corporate Website, Webspecial, Portal oder Online-Kampagne: Wir lieben, was wir tun.

The SYZYGY teams in Bad Homburg (near Frankfurt/Main) and London create and realise digital worlds of experience that touch people's hearts and simplify processes. We tell stories, charm and ensnare users, surprise and inspire them. We showcase brands and make use of all the right channels to reach and capture their respective audiences. Whether it's a corporate website, web special, web portal or online campaign: we love what we do!

TÄTIGKEITSFELDER — DISCIPLINES
Strategische Beratung und Markenführung. Entwicklung von Kommunikationsideen. Design und Realisierung komplexer Internet-Anwendungen. Intelligent, benutzerfreundlich, kreativ.

Strategic consulting and brand management. Development of communication ideas. Design and implementation of complex internet applications. Intelligent, user-friendly, creative.

REFERENZEN — REFERENCES
ADC Germany, Allianz, Avis, Chanel, Commerzbank, Daimler, Dolce & Gabbana, Ferrero, Fleurop, Fujifilm, Henkel, HSBC, Jägermeister, Mazda, Telefónica Germany, ZDF

KREATIVDIREKTOREN — CREATIVE DIRECTORS
Dominik Lammer
Katharina Schlungs
Victor Sahate

GRÜNDUNGSDATUM — FOUNDATION
1995

MITARBEITER — EMPLOYEES
160

AUSZEICHNUNGEN — AWARDS

ANSCHRIFT — ADDRESS
SYZYGY Deutschland GmbH
Im Atzelnest 3
61352 Bad Homburg
Deutschland
T +49 (0) 61 72 94 88 100
info@syzygy.de
www.syzygy.de

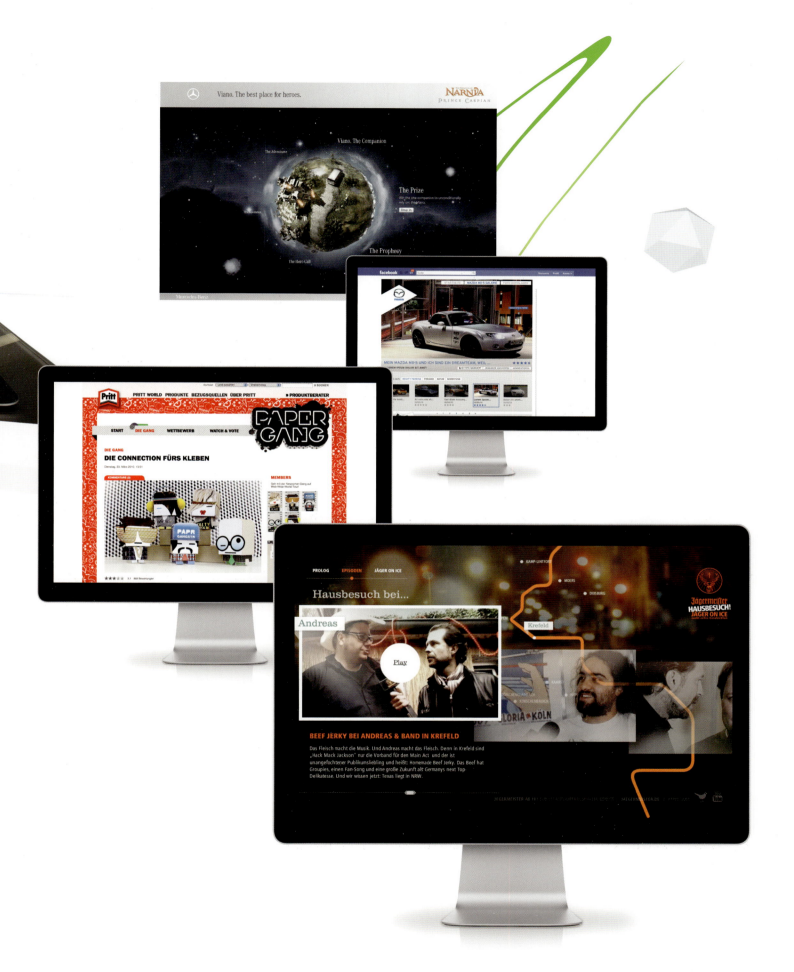

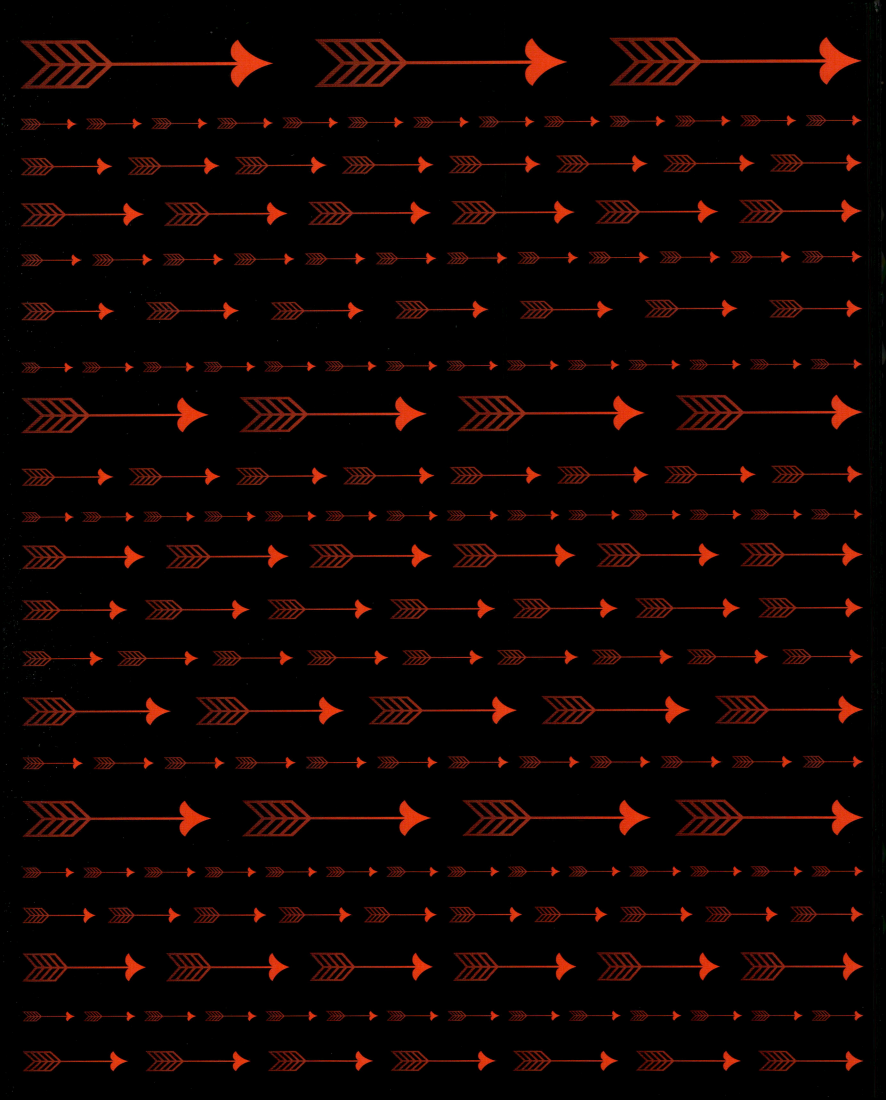

INDEX
ALPHABETICAL
FIELDS OF ACTIVITY
AWARDS

ALPHABETICAL

1

VOL. 1 140-141
100% INTERIOR SYLVIA LEYDECKER
Stammheimerstraße 113
D-50735 Köln
T +49 (0) 221 5708000
info@100interior.de
www.100interior.de

A

VOL. 2 36-37
ABERHAM
Hansaallee 42
D-40547 Düsseldorf
T +49 (0) 211 5577510
F +49 (0) 211 5577520
info@aberham-design.de
www.aberham-design.de

VOL. 2 38-39
ALLDESIGN
Schillerstraße 47
D-41061 Mönchengladbach
T +49 (0) 2161 293080
F +49 (0) 2161 2930870
info@alldesign.de
www.alldesign.de

VOL. 1 28-37
ARTEFAKT
Alte Fabrik, Liebigstraße 50-52
D-64293 Darmstadt
T +49 (0) 6151 396700
F +49 (0) 6151 3967020
public@artefakt.de
www.artefakt.de

VOL. 1 38-41
AT-DESIGN
Flugplatzstraße 111
D-90768 Fürth
T +49 (0) 911 239808-10
F +49 (0) 911 239808-29
info@atdesign.de
www.atdesign.de

B

VOL. 2 40-41
BAGGENDESIGN GMBH
Martinstraße 47-55, Haus F
D-40223 Düsseldorf
T +49 (0) 211 61717627
F +49 (0) 211 61717621
info@baggendesign.de
www.baggendesign.de

VOL. 2 42-43
BEAU BUREAU DESIGN
Händelstraße 26
D-50674 Köln
T +49 (0) 221 1686706
F +49 (0) 221 1686707
form@beau-bureau.de
www.beau-bureau.de

VOL. 1 42-43
BEGER DESIGN
Im Zollhafen 12
D-50678 Köln
T +49 (0) 221 7392366
F +49 (0) 221 7392386
info@begerdesign.de
www.begerdesign.de

VOL. 1 44-45
LOTHAR BÖHM GMBH
Große Elbstraße 281
D-22767 Hamburg
T +49 (0) 40 3910080
F +49 (0) 40 39100844
steffi.worgall@boehm-design.com
www.boehm-design.com

VOL. 2 46-47
BOTSCHAFT PROF. GERTRUD NOLTE VISUELLE KOMMUNIKATION UND BERATUNG
Talstraße 24
D-40217 Düsseldorf
T +49 (0) 211 159235-28
F +49 (0) 211 159235-46
info@botschaftnolte.de
www.botschaftnolte.de

VOL. 2 102-103
BRANDTOUCH GMBH
Holstenwall 7
D-20355 Hamburg
T +49 (0) 40 35019300
F +49 (0) 40 350193029
contact@brandtouch.com
www.brandtouch.com

VOL. 1 142-143
BRAUNWAGNER GMBH
Krefelder Straße 147
D-52070 Aachen
T +49 (0) 241 4010720
F +49 (0) 241 4010722
info@braunwagner.de
www.braunwagner.de

VOL. 2 48-49
BRÖSSKE, MEYER & RUF GMBH
Steinstraße 20
D-40212 Düsseldorf
T +49 (0) 211 17970
F +49 (0) 211 1797111
hello@bmr-design.de
www.bmr-design.de

VOL. 1 46-49
BUDDE INDUSTRIE DESIGN GMBH
Dülmener Starße 67
D-48163 Münster
T +49 (0) 2536 33060
F +49 (0) 2536 330633
info@budde-design.de
www.budde-design.de

VOL. 2 104-105
BURKARDT / HOTZ, BÜRO FÜR GESTALTUNG
Luisenstraße 83
D-63067 Offenbach
T +49 (0) 69 881424
F +49 (0) 69 881423
mail@burkardt-hotz.de
www.burkardt-hotz.de

VOL. 2 106-107
BÜRO BENSELER
Eckener Straße 10
D-86415 Mering
T +49 (0) 8233 4388
F +49 (0) 8233 1599
buero.benseler@t-online.de

VOL. 2 50-51
BÜRO GROTESK
Wissmannstraße 15
D-40219 Düsseldorf
T +49 (0) 211 1372796
hacker@buero-grotesk.de
www.buero-grotesk.de

C

VOL. 1 144-145
VOL. 2 52-53
CHRISTIAN WEISSER AGENTURGRUPPE
Marienstraße 37
D-70178 Stuttgart
T +49 (0) 711 99339130
F +49 (0) 711 99339133
info@christianweisser.de
www.christianweisser.de

VOL. 2 54-55
C & N DESIGN-AGENTUR GMBH
Wiesenau 27-29
D-60323 Frankfurt am Main
T +49 (0) 69 170085-0
F +49 (0) 69 17008520
info@c-u-n.de
www.c-u-n.de

VOL. 2 56-57
CREDO CONCEPT. COMMUNICATION
Bischof-Wolfger-Straße 30
D-94032 Passau
T +49 (0) 851 9520234
F +49 (0) 851 9520235
info@credo-concept.com
www.credo-concept.com

VOL. 2 58-59
CYCLOS DESIGN GMBH
Hafenweg 24
D-48155 Münster
T +49 (0) 251 915998-0
F +49 (0) 251 915998-10
info@cyclos-design.de
www.cyclos-design.de

D

VOL. 1 50-51
DEMAT GMBH
Carl-von-Noorden Platz 5
D-60596 Frankfurt am Main
T +49 (0) 69 2740030
F +49 (0) 69 27400340
info@demat.com
www.demat.com

VOL. 2 108-109
DESIGNSHIP
Heimstraße 29
D-89073 Ulm
T +49 (0) 731 28046
F +49 (0) 731 27380
info@designship.de
www.designship.de

VOL. 1 52-53
DIALOGFORM GMBH
Wallbergstraße 3
D-82024 Taufkirchen/Potzham
T +49 (0) 89 6128251
F +49 (0) 89 6128253
info@dialogform.de
www.dialogform.de

VOL. 2 60-61
DISEGNO GBR VISUELLE KOMMUNIKATION
Seydlitzstraße 9
D-42281 Wuppertal
T +49 (0) 202 86435
F +49 (0) 202 2802074
hallo@disenjo.de
www.disenjo.de

E

VOL. 1 54-55
EINMALEINS BÜRO FÜR GESTALTUNG
Im Weitblick 1
D-88483 Burgrieden bei Ulm
T +49 (0) 7392 969611
F +49 (0) 7392 969622
info@einmaleins.net
www.einmaleins.net

VOL. 2 62-63
ELBEDESIGNCREW GMBH
Bernhard-Nocht-Straße 99
D-20359 Hamburg
T +49 (0) 40 899690-0
F +49 (0) 40 899690-44
j.heise@elbedesigncrew.de
www.elbedesigncrew.de

VOL. 1 56-57
ENTHOVEN ASSOCIATES DESIGN CONSULTANTS
Lange Lozanastraat 254
B-2018 Antwerp
T +32 (0) 3 2035300
F +32 (0) 3 2035303
eadc@ea-dc.com
www.ea-dc.com

F

VOL. 1 58-59
HEINRICH FIEDELER INDUSTRIAL DESIGN
Adolfsallee 12
D-65185 Wiesbaden
T +49 (0) 611 9406655
F +49 (0) 611 9406654
fiedeler@heinrich-fiedeler.com
www.heinrich-fiedeler.com

VOL. 1 60-61
FRACKENPOHL POULHEIM GMBH
Luxemburger Straße 72
D-50674 Köln
T +49 (0) 221 78950550
F +49 (0) 221 78950559
info@frackenpohl-poulheim.de
www.frackenpohl-poulheim.de

H

VOL. 1 62-63
H-DESIGN
Hauptstraße 66
D-01465 Langebrück
T +49 (0) 35201 70872
F +49 (0) 35201 71314
hartig@h-design.de
www.h-design.de

VOL. 1 64-67
HENSSLER UND SCHULTHEISS FULLSERVICE PRODUCTDESIGN GMBH
Weissensteiner Straße 28
D-73525 Schwäbisch Gmünd
T +49 (0) 7171 927420
F +49 (0) 7171 9274242
info@henssler-schultheiss.de
www.henssler-schultheiss.de

VOL. 1 68-69
HUMAN INTERFACE DESIGN
Schulweg 34-36
D-20259 Hamburg
T +49 (0) 40 27877032
F +49 (0) 40 27877031
mail@human-interface.de
www.human-interface.de

VOL. 1 70-71
HYVE AG
Schellingstraße 45
D-80799 München
T +49 (0) 89 189081-100
F +49 (0) 89 189081-400
info@hyve.de
www.hyve.de

I

VOL. 1 72-73
ID DESIGN AGENTUR
Pentenrieder Straße 39
D-82152 Krailling/München
T +49 (0) 89 8571007
F +49 (0) 89 8574069
info@id-design.de
www.id-design.de

VOL. 2 64-65
IDENTIS GMBH, DESIGN-GRUPPE JOSEPH PLÖZELBAUER
Bötzinger Straße 36
D-79111 Freiburg
T +49 (0) 761 401379-0
F +49 (0) 761 42030
info@identis.de
www.identis.de

VOL. 2 110-111
IFP. INSTITUT FÜR MARKEN-, PACKUNGS- UND CORPORATE DESIGN GMBH
Poststraße 14-16
D-20354 Hamburg
T +49 (0) 40 30039210
ribbe@ifp-design.de
www.ifp-design.de

VOL. 1 74-75
INDEED INNOVATION GMBH
Holstenwall 5
D-20355 Hamburg
T +49 (0) 40 284674400
F +49 (0) 40 284674067
info@indeed-innovation.com
www.indeed-innovation.com

VOL. 2 66-67
INDEPENDENT MEDIEN-DESIGN
Widenmayerstraße 16
D-80538 München
T +49 (0) 89 2900150
F +49 (0) 89 29001515
info@independent-medien-design.de
www.independent-medien-design.de

VOL. 2 112-113
INTERBRAND
Kirchenweg 5
CH-8008 Zürich
T +41 (0) 44 3887878
F +41 (0) 44 3887790
cee.contact@interbrand.com
www.interbrand.com

J

VOL. 2 68-69
JUNGEPARTNER
Wullener Feld 60
D-58454 Witten
T +49 (0) 2302 9140910
F +49 (0) 2302 9140911
info@jungepartner.de
www.jungepartner.de

K

VOL. 1 76-77
VOL. 2 70-71
KISKA
St. Leonharder-Straße 4
A-5081 Anif-Salzburg
T +43 (0) 6246 734880
F +43 (0) 6246 734881044
office@kiska.com
www.kiska.com

VOL. 1 78-79
KORB + KORB
Schartenstrasse 3
CH-5400 Baden
T +41 (0) 56 2001420
F +41 (0) 56 2001424
info@korb-korb.ch
www.korb-korb.ch

VOL. 2 72-73
KOREFE - KOLLE REBBE FORM UND ENTWICKLUNG
Dienerreihe 2
D-20457 Hamburg
T +49 (0) 40 3254230
F +49 (0) 40 32542323
info@kolle-rebbe.de
www.korefe.de

VOL. 1 80-83
KURZ KURZ DESIGN
Engelsberg 44
D-42697 Solingen
T +49 (0) 212 336983
F +49 (0) 212 337198
info@kurz-kurz-design.de
www.kurz-kurz-design.de

VOL. 2 114-117
KW43 BRANDDESIGN
Platz der Ideen 1
D-40476 Düsseldorf
T +49 (0) 211 5577830
F +49 (0) 211 55778333
contact@kw43.de
www.kw43.de

L

VOL. 1 84-85
LSG SKY CHEFS CATERING LOGISTICS GMBH
Dornhofstraße 40
D-63263 Neu-Isenburg
T +49 (0) 6102 240609
F +49 (0) 6102 240603
design@lsgskychefs.com
www.lsgskychefs.com

M

VOL. 2 134-135
MEDIEN|DESIGN
Bartholomäusstraße 26
D-90489 Nürnberg
T +49 (0) 911 393600
F +49 (0) 911 3936024
info@mediendesign.de
www.mediendesign.de

VOL. 1 86-87
VOL. 2 118-119
MEYER-HAYOZ DESIGN ENGINEERING GROUP
Zollernstraße 26
D-78462 Konstanz
T +49 (0) 7531 90930
F +49 (0) 7531 909390
info.de@meyer-hayoz.com
www.meyer-hayoz.com

VOL. 1 86-87
VOL. 2 118-119
MEYER-HAYOZ DESIGN ENGINEERING GROUP
Jägerstrasse 2
CH-8406 Winterthur
T +41 (0) 52 2090101
F +41 (0) 52 2090109
info.ch@meyer-hayoz.com
www.meyer-hayoz.com

VOL. 1 88-89
DESIGNBÜRO WOLFGANG C.R. MEZGER
Olgastraße 12
D-73033 Göppingen
T +49 (0) 7161 89998
F +49 (0) 7161 89988
info@design-mezger.com
www.design-mezger.com

VOL. 1 146-147
MILLA & PARTNER
Heusteigstraße 44
D-70180 Stuttgart
T +49 (0) 711 9667372
F +49 (0) 711 6075076
c.scholl@milla.de
www.milla.de

VOL. 2 74-75
MOSKITO KOMMUNIKATION UND DESIGN
Hoerneckestraße 25-31, Schuppen 2
D-28217 Bremen
T +49 (0) 421 33558-701
F +49 (0) 421 33558-729
agentur@moskito.de
www.moskito.de

VOL. 2 120-123
MOYSIG RETAIL DESIGN GMBH
Vilsendorferstraße 62
D-32049 Herford
T +49 (0) 5221 9944610
F +49 (0) 5221 99446911
michael-bonschenk@moysig.de
www.moysig.de

VOL. 2 124-125
MUTHMARKEN GMBH
Bockenheimer Landstraße 31
D-60325 Frankfurt am Main
T +49 (0) 69 17007172
F +49 (0) 69 17007133
info@muthmarken.de
www.muthmarken.de

N

VOL. 1 90-91
NEXUS PRODUCT DESIGN
Muerfeldstraße 22
D-33719 Bielefeld
T +49 (0) 521 333352
F +49 (0) 521 333382
info@nexusproductdesign.de
www.nexusproductdesign.de

VOL. 2 76-77
NODESIGN
Mintropstraße 61
D-45239 Essen
T +49 (0) 201 766569
F +49 (0) 201 7509009
design@nodesign.com
www.nodesign.com

P

VOL. 1 92-95
PEARL CREATIVE
Königsallee 57
D-71638 Ludwigsburg
T +49 (0) 7141 4887490
F +49 (0) 7141 4887499
info@pearlcreative.com
www.pearlcreative.com

VOL. 2 126-127
PETER SCHMIDT GROUP
ABC-Straße 47
D-20354 Hamburg
T+ 49 (0) 40 4418040
F+ 49 (0) 40 44180470
info@peter-schmidt-group.de
www.peter-schmidt-group.de

VOL. 1 96-97
INDUSTRIEFORMEN PIOREK
Bahnhofstraße 50
D-65185 Wiesbaden
T +49 (0) 611 373925
F +49 (0) 611 375418
pio@piorek.com
www.piorek.com

VOL. 2 128-129
POLYFORM
Brunnenstraße 196
D-10119 Berlin
T +49 (0) 30 28049790
info@polyform-net.de
www.polyform-net.de

VOL. 2 130-131
PROFORMA
Bülowstraße 66
D-10783 Berlin
T +49 (0) 30 780976-0
F +49 (0) 30 780976-77
proforma@proforma.de
www.proforma.de

VOL. 1 98-101
**PRO INDUSTRIA
BÜRO FÜR INDUSTRIAL DESIGN MANFRED LANG**
Oberwiehler Straße 92
D-51674 Wiehl
T +49 (0) 2262 72750
F +49 (0) 2262 727520
info@proindustria.de
www.produstria.de

VOL. 1 102-103
PULS PRODUKT DESIGN
Nieder-Ramstädter-Straße 247
D-64285 Darmstadt
T +49 (0) 6151 42876813
F +49 (0) 6151 42876820
info@puls-design.de
www.puls-design.de

VOL. 2 78-79
PURE COMMUNICATIONS
Sägenstrasse 4
CH-7007 Chur
T +41 (0) 81 2522420
info@purecommunications.ch
www.purecommunications.ch

VOL. 2 78-79
PURE COMMUNICATIONS
Seebahnstrasse 85
CH-8003 Zürich
T +41 (0) 44 4504700
info@purecommunications.ch
www.purecommunications.ch

Q

VOL. 1 104-105
QUADESIGN PARTNER AG
Untermüli 5
CH-6300 Zug
T +41 (0) 41 7608670
F +41 (0) 41 7608673
design@quadesign.ch
www.quadesign.ch

R

VOL. 1 106-107
REALDESIGN GMBH
Käthe-Kollwitz-Straße 80
D-04275 Leipzig
T +49 (0) 341 9832026
F +49 (0) 341 9832027
info@realdesign.de
www.realdesign.de

VOL. 2 80-81
RINCÓN2 MEDIEN GMBH
Gilbachstraße 29a
D-50672 Köln
T +49 (0) 221 9216360
F +49 (0) 221 92163610
info@rincon.de
www.rincon.de

S

VOL. 1 108-109
SCALA DESIGN TECHNISCHE PRODUKTENTWICKLUNG GMBH
Wolf-Hirth-Straße 23
D-71034 Böblingen
T +49 (0) 7031 226908
F +49 (0) 7031 227809
scala@scala-design.de
www.scala-design.de

VOL. 1 110-111, 148-149
MARIUS SCHREYER DESIGN
Rechenbergallee 9
D-90491 Nürnberg
T +49 (0) 911 2878120
F +49 (0) 911 2878122
info@marius-schreyer-design.de
www.marius-schreyer-design.de

VOL. 2 82-83
BÜRO SIEBER
Parlerstraße 34
D-73525 Schwäbisch Gmünd
T +49 (0) 7171 30040
F +49 (0) 7171 30052
info@buero-sieber.de
www.buero-sieber.de

ALPHABETICAL

VOL. 2 84-85
SIGN KOMMUNIKATION GMBH
Oskar-von Miller-Straße 14
D-60314 Frankfurt am Main
T +49 (0) 69 9443240
F +49 (0) 69 94432450
info@sign.de
www.sign.de

VOL. 1 112-113
UWE SPANNAGEL ™
Engelbertstraße 21
D-50674 Köln
T +49 (0) 221 2400497
F +49 (0) 221 2400498
office@uwespannagel.com
www.uwespannagel.com

VOL. 1 114-115
STRUPPLER INDUSTRIEDESIGN
Senftlstraße 7
D-81541 München
T +49 (0) 89 8905870
F +49 (0) 89 89058725
info@strupplerdesign.de
www.strupplerdesign.de

VOL. 2 86-87
STUDIO LAEIS
Lindenallee 43
D-50968 Köln
T +49 (0) 221 8887870
F +49 (0) 221 8887878
info@laeis.com
www.laeis.com

VOL. 2 88-89
**STUDIO 38
PURE COMMUNICATION GMBH**
Rosenthaler Straße 38
D-10178 Berlin
T +49 (0) 30 2851870
F +49 (0) 30 28518718
contact@studio38.de
www.studio38.de

VOL. 1 116-117
**HEINRICH STUKENKEMPER
INDUSTRIAL DESIGN TEAM**
Am Foederturm 8
D-44575 Castrop-Rauxel
T +49 (0) 2305 43495
F +49 (0) 2305 922110
stukenkemper@t-online.de
www.stukenkemper.com

VOL. 1 118-119
SYNAPSIS DESIGN GMBH
Teckstraße 56
D-70190 Stuttgart
T +49 (0) 711 2621131
F +49 (0) 711 2622670
mail@synapsisdesign.com
www.synapsisdesign.com

VOL. 1 120-121
SYNPRO DESIGN
Groß-Buchholzer Straße 33b
D-30655 Hannover
T +49 (0) 511 5414411
F +49 (0) 511 5414414
info@synpro-design.de
www.synpro-design.de

VOL. 2 136-137
SYZYGY DEUTSCHLAND GMBH
Im Atzelnest 3
D-61352 Bad Homburg
T +49 (0) 6172 9488100
F +49 (0) 6172 9488270
info@syzygy.net
www.syzygy.net

T

VOL. 1 122-123
TEAGUE GMBH
Oskar-Schlemmer-Straße 15
D-80807 München
T +49 (0) 89 3866790
F +49 (0) 89 38667910
info.europe@teague.com
www.teague.com

VOL. 1 124-125
TEAMS-DESIGN GMBH
Kollwitzstraße 1
D-73728 Esslingen am Neckar
T +49 (0) 711 3517650
F +49 (0) 711 35176525
info@teams-design.de
www.teamsdesign.com

VOL. 1 126-127
**TINZ. *DCC*
DESIGN CREATIVE CENTER
TOMORROW´S INNOVATION
NEEDS ZEST!**
Ferdinand-Lassalle-Straße 16
D-72770 Reutlingen
T +49 (0) 7121 958810
F +49 (0) 7121 958812
bhtinz@yahoo.de
www.tinzdcc.de

VOL. 2 90-91
**TRAWNY / QUASS VON DEYEN,
KONZEPTION + DESIGN**
Hohenstaufenring 42
D-50674 Köln
T +49 (0) 221 9216210
F +49 (0) 221 92162121
schueller@kdkoeln.de
www.kdkoeln.de

VOL. 1 128-131
TRICON DESIGN AG
Bahnhofstraße 26
D-72138 Kirchentellinsfurt
T +49 (0) 7121 680870
F +49 (0) 7121 6808720
info@tricon-design.de
www.tricon-design.de

VOL. 1 126-127
**T.V.T SWISSCONSULT GMBH
TARGETED VALUE ON TIME**
Chaltenbodenstrasse 4B
CH-8834 Schindellegi
T +41 (0) 43 8881040
F +41 (0) 43 8881044
mail@tvtswiss.com
www.tvtswiss.com

V

VOL. 2 92-93
VISUPHIL® DESIGN STUDIOS
Konkordiastraße 20
D-40219 Düsseldorf
T +49 (0) 211 3036007
F +49 (0) 211 3036221
look@visuphil.com
www.visuphil.com

W

VOL. 1 150-153
WALBERT-SCHMITZ
Gut-Knapp-Straße 8-14
D-52080 Aachen
T +49 (0) 2405 60020
F +49 (0) 2405 600290
info@walbert-schmitz.de
www.walbert-schmitz.de

VOL. 2 94-95
**BÜRO FÜR GESTALTUNG
WANGLER & ABELE**
Hohenzollernstraße 89
D-80796 München
T +49 (0) 89 27370260
F +49 (0) 89 27370280
info@bfgest.de
www.bfgest.de

VOL. 1 132-133
ANDREAS WEBER DESIGN
Madeleine-Rouff-Straße 26a
D-82211 Herrsching am
Ammersee
T +49 (0) 8152 90980
F +49 (0) 8152 90989
info@andreasweberdesign.de
www.andreasweberdesign.de

VOL. 2 96-97
**REGELINDIS WESTPHAL
GRAFIK-DESIGN**
Willdenowstraße 5
D-13353 Berlin
T +49 (0) 30 4624006
F +49 (0) 30 4622728
mail@westphalgrafikdesign.de
www.westphalgrafikdesign.de

VOL. 1 134-135
WHITE ID
Vordere Schmiedgasse 36-1
D-73525 Schwäbisch Gmünd
T +49 (0) 7171 877184
F +49 (0) 7171 877185
info@white-id.com
www.white-id.com

VOL. 1 136-137
**WIEGE ENTWICKLUNGS-
GESELLSCHAFT MBH**
Hauptstraße 81
D-31848 Bad Münder
T +49 (0) 5042 999900
G +49 (0) 5042 999901
wiege@wiege.com
www.wiege.com

Z

VOL. 2 98-99
ZWÖLFTON DESIGN
Sonnenberger Straße 21
D-65193 Wiesbaden
T +49 (0) 611 1885353
F +49 (0) 611 1885354
projekt@zwoelfton.de
www.zwoelfton.com

FIELDS OF ACTIVITY

				INDUSTRIEDESIGN	ACCESSOIRES, SCHMUCK	BÜRO, OBJEKT	FREIZEIT, SPORT, SPIEL	GEBÄUDETECHNIK	HANDWERK, INDUSTRIE	HAUSHALT, KÜCHE, BAD	MEDIEN, KOMMUNIKATION	MEDIZIN, REHABILITATION	PUBLIC DESIGN	TRANSPORT	WOHNEN	GRAFIKDESIGN	ARCHITEKTUR	CORPORATE DESIGN	ILLUSTRATION	INFORMATIONSSYSTEME	KULTUR UND INSTITUTIONEN
AUSTRIA																					
5000	**KISKA**	St. Leonharder-Straße 4 A-5081 Anif-Salzburg	VOL. 1 76–77 VOL. 2 70–71				X	X	X	X	X	X		X				X			
BELGIUM																					
2000	**ENTHOVEN ASSOCIATES DESIGN CONSULTANTS**	Lange Lozanastraat 254 B-2018 Antwerp	VOL. 1 56–57	X		X	X	X	X	X	X	X	X	X	X						
GERMANY																					
00000	**H-DESIGN**	Hauptstraße 66 D-01465 Langebrück	VOL. 1 62–63				X	X	X	X		X	X	X				X	X	X	X
	REALDESIGN GMBH	Käthe-Kollwitz-Straße 80 D-04275 Leipzig	VOL. 1 106–107	X												X					
10000	**POLYFORM**	Brunnenstraße 196 D-10119 Berlin	VOL. 2 128–129									X				X		X		X	X
	STUDIO 38 PURE COMMUNICATION GMBH	Rosenthaler Straße 38 D-10178 Berlin	VOL. 2 88–89	X												X		X	X		
	PROFORMA	Bülowstraße 66 D-10783 Berlin	VOL. 2 130–131															X		X	X
	REGELINDIS WESTPHAL GRAFIK-DESIGN	Willdenowstraße 5 D-13353 Berlin	VOL. 2 96–97													X	X	X	X	X	X
20000	**HUMAN INTERFACE DESIGN**	Schulweg 34–36 D-20259 Hamburg	VOL. 1 68–69	X				X	X	X	X					X		X			
	IFP. INSTITUT FÜR MARKEN-, PACKUNGS- UND CORPORATE DESIGN GMBH	Poststraße 14–16 D-20354 Hamburg	VOL. 2 110–111															X			
	PETER SCHMIDT GROUP	ABC-Straße 47 D-20354 Hamburg	VOL. 2 126–127													X		X		X	X
	BRANDTOUCH GMBH	Holstenwall 7 D-20355 Hamburg	VOL. 2 102–103													X		X		X	
	INDEED INNOVATION GMBH	Holstenwall 5 D-20355 Hamburg	VOL. 1 74–75	X		X	X	X	X	X	X	X	X	X	X						

Kategorie	1	2	3	4	5	6	7	8	9
PRODUKTKOMMUNIKATION	X	X		X	X		X		
UNTERNEHMENSKOMMUNIKATION	X	X		X	X				
VERLAGSWESEN	X								
VERPACKUNG	X	X		X				X	
WERBUNG	X	X		X					X
LOGISTIK UND ORGANISATION									
AUSSTELLUNGSDESIGN		X		X	X	X			
FULL SERVICE MESSEAUFTRITTE							X		
NORM/SYSTEM MESSESTÄNDE					X				
INDIVIDUELLE MESSESTÄNDE	X			X		X			
SONDERARCHITEKTUR [MEHRSTÖCKIG]	X								
DISPLAYS	X			X	X	X			
MÖBLIERUNG UND DEKORATION					X				
BELEUCHTUNG, TON, AV									
EVENTS/VERANSTALTUNGEN (KONZEPT, PLANUNG, DURCHFÜHRUNG)									
AUSSTELLUNGEN FLÄCHENVERMITTLUNG (KONZEPT, PLANUNG, DURCHFÜHRUNG)				X	X				
UNTERHALTUNGSELEKTRONIK									
MULTIMEDIA	X			X	X			X	
ANIMATION			X						X
AUDIVISUELLE MEDIEN									X
CD ROM					X	X			
INFORMATIONSDESIGN	X	X		X	X	X			X
WEB DESIGN	X	X		X	X	X			X
MODE/TEXTIL DESIGN									
BEKLEIDUNG			X		X				
BEKLEIDUNGSSTOFFE			X						
HEIMTEXTILIEN			X						
LABELS									
MOTIVDRUCK, STICKEREI					X				
SCHNITTGESTALTUNG					X				
FOTO DESIGN									
ARCHITEKTUR									
EINRICHTUNGEN									
LANDSCHAFTEN									
MENSCHEN									
MODE									
NAHRUNGSMITTEL									
REDAKTION			X						
STILLLEBEN			X						
TRANSPORT									

FIELDS OF ACTIVITY

Company	Ref	INDUSTRIEDESIGN	ACCESSOIRES, SCHMUCK	BÜRO, OBJEKT	FREIZEIT, SPORT, SPIEL	GEBÄUDETECHNIK	HANDWERK, INDUSTRIE	HAUSHALT, KÜCHE, BAD	MEDIEN, KOMMUNIKATION	MEDIZIN, REHABILITATION	PUBLIC DESIGN	TRANSPORT	WOHNEN	GRAFIKDESIGN	ARCHITEKTUR	CORPORATE DESIGN	ILLUSTRATION	INFORMATIONSSYSTEME	KULTUR UND INSTITUTIONEN
ELBEDESIGNCREW GMBH Bernhard-Nocht-Straße 99, D-20359 Hamburg	VOL. 2 62–63													X		X			
KOREFE – KOLLE REBBE FORM UND ENTWICKLUNG Dienerreihe 2, D-20457 Hamburg	VOL. 2 72–73							X	X					X		X		X	
LOTHAR BÖHM GMBH Große Elbstraße 281, D-22767 Hamburg	VOL. 1 44–45	X					X	X			X			X			X		
MOSKITO KOMMUNIKATION UND DESIGN Hoerneckestraße 25–31, Schuppen 2, D-28217 Bremen	VOL. 2 74–75													X		X			
SYNPRO DESIGN Groß-Buchholzer Straße 33b, D-30655 Hannover	VOL. 1 120–121	X														X	X		
WIEGE ENTWICKLUNGSGESELLSCHAFT MBH Hauptstraße 81, D-31848 Bad Münder	VOL. 1 136–137	X																	
MOYSIG RETAIL DESIGN GMBH Vilsendorferstraße 62, D-32049 Herford	VOL. 2 120–123														X	X			
NEXUS PRODUCT DESIGN Muerfeldstraße 22, D-33719 Bielefeld	VOL. 1 90–91	X		X		X	X	X		X		X							
BRÖSSKE, MEYER & RUF GMBH Steinstraße 20, D-40212 Düsseldorf	VOL. 2 48–49															X			
BOTSCHAFT PROF. GERTRUD NOLTE VISUELLE KOMMUNIKATION UND BERATUNG Talstraße 24, D-40217 Düsseldorf	VOL. 2 46–47															X		X	
BÜRO GROTESK Wissmannstraße 15, D-40219 Düsseldorf	VOL. 2 50–51													X		X		X	
VISUPHIL® DESIGN STUDIOS Konkordiastraße 20, D-40219 Düsseldorf	VOL. 2 92–93													X		X		X	
BAGGENDESIGN GMBH Martinstraße 47–55, Haus F, D-40223 Düsseldorf	VOL. 2 40–41													X		X		X	
KW43 BRANDDESIGN Platz der Ideen 1, D-40476 Düsseldorf	VOL. 2 114–117															X			
ABERHAM Hansaallee 42, D-40547 Düsseldorf	VOL. 2 36–37														X	X		X	

	C1	C2	C3	C4	C5	C6	C7	C8
PRODUKTKOMMUNIKATION	X	X		X		X		X
UNTERNEHMENSKOMMUNIKATION	X	X	X	X		X	X	
VERLAGSWESEN		X				X		
VERPACKUNG	X	X		X		X		X
WERBUNG	X			X		X	X	
LOGISTIK UND ORGANISATION								
AUSSTELLUNGSDESIGN		X					X	
FULL SERVICE MESSEAUFTRITTE								
NORM / SYSTEM MESSESTÄNDE								
INDIVIDUELLE MESSESTÄNDE		X		X				
SONDERARCHITEKTUR (MEHRSTÖCKIG)								
DISPLAYS								X
MÖBLIERUNG UND DEKORATION								
BELEUCHTUNG, TON, AV								
EVENTS/VERANSTALTUNGEN (KONZEPT, PLANUNG, DURCHFÜHRUNG)								
AUSSTELLUNGEN FLÄCHENVERMITTLUNG (KONZEPT, PLANUNG, DURCHFÜHRUNG)								
UNTERHALTUNGSELEKTRONIK								
MULTIMEDIA		X					X	
ANIMATION								
AUDIVISUELLE MEDIEN								
CD ROM								
INFORMATIONSDESIGN							X	
WEB DESIGN		X					X	
MODE / TEXTIL DESIGN								
BEKLEIDUNG								
BEKLEIDUNGSSTOFFE								
HEIMTEXTILIEN								
LABELS								
MOTIVDRUCK, STICKEREI								
SCHNITTGESTALTUNG								
FOTO DESIGN								
ARCHITEKTUR								
EINRICHTUNGEN								
LANDSCHAFTEN								
MENSCHEN								
MODE								
NAHRUNGSMITTEL								
REDAKTION								
STILLLEBEN								
TRANSPORT								

FIELDS OF ACTIVITY

Company	Ref	INDUSTRIEDESIGN	ACCESSOIRES, SCHMUCK	BÜRO, OBJEKT	FREIZEIT, SPORT, SPIEL	GEBÄUDETECHNIK	HANDWERK, INDUSTRIE	HAUSHALT, KÜCHE, BAD	MEDIEN, KOMMUNIKATION	MEDIZIN, REHABILITATION	PUBLIC DESIGN	TRANSPORT	WOHNEN	GRAFIKDESIGN	ARCHITEKTUR	CORPORATE DESIGN	ILLUSTRATION	INFORMATIONSSYSTEME	KULTUR UND INSTITUTIONEN
ALLDESIGN Schillerstraße 47, D-41061 Mönchengladbach	VOL. 2 38-39										X			X	X	X	X	X	X
DISEGNO GBR VISUELLE KOMMUNIKATION Seydlitzstraße 9, D-42281 Wuppertal	VOL. 2 60-61													X		X	X	X	
KURZ KURZ DESIGN Engelsberg 44, D-42697 Solingen	VOL. 1 80-83	X		X	X	X	X	X		X		X	X	X		X	X		
HEINRICH STUKENKEMPER INDUSTRIAL DESIGN TEAM Am Foederturm 8, D-44575 Castrop-Rauxel	VOL. 1 116-117				X			X	X			X	X						
NODESIGN Mintropstraße 61, D-45239 Essen	VOL. 2 76-77													X	X	X	X	X	X
CYCLOS DESIGN GMBH Hafenweg 24, D-48155 Münster	VOL. 2 58-59													X	X	X	X	X	X
BUDDE INDUSTRIE DESIGN GMBH Dülmener Staße 67, D-48163 Münster	VOL. 1 46-49	X		X	X	X		X	X	X		X				X	X		
RINCÓN2 MEDIEN GMBH Gilbachstraße 29a, D-50672 Köln	VOL. 2 80-81													X		X			
BEAU BUREAU DESIGN Händelstraße 26, D-50674 Köln	VOL. 2 42-43													X			X	X	
FRACKENPOHL POULHEIM GMBH Luxemburger Straße 72, D-50674 Köln	VOL. 1 60-61	X			X	X		X	X	X									
UWE SPANNAGEL TM Engelbertstraße 21, D-50674 Köln	VOL. 1 112-113			X				X	X	X	X		X						
TRAWNY / QUASS VON DEYEN, KONZEPTION + DESIGN Hohenstaufenring 42, D-50674 Köln	VOL. 2 90-91													X		X			
BEGER DESIGN Im Zollhafen 12, D-50678 Köln	VOL. 1 42-43	X		X	X	X	X	X	X			X				X	X		
100% INTERIOR SYLVIA LEYDECKER Stammheimerstraße 113, D-50735 Köln	VOL. 1 140-141	X	X										X	X	X				
STUDIO LAEIS Lindenallee 43, D-50968 Köln	VOL. 2 86-87													X		X	X	X	X

	C1	C2	C3	C4	C5	C6	C7	C8
PRODUKTKOMMUNIKATION	X			X				X
UNTERNEHMENSKOMMUNIKATION	X	X		X	X		X	X
VERLAGSWESEN	X	X		X	X			X
VERPACKUNG	X			X				X
WERBUNG				X	X	X		X
LOGISTIK UND ORGANISATION				X				X
AUSSTELLUNGSDESIGN								
FULL SERVICE MESSEAUFTRITTE	X			X		X		
NORM/SYSTEM MESSESTÄNDE	X							
INDIVIDUELLE MESSESTÄNDE	X			X		X	X	
SONDERARCHITEKTUR (MEHRSTÖCKIG)								
DISPLAYS	X				X			X
MÖBLIERUNG UND DEKORATION					X			
BELEUCHTUNG, TON, AV								
EVENTS/VERANSTALTUNGEN (KONZEPT, PLANUNG, DURCHFÜHRUNG)					X		X	
AUSSTELLUNGEN FLÄCHENVERMITTLUNG (KONZEPT, PLANUNG, DURCHFÜHRUNG)								
UNTERHALTUNGSELEKTRONIK								X
MULTIMEDIA			X	X	X		X	X
ANIMATION		X	X	X	X		X	X
AUDIVISUELLE MEDIEN					X			X
CD ROM					X			X
INFORMATIONSDESIGN	X			X	X		X	X
WEB DESIGN	X			X	X	X	X	X
MODE/TEXTIL DESIGN	X							
BEKLEIDUNG							X	
BEKLEIDUNGSSTOFFE								
HEIMTEXTILIEN	X							
LABELS								
MOTIVDRUCK, STICKEREI								
SCHNITTGESTALTUNG								
FOTO DESIGN							X	X
ARCHITEKTUR					X			
EINRICHTUNGEN					X			
LANDSCHAFTEN					X			
MENSCHEN					X			
MODE					X			
NAHRUNGSMITTEL					X			
REDAKTION								
STILLLEBEN					X		X	
TRANSPORT								

150
FIELDS OF ACTIVITY

			INDUSTRIEDESIGN	ACCESSOIRES, SCHMUCK	BÜRO, OBJEKT	FREIZEIT, SPORT, SPIEL	GEBÄUDETECHNIK	HANDWERK, INDUSTRIE	HAUSHALT, KÜCHE, BAD	MEDIEN, KOMMUNIKATION	MEDIZIN, REHABILITATION	PUBLIC DESIGN	TRANSPORT	WOHNEN	GRAFIKDESIGN	ARCHITEKTUR	CORPORATE DESIGN	ILLUSTRATION	INFORMATIONSSYSTEME	KULTUR UND INSTITUTIONEN
	PRO INDUSTRIA BÜRO FÜR INDUSTRIAL DESIGN MANFRED LANG Oberwiehler Straße 92 D-51674 Wiehl	VOL. 1 98-101	X	X	X	X	X	X	X	X	X	X	X							
	BRAUNWAGNER GMBH Krefelder Straße 147 D-52070 Aachen	VOL. 1 142-143	X				X			X	X	X			X	X	X		X	
	WALBERT-SCHMITZ Gut-Knapp-Straße 8 - 14 D-52080 Aachen	VOL. 1 150-153																		
	JUNGEPARTNER Wullener Feld 60 D-58454 Witten	VOL. 2 68-69													X		X			X
60000	**SIGN KOMMUNIKATION GMBH** Oskar-von-Miller-Straße 14 D-60314 Frankfurt am Main	VOL. 2 84-85													X	X	X			X
	C & N DESIGN-AGENTUR GMBH Wiesenau 27 - 29 D-60323 Frankfurt am Main	VOL. 2 54-55													X		X			
	MUTHMARKEN GMBH Bockenheimer Landstraße 31 D-60325 Frankfurt am Main	VOL. 2 124-125													X		X			
	DEMAT GMBH Carl-von-Noorden Platz 5 D-60596 Frankfurt am Main	VOL. 1 50-51																		
	SYZYGY DEUTSCHLAND GMBH Im Atzelnest 3 D-61352 Bad Homburg	VOL. 2 136-137																		
	BURKARDT / HOTZ, BÜRO FÜR GESTALTUNG Luisenstraße 83 D-63067 Offenbach	VOL. 2 104-105													X		X	X	X	
	LSG SKY CHEFS CATERING LOGISTICS GMBH Dornhofstraße 40 D-63263 Neu-Isenburg	VOL. 1 84-85		X		X		X				X			X		X	X		
	PULS PRODUKT DESIGN Nieder-Ramstädter-Straße 247 D-64285 Darmstadt	VOL. 1 102-103	X		X			X		X	X	X					X		X	
	ARTEFAKT Alte Fabrik, Liebigstraße 50-52 D-64293 Darmstadt	VOL. 1 28-37	X		X	X		X		X	X	X	X							
	HEINRICH FIEDELER INDUSTRIAL DESIGN Adolfsallee 12 D-65185 Wiesbaden	VOL. 1 58-59	X	X		X	X	X		X	X	X	X		X		X			
	INDUSTRIEFORMEN PIOREK Bahnhofstraße 50 D-65185 Wiesbaden	VOL. 1 96-97	X		X	X	X	X			X	X	X	X						

Category	C1	C2	C3	C4	C5	C6	C7	C8	C9	C10
PRODUKTKOMMUNIKATION										X
UNTERNEHMENSKOMMUNIKATION						X		X		X
VERLAGSWESEN		X						X		
VERPACKUNG		X						X		
WERBUNG								X		
LOGISTIK UND ORGANISATION		X						X		
AUSSTELLUNGSDESIGN	X	X				X	X	X		X
FULL SERVICE MESSEAUFTRITTE		X	X			X	X			
NORM/SYSTEM MESSESTÄNDE		X	X				X	X		
INDIVIDUELLE MESSESTÄNDE	X	X	X			X	X	X		X
SONDERARCHITEKTUR (MEHRSTÖCKIG)		X	X				X			
DISPLAYS		X	X			X		X		
MÖBLIERUNG UND DEKORATION		X	X							X
BELEUCHTUNG, TON, AV		X								
EVENTS/VERANSTALTUNGEN (KONZEPT, PLANUNG, DURCHFÜHRUNG)		X				X	X			X
AUSSTELLUNGEN FLÄCHENVERMITTLUNG (KONZEPT, PLANUNG, DURCHFÜHRUNG)						X				X
UNTERHALTUNGSELEKTRONIK		X								
MULTIMEDIA		X						X		
ANIMATION		X								
AUDIVISUELLE MEDIEN		X								
CD ROM					X					
INFORMATIONSDESIGN		X						X		X
WEB DESIGN					X			X		X
MODE/TEXTIL DESIGN										X
BEKLEIDUNG										X
BEKLEIDUNGSSTOFFE										
HEIMTEXTILIEN										X
LABELS										
MOTIVDRUCK, STICKEREI										
SCHNITTGESTALTUNG										
FOTO DESIGN										
ARCHITEKTUR										
EINRICHTUNGEN										
LANDSCHAFTEN										
MENSCHEN										
MODE										
NAHRUNGSMITTEL										X
REDAKTION										
STILLLEBEN										X
TRANSPORT										

FIELDS OF ACTIVITY

			INDUSTRIEDESIGN	ACCESSOIRES, SCHMUCK	BÜRO, OBJEKT	FREIZEIT, SPORT, SPIEL	GEBÄUDETECHNIK	HANDWERK, INDUSTRIE	HAUSHALT, KÜCHE, BAD	MEDIEN, KOMMUNIKATION	MEDIZIN, REHABILITATION	PUBLIC DESIGN	TRANSPORT	WOHNEN	GRAFIKDESIGN	ARCHITEKTUR	CORPORATE DESIGN	ILLUSTRATION	INFORMATIONSSYSTEME	KULTUR UND INSTITUTIONEN
	ZWÖLFTON DESIGN Sonnenberger Straße 21 D-65193 Wiesbaden	VOL. 2 98-99													X		X	X	X	X
70000	**CHRISTIAN WEISSER AGENTURGRUPPE** Marienstraße 37 D-70178 Stuttgart	VOL. 1 144-145 VOL. 2 52-53													X		X		X	
	MILLA & PARTNER Heusteigstraße 44 D-70180 Stuttgart	VOL. 1 146-147																		
	SYNAPSIS DESIGN GMBH Teckstraße 56 D-70190 Stuttgart	VOL. 1 118-119	X	X	X	X	X	X	X	X	X	X	X	X			X	X		
	SCALA DESIGN TECHNISCHE PRODUKTENTWICKLUNG GMBH Wolf-Hirth-Straße 23 D-71034 Böblingen	VOL. 1 108-109	X		X	X	X	X		X	X	X	X				X	X		
	PEARL CREATIVE Königsallee 57 D-71638 Ludwigsburg	VOL. 1 92-95	X		X	X	X	X	X	X	X	X	X	X			X			
	TRICON DESIGN AG Bahnhofstraße 26 D-72138 Kirchentellinsfurt	VOL. 1 128-131									X	X								
	TINZ. DCC. DESIGN CREATIVE CENTER. TOMORROW'S INNOVATION NEEDS ZEST! Ferdinand-Lassalle-Straße 16 D-72770 Reutlingen	VOL. 1 126-127																		
	DESIGNBÜRO WOLFGANG C.R. MEZGER Olgastraße 12 D-73033 Göppingen	VOL. 1 88-89			X				X					X						
	HENSSLER UND SCHULTHEISS FULLSERVICE PRODUCTDESIGN GMBH Weissensteiner Straße 28 D-73525 Schwäbisch Gmünd	VOL. 1 64-67	X			X		X	X		X		X							
	BUERO-SIEBER.DE Parlerstraße 34 D-73525 Schwäbisch Gmünd	VOL. 2 82-83													X		X	X	X	X
	WHITE ID Vordere Schmiedgasse 36-1 D-73525 Schwäbisch Gmünd	VOL. 1 134-135	X																	
	TEAMS-DESIGN GMBH Kollwitzstraße 1 D-73728 Esslingen am Neckar	VOL. 1 124-125	X			X	X	X	X	X	X	X			X		X	X	X	X
	MEYER-HAYOZ DESIGN ENGINEERING GROUP Zollernstraße 26 D-78462 Konstanz	VOL. 1 86-87 VOL. 2 118-119	X		X	X	X	X		X	X	X	X		X	X	X		X	X
	IDENTIS GMBH, DESIGN-GRUPPE JOSEPH PLÖZELBAUER Bötzinger Straße 36 D-79111 Freiburg	VOL. 2 64-65													X	X	X		X	

Service Category	C1	C2	C3	C4	C5	C6	C7	C8	C9
PRODUKTKOMMUNIKATION	X						X	X	
UNTERNEHMENSKOMMUNIKATION	X						X	X	X
VERLAGSWESEN	X						X		
VERPACKUNG	X						X		X
WERBUNG	X						X		X
LOGISTIK UND ORGANISATION	X								
AUSSTELLUNGSDESIGN	X	X			X	X	X		X
FULL SERVICE MESSEAUFTRITTE			X			X	X		
NORM/SYSTEM MESSESTÄNDE	X					X			
INDIVIDUELLE MESSESTÄNDE	X				X	X	X	X	
SONDERARCHITEKTUR [MEHRSTÖCKIG]	X					X			
DISPLAYS	X				X		X	X	
MÖBLIERUNG UND DEKORATION	X								
BELEUCHTUNG, TON, AV						X		X	
EVENTS/VERANSTALTUNGEN (KONZEPT, PLANUNG, DURCHFÜHRUNG)						X	X	X	
AUSSTELLUNGEN FLÄCHENVERMITTLUNG (KONZEPT, PLANUNG, DURCHFÜHRUNG)							X		
UNTERHALTUNGSELEKTRONIK									
MULTIMEDIA	X					X			X
ANIMATION	X								
AUDIVISUELLE MEDIEN	X					X			
CD ROM	X								
INFORMATIONSDESIGN	X							X	X
WEB DESIGN	X		X					X	X
MODE/TEXTIL DESIGN									
BEKLEIDUNG									
BEKLEIDUNGSSTOFFE									
HEIMTEXTILIEN									
LABELS									
MOTIVDRUCK, STICKEREI									
SCHNITTGESTALTUNG									
FOTO DESIGN	X								
ARCHITEKTUR	X								
EINRICHTUNGEN									
LANDSCHAFTEN									
MENSCHEN									
MODE									
NAHRUNGSMITTEL									
REDAKTION									
STILLLEBEN									
TRANSPORT									

FIELDS OF ACTIVITY

				INDUSTRIEDESIGN	ACCESSOIRES, SCHMUCK	BÜRO, OBJEKT	FREIZEIT, SPORT, SPIEL	GEBÄUDETECHNIK	HANDWERK, INDUSTRIE	HAUSHALT, KÜCHE, BAD	MEDIEN, KOMMUNIKATION	MEDIZIN, REHABILITATION	PUBLIC DESIGN	TRANSPORT	WOHNEN	GRAFIKDESIGN	ARCHITEKTUR	CORPORATE DESIGN	ILLUSTRATION	INFORMATIONSSYSTEME	KULTUR UND INSTITUTIONEN
80000	**INDEPENDENT MEDIEN-DESIGN** Widenmayerstraße 16 D-80538 München		VOL. 2 66-67															X	X		X
	BÜRO FÜR GESTALTUNG WANGLER & ABELE Hohenzollernstraße 89 D-80796 München		VOL. 2 94-95	X							X		X								
	HYVE AG Schellingstraße 45 D-80799 München		VOL. 1 70-71	X		X	X		X	X	X	X									
	TEAGUE GMBH Oskar-Schlemmer-Straße 15 D-80807 München		VOL. 1 122-123	X	X	X	X		X	X	X	X	X	X				X			
	STRUPPLER INDUSTRIEDESIGN Senftlstraße 7 D-81541 München		VOL. 1 114-115	X	X	X	X	X	X	X	X	X	X	X							
	DIALOGFORM GMBH Wallbergstraße 3 D-82024 Taufkirchen/Potzham		VOL. 1 52-53			X	X		X					X	X			X	X	X	
	ID DESIGN AGENTUR Pentenrieder Straße 39 D-82152 Krailling/München		VOL. 1 72-73	X		X	X	X	X	X	X	X	X	X	X	X	X	X	X	X	X
	ANDREAS WEBER DESIGN Madeleine-Rouff-Straße 26a D-82211 Herrsching am Ammersee		VOL. 1 132-133	X		X			X					X	X		X				
	BÜRO BENSELER Eckener Straße 10 D-86415 Mering		VOL. 2 106-107													X		X			
	EINMALEINS BÜRO FÜR GESTALTUNG Im Weitblick 1 D-88483 Burgrieden bei Ulm		VOL. 1 54-55	X			X	X	X			X			X		X	X	X	X	
	DESIGNSHIP Heimstraße 29 D-89073 Ulm		VOL. 2 108-109																		
90000	**MEDIEN|DESIGN** Bartholomäusstraße 26 D-90489 Nürnberg		VOL. 2 134-135												X		X		X	X	
	MARIUS SCHREYER DESIGN Rechenbergallee 9 D-90491 Nürnberg		VOL. 1 110-111 VOL. 1 148-149	X		X		X	X		X		X	X	X						
	AT-DESIGN Flugplatzstraße 111 D-90768 Fürth		VOL. 1 38-41	X					X			X	X	X				X			
	CREDO CONCEPT.COMMUNICATION Bischof-Wolfger-Straße 30 D-94032 Passau		VOL. 2 56-57													X		X	X		

Kategorie	1	2	3	4	5	6	7	8
PRODUKTKOMMUNIKATION		X			X			X
UNTERNEHMENSKOMMUNIKATION	X	X			X	X	X	
VERLAGSWESEN	X				X			
VERPACKUNG		X		X	X			X
WERBUNG		X		X	X		X	X
LOGISTIK UND ORGANISATION					X			
AUSSTELLUNGSDESIGN	X	X	X	X	X			
FULL SERVICE MESSEAUFTRITTE	X				X			
NORM/SYSTEM MESSESTÄNDE					X			
INDIVIDUELLE MESSESTÄNDE	X			X	X			
SONDERARCHITEKTUR (MEHRSTÖCKIG)			X		X			
DISPLAYS	X		X		X			
MÖBLIERUNG UND DEKORATION	X		X		X			
BELEUCHTUNG, TON, AV					X			
EVENTS/VERANSTALTUNGEN (KONZEPT, PLANUNG, DURCHFÜHRUNG)					X			
AUSSTELLUNGEN FLÄCHENVERMITTLUNG (KONZEPT, PLANUNG, DURCHFÜHRUNG)					X			
UNTERHALTUNGSELEKTRONIK								
MULTIMEDIA	X				X	X		
ANIMATION	X				X			
AUDIVISUELLE MEDIEN	X				X			
CD ROM	X				X			
INFORMATIONSDESIGN	X			X	X			
WEB DESIGN	X	X			X			
MODE/TEXTIL DESIGN					X			
BEKLEIDUNG					X			
BEKLEIDUNGSSTOFFE					X			
HEIMTEXTILIEN					X			
LABELS					X			
MOTIVDRUCK, STICKEREI					X			
SCHNITTGESTALTUNG					X			
FOTO DESIGN					X			
ARCHITEKTUR					X			
EINRICHTUNGEN					X			
LANDSCHAFTEN					X			
MENSCHEN					X			
MODE	X				X			
NAHRUNGSMITTEL					X			
REDAKTION					X			
STILLLEBEN					X			
TRANSPORT					X			

SWITZERLAND

			INDUSTRIEDESIGN	ACCESSOIRES, SCHMUCK	BÜRO, OBJEKT	FREIZEIT, SPORT, SPIEL	GEBÄUDETECHNIK	HANDWERK, INDUSTRIE	HAUSHALT, KÜCHE, BAD	MEDIEN, KOMMUNIKATION	MEDIZIN, REHABILITATION	PUBLIC DESIGN	TRANSPORT	WOHNEN	GRAFIKDESIGN	ARCHITEKTUR	CORPORATE DESIGN	ILLUSTRATION	INFORMATIONSSYSTEME	KULTUR UND INSTITUTIONEN
5000	**KORB + KORB** Schartenstrasse 3 CH-5400 Baden	VOL.1 78-79	X		X		X		X			X		X	X	X	X	X	X	
6000	**QUADESIGN PARTNER AG** Untermüli 5 CH-6300 Zug	VOL.1 104-105		X	X	X	X	X	X	X	X	X	X	X			X	X	X	
7000	**PURE COMMUNICATIONS** Sägenstrasse 4 CH-7007 Chur	VOL.2 78-79														X	X	X	X	X
8000	**PURE COMMUNICATIONS** Seebahnstrasse 85 CH-8003 Zürich	VOL.2 78-79														X	X	X	X	X
	INTERBRAND Kirchenweg 5 CH-8008 Zürich	VOL.2 112-113													X					
	MEYER-HAYOZ DESIGN ENGINEERING GROUP Jägerstrasse 2 CH-8406 Winterthur	VOL.1 86-87 VOL.2 118-119																		
	T.V.T SWISSCONSULT GMBH. TARGETED VALUE ON TIME Chaltenbodenstrasse 4B CH-8834 Schindellegi	VOL.1 126-127	X												X					

Category	1	2	3	4
PRODUKTKOMMUNIKATION	X			
UNTERNEHMENSKOMMUNIKATION	X	X	X	
VERLAGSWESEN		X	X	
VERPACKUNG	X	X	X	
WERBUNG	X	X	X	
LOGISTIK UND ORGANISATION				
AUSSTELLUNGSDESIGN	X			X
FULL SERVICE MESSEAUFTRITTE		X	X	
NORM/SYSTEM MESSESTÄNDE				
INDIVIDUELLE MESSESTÄNDE	X	X	X	
SONDERARCHITEKTUR [MEHRSTÖCKIG]	X	X	X	
DISPLAYS		X	X	
MÖBLIERUNG UND DEKORATION	X	X	X	
BELEUCHTUNG, TON, AV				
EVENTS/VERANSTALTUNGEN (KONZEPT, PLANUNG, DURCHFÜHRUNG)		X	X	
AUSSTELLUNGEN FLÄCHENVERMITTLUNG (KONZEPT, PLANUNG, DURCHFÜHRUNG)				
UNTERHALTUNGSELEKTRONIK				
MULTIMEDIA	X			X
ANIMATION				
AUDIVISUELLE MEDIEN				
CD ROM	X			
INFORMATIONSDESIGN	X	X		
WEB DESIGN	X	X		
MODE/TEXTIL DESIGN	X			
BEKLEIDUNG	X			
BEKLEIDUNGSSTOFFE	X			
HEIMTEXTILIEN				
LABELS				
MOTIVDRUCK, STICKEREI				
SCHNITTGESTALTUNG				
FOTO DESIGN				X
ARCHITEKTUR				
EINRICHTUNGEN				
LANDSCHAFTEN				
MENSCHEN	X			
MODE				
NAHRUNGSMITTEL				
REDAKTION				
STILLLEBEN				
TRANSPORT				

1

100% INTERIOR SYLVIA LEYDECKER
IF PRODUCT DESIGN AWARD: 2009; für Wandbelag ccflex, Stardust
GUTE GESTALTUNG: 2009; Bronze Medaille für Wandbelag ccflex, Stardust
DESIGN PLUS: 2009; Auszeichnung zur Material Vision für Wandbelag ccflex, Stardust
DESIGNPREIS DER BUNDESREPUBLIK DEUTSCHLAND: 2010; Nominierung für Wandbelag ccflex, Stardust

A

ARTEFAKT
Auszug Preise 2009 und 2008
RED DOT DESIGN AWARD: 2009 für Duschabläufe Viega „Tempoplex"; 2009 für Türbeschlagserie Jado „ID-9"; 2009 für Türbeschlagserie Jado „Loop"; 2009 für Glastürbeschlagserie Dorma DSign beta; 2009 für Glastürbeschlagserie Dorma DSign alpha; 2009 für Betätigungsplatten Viega Visignforstyle „Modell 13+14"; 2008 für Waschplatzprogramm Ideal Standard SimplyU „dynamic"; 2008 für Betätigungsserie berührungslos Viega Visignformore; 2008 für Raumluftreiniger Asecos AirOne
IF PRODUCT DESIGN AWARD: 2009 für Waschplatzprogramm Ideal Standard SimplyU „dynamic"; 2009 für Waschplatzprogramm Ideal Standard SimplyU „natural"; 2009 für „integrierte" Armaturenserie Ideal Standard SimplyU; 2008 für Duschtrennwand system Glamü Diana Spin; 2008 für corporate productdesign Müsing; 2008 für Betätigungsserie Viega Visignformore; 2008 für Betätigungsserie berührungslos Viega Visignformore
DESIGN PLUS AWARD: 2009 für Viega „Multiplex Trio E"; 2009 für Flächenheizkörper Kermi „Fedon"
INNOVATIONSPREIS ARCHITEKTUR UND HEALTHCARE: 2009 für Betätigungsplatte Viega „Visign for care"

AT DESIGN
DESIGNPREIS DER BRD: 2011 nominiert Industrie PC SIMATIC IPC227D; 2011 nominiert Bedienpanel SINUMERIK 840D SL; 2006 nominiert Handbediengerät SIMATIC HT8
GOOD DESIGN JAPAN: 2007 für modularen Umrichter SINAMICS G120
IDEA USA: 2005 für modularen Antrieb SINAMICS S120
IF PRODUCT DESIGN AWARD:
2011 für Industrie PC SIMATIC IPC227D; 2011 für Bedienpanel SINUMERIK 840D SL; 2010 für Steuerung SIMATIC S7-1200; 2010 für Stellungsregler SITRANS VP300; 2009 für mobiles Handbediengerät SIMATIC MP277B 10»; 2006 für mobiles Handbediengerät SIMATIC HT8; 2006 für mobiles Handbediengerät SIMATIC MP277B; 2004 für modularen Antrieb SINAMICS S120; 2004 für Frequenzumrichter SINAMICS G110; 2004 für Steuerung SIMATIC ET200X; 2004 für Maschinensteuertafel SINUMERIK 840D; 2004 für Vision Sensor SIMATIC VS120; 2001 für mobiles Handbediengerät SINUMERIK HT6; 1999 für Industrie Monitor Panel SICOMP IMC 01
MATERIALICA DESIGN AWARD 2003 für „Die neue Ästhetik des Spitzens"
RED DOT 2004 für Frequenzumrichter SINAMICS G110; 2004 für modularen Antrieb SINAMICS S120 (best of the best)

B

BEAU BUREAU DESIGN
EULDA: 2006 (Award winner) für Markenentwicklung Pro Sky Travel GmbH
IF COMMUNICATION DESIGN AWARD: 2007 für Imagebroschüre Fairtrade International e.V.
MFG AWARD: 2006 Nachwuchswettbewerb Geschäftsausstattung Pro Sky Travel GmbH; Shortlist Eigene Geschäftspapierausstattung; 2007 2. Preis für Formularfamilie Wohnen für Hilfe, Köln; 2008 Shortlist: Formularfamilie Polaris
NOMINIERT FÜR DEN DESIGNPREIS DER BRD: 2009 für Formularfamilie Wohnen für Hilfe, Köln und Imagebroschüre Fairtrade International e.V.; 2008 für Geschäftsausstattung Pro Sky Travel GmbH
WOLDA: 2009 (Award winner) für Markenentwicklung Universität des Saarlandes / Fachbereich Physik

BEGER DESIGN
IF PRODUCT DESIGN AWARD: 2002 für OPserver Integrierter Systemarbeitsplatz für die chirurgische Endoskopie
BUNDESPREIS PRODUKTDESIGN: 2003 für OPserver
ANIMAGO AWARD: 2005 1. Preis für das interactive Spiel „Nutritopia"

LOTHAR BÖHM GMBH
RED DOT DESIGN AWARD: winner 2008 für Osram energy saver packaging; winner 2009 für BSN Actimove Bandage
IF PRODUCT AWARD: Gold 2009 für BSN Actimove Bandage
NOMINIERT FÜR DEN DESIGNPREIS DER BRD: 2010 für BSN Actimove Bandage

BOTSCHAFT PROF. GERTRUD NOLTE VISUELLE KOMMUNIKATION UND BERATUNG
100 BESTE PLAKATE: 1999, 2000, 2001 (Ehrendiplom), 2002, 2003, 2006/07
POSTER-TRIENNIAL OF TRNAVA: 2003 (Major Award); 2006, 2009
RED DOT DESIGN AWARD/DEUTSCHER PREIS FÜR KOMMUNIKATIONSDESIGN: 2008, 2003, 2001, 2000, 1999
TDC NEW YORK: 1998, 2002
ADC NEW YORK: (Merit Award 2001/02)
ADC GERMANY: 1998, 1999, 2001
DIE SCHÖNSTEN BÜCHER DEUTSCHLANDS, STIFTUNG BUCHKUNST: 2001 and 2002
3RD AND 4TH BIENNIAL OF BOOK ART MARTIN BBA, TSCHECHIE: (Merit Award) 1999, 2001/02
NOMINIERUNG FÜR DEN DESIGN PREIS DER BUNDESREPUBLIK DEUTSCHLAND: 2009 und 2010
Ausgewählt:
1ST AND 2ND POSTER BIENNIAL OF KOREA: 2002, 2004/05
18TH INTERNATIONAL POSTER BIENNALE WARSAW: 2002, 2004
INTERNATIONAL BIENNIAL OF GRAPHIC DESIGN BRNO, TSCHECHIEN: 2000
POSTER BIENNIAL HANGZHOU: 2005, 2007
CHINA INTERNATIONAL POSTER BIENNIAL
INTERNATIONAL POSTER TRIENNIAL TOYAMA (JAPAN)
FESTIVAL D'AFFICHES DE CHAUMONT: 1996, 2007
LAHTI POSTER BIENNALE XVI: 2007

BRANDTOUCH
DESIGNPREIS DER BUNDESREPUBLIK DEUTSCHLAND: 2012 Nominee (Communication Design), 2010 Nominee (Internet Films, Print Campaign)
RED DOT DESIGN AWARD: 2011 2x Winner (Advertising, Editorial), 2010 Best of the Best (Advertising), 2x Winner (Editorial, Online Communication)
IF COMMUNICATION DESIGN AWARD: 2011 2x Gold (Print, Print Campaign), Award (Self Promotion), 2010 Gold (Calendars)
THE NEW YORK FESTIVALS: 2010 Gold (Calendars)
CREATIVITY INTERNATIONAL AWARDS: 2010 3x Platinum (Calendars, Photography, Consumer Campaign), Gold (Single Unit), Certificate (Logo & Trademarks)
DDC – DEUTSCHER DESIGNERCLUB: 2009 Gold (Foto & Film), Silver (Advertising)
CORPORATE DESIGN AWARD: 2010 Award (Corporate Design / Corporate Identity)
GOOD DESIGN – CHICAGO ATHENAEUM MUSEUM OF ARCHITECTURE AND DESIGN: 2010 Award (Graphic Design)
THE ONE SHOW FESTIVAL: 2010: Bronze (Collateral Promotion)
INTERNATIONAL CALENDAR SHOW: 2010 Bronze (Calendars)

BRAUNWAGNER
DESIGN PREIS DER BRD: 2007 Silber für Loewe IFA 2005
NOMINIERT FÜR DEN DESIGNPREIS DER BRD: 2012 für smart urban stage, smart IAA 2009; 2011 für smart lane Exhibition Concept, Nespresso CitiZ Showroom; 2007 für smart Hospitality Pavillon 2005; 2006 für Loewe IFA 2003; 2006 für smart IAA 2003; 2004 für Loewe IFA 2003; 2004 für smart IAA 2003
IF COMMUNICATION DESIGN AWARD: 2009 für smart lane Exhibition Concept 2008–2010
IF PRODUCT DESIGN AWARD: 2006 für smart Hospitality Pavillon 2005; 2004 für Loewe IFA 2003
IF PUBLIC DESIGN AWARD: 2004 für smart IAA 2003; 2003 für Loewe Forum 2002
DP3D DIE GOLDENE FLAMME: 2006 Prädikat: Herausragend für Loewe IFA 2005
RED DOT AWARD COMMUNICATION DESIGN: 2010 für smart urban stage, smart IAA 2009; 2009 für Nespresso CitiZ Showroom
RED DOT AWARD PRODUCT DESIGN: 2006 für Loewe IFA 2005; 2004 für smart IAA 2003
ADC AWARD: 2011 Bronze für smart urban stage; 2004 Auszeichnung für smart IAA 2003
ADAM AWARD DER AUSGEZEICHNETEN MESSEAUFTRITTE: 2006 Gold in Kategorie XXL: Loewe IFA 2005; 2004 2. Platz Kategorie 1500m2: Loewe IFA 2003
GOOD DESIGN: 2010 für smart urban stage; 2009 für smart lane Exhibition Concept
EXHIBIT DESIGN AWARDS: 2009 Silver für smart IAA 2009

BUDDE INDUSTRIE DESIGN GMBH
RED DOT DESIGN AWARD: 2000 für das Koffertransportsystem „autover system" der Fa. BEUMER Maschinenfabrik KG aus Beckum
IF PRODUCT DESIGN AWARD: 2008 für den Mähdrescher „TUCANO" der Fa. CLAAS SE GmbH aus Harsewinkel
STAATSPREIS FÜR DESIGN: 2009 für den Feldhäcksler „JAGUAR" der Fa. CLAAS SE GmbH aus Harsewinkel
FVK KUNSTSTOFFPREIS: 1997 für die CD BOX „MÄX 6" der Fa. HAN BÜROGERÄTE GmbH & Co. KG aus Herford
STAHLINNOVATIONSPREIS: 2009 für die Heckklappe des Mähdreschers „TUCANO" der Fa. CLAAS SE GmbH aus Harsewinkel
STAATSPREIS DES LANDES NRW: 1989 für den Getränkecontainer „keggy" der Fa. SCHÄFER WERKE GMBH aus Neuenkirchen
DESIGNAUSWAHL STUTTGART: 1990 für den Getränkecontainer „keggy" der Fa. SCHÄFER WERKE GMBH aus Neuenkirchen

BÜRO FÜR GESTALTUNG WANGLER & ABELE
RED DOT DESIGN AWARD COMMUNICATION DESIGN: 2010 für Green Point Stadium Cape Town, Visuelle Kommunikation, Leit- und Orientierungssystem; 2009 für Leibniz Universität Hannover, Visuelle Kommunikation, Leit- und Orientierungssystem; 2007 für Kapelle im Olympiastadion Berlin, Wandgestaltung; 2005 für „gestalten drei" und „gestalten vier", Bürobroschüren; 2003 für „gestalten eins" und „gestalten zwei", Bürobroschüren
IF COMMUNICATION DESIGN AWARD: 2010 für Moses Mabhida Stadium Durban, Visuelle Kommunikation, Leit- und Orientierungssystem; 2007 Gold Award für Kapelle im Olympiastadion Berlin, Wandgestaltung
NOMINIERUNG FÜR DEN DESIGNPREIS DER BRD: 2011 Leibniz Universität Hannover, Visuelle Kommunikation, Leit- und Orientierungssystem; 2009 für „Kapelle im Olympiastadion Berlin", Wandgestaltung; 2007 für „gestalten drei" und „gestalten vier", Bürobroschüren
DIE SCHÖNSTEN DEUTSCHEN BÜCHER: 2005 Auszeichnung, Stiftung Buchkunst, Frankfurt am Main für „gestalten drei" und „gestalten vier", Bürobroschüren; 2002 „Lobende Anerkennung", Stiftung Buchkunst
NOMINIERUNG DEUTSCHER DESIGNPREIS: 2012 für Moses Mabhida Stadium Durban, Visuelle Kommunikation, Leit- und Orientierungssystem; 2012 für Green Point Stadion Cape Town, Visuelle Kommunikation, Leit- und Orientierungssystem

BÜRO GROTESK
ADC DEUTSCHLAND: 1999 Bronze für Plakate Alexander Rodtschenko
ADC NY: 1998 für Ausstellungskatalog '68 Design und Alltagskultur zwischen Konsum und Konflikt
DEUTSCHER PREIS FÜR KOMMUNIKATIONSDESIGN: 1999 für Plakate Alexander Rodtschenko
DEUTSCHER PLAKAT GRAND PRIX: 1998 für Plakate Alexander Rodtschenko
TDC NY: 2003 Plakate Kunstverein Region Heinsberg; 1998 für Plakate Alexander Rodtschenko
100 BESTE PLAKATE: 2004 für Kunstverein Region Heinsberg; 1999 für Plakate Alexander Rodtschenko

C

CHRISTIAN WEISSER AGENTURGRUPPE
100 BESTE PLAKATE E.V.: 1 x Aufnahme
ANNUAL MULTIMEDIA JAHRBUCH: 3 x Aufnahme Multimedia
ART DIRECTORS CLUB DEUTSCHLAND: 1 x Silber Interaktive Medien
DIE SCHÖNSTEN DEUTSCHEN BÜCHER: 1 x Prämierung
DESIGNPREIS DER BUNDESREPUBLIK DEUTSCHLAND: 8 x Nominierung
DESIGN ZENTRUM NORDRHEIN-WESTFALEN: 1 x best of the best
RED DOT COMMUNICATION DESIGN: 5 x
DEUTSCHER DESIGNER CLUB: 1 x Gold, 6 x Bronze, 2 x Auszeichnung [Das Gute Stück / Das Gute Netzwerk]
IF INTERNATIONAL FORUM DESIGN: 3 x Silber, 6 x Auszeichnung Communication Design
IWPA SAN JOSÉ USA: 1 x International Web Page Award Corporate Communication
JAHRBUCH DER WERBUNG: 6 x Aufnahme Kulturmarketing, Internet
KOMMUNIKATIONSVERBAND DMMV: 1 x Deutscher Multimedia Award Winner
KOMMUNIKATIONSVERBAND: 1 x B-to-B Silver Award Multimedia
LONDON INTERNATIONAL ADVERTISING AWARDS: 1 x Finalist Interactive Media
MERCEDES-BENZ STAR AWARD: Silver, Shows & Exhibitions – National
THE NEW YORK FESTIVALS: 1 x Gold World Medal Best Website Design
THE ONE CLUB: 1 x Merit Award One Show Interactive

CREDO CONCEPT.COMMUNICATION
BDG:LOGOWETTBEWERB: 2000 1. Preis für Kunden HGP audioelektronik; 2. Preis für „eyedentity" und 2. Preis „ScharfrichterHaus"

CYCLOS DESIGN GMBH
RED DOT DESIGN AWARD COMMUNICATION DESIGN: 2011 für die Markenentwicklung von Laib und Seele, für den Marken-Relaunch der Gärtner von Eden sowie für den Markenauftritt und den Messestand von blomus
GOLDEN EYE BTOB PHOTO AWARD: 2011
DEUTSCHE POST UND SIEGFRIED VÖGELE INSTITUT MAILING WETTBEWERB: 2008 3. Sieger bundesweit für die 3-stufige Mailingstrecke SEHEN – RIECHEN – FÜHLEN der Gebrüder Wilke GmbH mit einer Responsequote von 30%
JAPAN CALENDAR AWARD: 2011 mit dem Special Prize für den Image-Kalender „Wand-Geschichten"
INTERNATIONALE KALENDERSCHAU: 2011 mit dem Prädikat Silber sowie dem Award of Excellence in der Kategorie „Best Use Of Paper" für den Image-Kalender „Wand-Geschichten"
MÜNSTER-MARATHON: 2008 Erfolgreiche Teilnahme von cyclos design als „Die Hafenarbeiter" mit einer Zeit von 3:56:55 h.

D

DESIGNSHIP
RED DOT DESIGN AWARD HONORABLE MENTION: 2011 Anti-Schlingerkupplung AL-KO GmbH
IF PRODUCT DESIGN AWARD: 2011 Antriebssystem Mammut AL-KO GmbH
CARAVANING DESIGN AWARD: 2011 Antriebssystem Mammut AL-KO GmbH
RED DOT DESIGN AWARD: 2009 Drehstuhl Meet-Chair Sedus AG
IF DESIGN AWARD: 2009 Drehstuhl Meet-Chair Sedus AG
IF DESIGN AWARD: 2009 Verpackungsmaschine FlexiSEAL Köra-Packmat Maschinenbau GmbH
IF DESIGN AWARD: 2007 Blister Express Center BEC Uhlmann Pac-Systeme
TOP 100 RANKING DESIGN: 2006
RED DOT DESIGN AWARD: 2005 Verpackungsmaschine b 1880 Uhlmann Pac-Systeme
IF DESIGN AWARD: 2005 Wellrohrextruder Drossbach GmbH & Co. KG
DEUTSCHER VERPACKUNGSPREIS: 2005 Verpackungsmaschine b 1880 Uhlmann Pac System
FOCUS LEBENSART: 2002 Stuhl Thira / Klöber GmbH
AWARD OF EXCELLENCE: 2000 PPMA Tubenfüller TFS 80 IWKA
DESIGN-INNOVATION ESSEN: 1999 Stuhl Senzo Wilkhahn
DESIGN-INNOVATION ESSEN: 1998 Stuhl Bingo Bisterfeld + Weiss
IF DESIGN AWARD: 1997 Präsentationssystem CARL ZEISS
GOOD DESIGN CHICAGO: 1995 Stuhl El Toro Bisterfeld + Weiss
KUNSTGEWERBEMUSEUM BERLIN: 1995 Stuhl El Toro Aufnahme ständige Sammlung
DESIGN CENTER STUTTGART: 1992 Thermoformmaschine UPS 1030 Uhlmann Pac-Systeme
YAMAHA DESIGN COMPETITION: 1990 Lautsprecherbox

DIALOGFORM GMBH
RED DOT DESIGN AWARD: 2007 für HAMM AG, HD-Compact Serie (kompakt Walzenzüge); 2004 für HAMM AG, DV Serie (Tandemwalzen); 2001 für HAMM AG, Serie 3000 (Walzenzüge) 1998 für rolly toys, Kinderschubkarre; 1996 für HAMM AG, Raco 550 (Asphaltrecycler)
IF PRODUCT DESIGN AWARD: 1996 rolly toys, MegaTrailer (Dreiseitenkipper); 1999 für HAMM AG, HD Serie (Tandemwalzen); 2002 für HAMM AG, Serie 3000 (Walzenzüge); 2005 für Gold Award HAMM AG, DV Serie (Tandemwalzen); 2006 Gold Award für HAMM AG, HD-Compact Serie (kompakt Walzenzüge); 2006 Joseph Vögele AG, Super 1900-2 / Super 2100-2 (Großfertiger Linie); 2009 für Joseph Vögele AG, Vision 5100-2 / 51003-2 (8ft class road paver); 2009 Joseph Vögele AG, Vision 5200-2 / 52003-2 (10ft class road paver)
NOMINIERT FÜR DEN DESIGNPREIS DER BRD: 2006 HAMM AG, DV Serie (Tandemwalzen); 2008 für HAMM AG, HD-Compact Serie (kompakt Walzenzüge); 2008 für Joseph Vögele AG, Super 1900-2 / Super 2100-2 (Großfertiger Linie)
UNIVERSAL DESIGN AWARD: 2008 für Joseph Vögele AG, MMI Bedienpult
GOOD DESING AWARD: 2008 Joseph Vögele AG, Vision 5100-2 / 51003-2 (8ft class road paver)

E

ENTHOVEN ASSOCIATES DESIGN CONSULTANTS
WALL PAPER DESIGN AWARDS: 2010 – Category best camping – Opera for YSIN
RED DOT – PRODUCT DESIGN: 2009 – Elan teak outdoor furniture (Gloster);
RED DOT – MESSE DÜSSELDORF – CARAVANING DESIGN AWARD: 2010 winner "best practice" – Opera (YSIN)
DESIGN PREIS DER BRD – NOMINIERT –: 2009 – bathroom furniture range "01 by Enthoven" für Dedecker
DESIGN PLUS: 2009 Material vision – Shinnoki (Decospan); 2009 ISH – "01 by Enthoven" für Dedecker;
IF GUTE INDUSTRIEFORM: 2009 Triplet Hawk magnifying glass (SwissAxe); 2009 Sublim'O watercooler (SipWell);
IF GUTEINDUSTRIEFORM CHINA: 2008 atmoVIT Classic (Vaillant); 2008 atmoCRAFT (Vaillant)
RAILWAY INTERIORS AWARD: 2008 Renovation – Thalys high speed train (Thalys)
OBSERVEUR DU DESIGN (APCI): 2009 – label für Elan teak outdoor furniture (Gloster); 2009 label für "01 by Enthoven" für Dedecker; 2008 label für seat for public transport (Fainsa); 2008 label für parking access and payment system (Amano); 2008 label für interior design LH Bank; 2008 label für Citadis tram Jerusalem (Alstom); 2008 label für Shinnoki (Decospan)
GOOD DESIGN – CHICAGO: 2007 – Sprinter EMU train (Bombardier)
HENRY VAN DE VELDE (DESIGN FLANDERS): 2009 Triplet Hawk magnifier (SwissAxe); 2008 Citadis tram for Jerusalem (Alstom); 2008 Bake Porter Line (houseware) (Prepco); 2007 Boa Metro Brussels (CAF); 2007 Flexity tram for Brussels (Bombardier)
GOURMET GOLD CONTEST (USA): 2008 finalist Bake Porter Line (Prepco)
WOOD AWARD (UK): 2009 winner in categories "furniture" and "outdoor" Elan (Gloster)

F

HEINRICH FIEDELER
IF PRODUCT DESIGN AWARD: 'Trasorter', 'Gin Bar Stool', 'Farbwerfer'
GOOD DESIGN AWARD: 'Barseries Loft'

FRACKENPOHL POULHEIM
IF PRODUCT DESIGN AWARD: 2010 für Mobiltelefon "Vodafone 545 Larry", 2010 für Mobiltelefon "Vodafone 540 Phil", 2009 für Lawinenschaufel "Cougar", 2008 "Mobile Connect 3G Modem"
GOOD DESIGN AWARD: 2010 für Smartphone "Vodafone 945", 2010 für Mobile Wi-Fi Router "Vodafone R201", "2010" für "Roboter Myon"
DESIGNPREIS DER BRD: 2007 nominiert für Snowboard Softboot „EMPIRE", 2010 nominiert für Mobiltelefon "Vodafone 545 Larry", 2010 nominiert für Mobiltelefon "Vodafone 540 Phil"
OBSERVEUR DU DESIGN: 2011 für Mobile Wi-Fi Router „Vodafone R201", 2010 für Smartphone „Vodafone 845"
UNIVERSAL DESIGN AWARD: 2011 Consumer Favorit für „Vodafone Webbox" VOLVO
SPORTS DESIGN AWARD: 2007, nominiert für Snowboard Softboot "EMPIRE"

H

H-DESIGN
SÄCHSISCHER STAATSPREIS FÜR DESIGN: Designpreis 1993 für Ziehspielzeug; Anerkennung 1993 für Fotostativ „Statik" Berlebach; Anerkennung 1996 für Fotostativ „Report" Berlebach; Anerkennung 1996 für Rotationslaser FG-L3; 3. Preis 2005 für Druckmaschine Rapida 105; 3. Preis 2009 für Verflüssigungssatz Ecostar-Unit
RED DOT DESIGN AWARD: 1994 für Ziehspielzeug
IF PACKAGING AWARD: Gold 2008 für Verpackungsmaschinen MCH / MCC
NOMINIERT FÜR DEN DESIGNPREIS DER BRD: 2009 für Verpackungsmaschinen MCH / MCC

HENSSLER UND SCHULTHEISS FULLSERVICE PRODUCTDESIGN GMBH
IF PRODUCT DESIGN AWARD: 2011 für D12 Dampfbad, Klafs GmbH & Co.; 2010 Gold Award für Pure Sauna, Klafs GmbH & Co; 2010 für PowerMax Elektro-Rasenmäher, Gardena; 2010 für SmallCut Rasentrimmer, Gardena; 2008 Gold Award für VISIONMES Teleszentrische Objektive Carl Zeiss; 2008 für byko-cut universal Lackprüfgerät BYK-Gardner GmbH; 2008 für SENSYS Scharnier mit Dämpfung Hettich Furn Tech GmbH & Co; 2006 für 380C Spindelmäher GARDENA; 2006 für ES500 Rasenlüfter GARDENA; 2006 für AS2 Wartungseinheit Bosch Rexroth AG; 2006 wave-scan dual Universalprüfgerät BYK-Gardner GmbH; 2006 F25 Koordinatenmessmaschine Carl Zeiss
RED DOT PRODUCT DESIGN AWARD: 2011 für i:Terminal Zentriersystem für Brillengläser; 2010 für Vmax Kommissioniersystem für Apotheken; Rowa; 2008 SENSYS Scharnier mit Dämpfung Hettich Furn Tech GmbH & Co.; 2008 für VENTANO Sauna Klafs GmbH & Co.; 2007 Bare- + Tabelware Set DESIGNHANSA; 2007 Werkzeugkoffer C. & E. Fein GmbH; 2006 ASM 9-2 Mittelhandgriffschrauber C. & E. Fein GmbH
NOMINIERT FÜR DEN DESIGNPREIS DEUTSCHLAND: 2010 für D12 Dampfbad; Klafs GmbH & Co.; 2011 für Pure system für Aoitgejebm Rowa; 2009 für VENTANO Sauna Klafs GmbH & Co.; 2006 für EVO Winkelschleifer C. & E. Fein GmbH; 2006 für PROTEO Sauna Klafs GmbH & Co.

HUMAN INTERFACE DESIGN
DESIGNPREIS DEUTSCHLAND 2012 „NOMINIERT": für das Vollflächen-Induktionskochfeld CX 480 | Markendesign Gaggenau; für Nutztierdatenverwaltung serv.it Rind | Vereinte Informationssysteme Tierhaltung; für das Energie-Managementsystem Busch-EnergyControl | Bush-Jaeger GmbH; für den Energiemonitor Busch-EnergyDisplay | Bush-Jaeger GmbH
2011
IF COMMUNICATION DESIGN AWARD 2011: Kategorie: „Produkt Interface" für das Vollflächen-Induktionskochfeld CX 480 | Markendesign Gaggenau; für Nutztierdatenverwaltung serv.it Rind | Vereinte Informationssysteme Tierhaltung
2010
RED DOT COMMUNICATION DESIGN
AWARD „BEST OF THE BEST" 2010: Kategorie: „Grafical User Interface"; für das Energie-Managementsystem Busch-EnergyControl | Bush-Jaeger GmbH; für den Energiemonitor Busch-EnergyDisplay | Bush-Jaeger GmbH
IF COMMUNICATION DESIGN AWARD 2010: Kategorie: „Produkt Interface" für das Energie-Managementsystem Busch-EnergyControl | Bush-Jaeger GmbH
DESIGNPREIS DER BUNDESREPUBLIK DEUTSCHLAND „NOMINIERT" 2010: für die Haussteurung Busch-ComfortPanel | Bush-Jaeger GmbH; für die Raumsteurung Busch-priOn | Bush-Jaeger GmbH
RED DOT COMMUNICATION DESIGN AWARD „BEST OF THE BEST" 2008: Kategorie: „Grafical User Interface" für die Haussteurung Busch-ComfortPanel | Bush-Jaeger GmbH für die Raumsteurung Busch-priOn | Bush-Jaeger GmbH

HYVE AG
RED DOT DESIGN AWARD HONOURABLE MENTION: 2010 für Stabmixer Styline MSM7 von B/S/H, 2010 für Performance Sport-Kompressionsstrümpfe von Sigvaris
RED DOT DESIGN AWARD WINNER: 2007 für MP3 Player Vibez von Trekstor; 2011 für Performance Sleeves and Socks von Sigvaris
RED DOT DESIGN AWARD BEST OF THE BEST: 2011 für Küchenmaschine Styline MUM5 von B/S/H
NOMINIERT FÜR DEN DESIGNPREIS DER BUNDESREPUBLIK DEUTSCHLAND: 2007 für MP3 Player Vibez von TrekStor
IF PRODUCT DESIGN AWARD: 2011 für Küchenmaschine Styline MUM5 von B/S/H
ISPO OUTDOOR AWARD: 2007 für Lawinenairbag Vario von ABS
BRAND NEW AWARD NOMINIERUNG: 2001 für Snowboardrucksack Diggit von Backtools

I

ID DESIGN AGENTUR
IF PRODUCT DESIGN AWARD: 1984 für Drucker WENGER 4/1; 1985 Einbruchmeldezentrale BBC; 1985 für Handetikettier gerät Meto GmbH; 1988 für Monitor Ritto Control RITTO-Werk; 1988 für Wohnsprechstelle RITTO-Werk; 1990 Aufstell-Tragebügel Rittal-Werk; 1991 Matrixdrucker Triathlon, Wenger AG; 1991 für Matrixdrucker, Wenger AG; 1993 für Satellite-Empfangsantenne, FUBA-Consumer Systems; 1995 für Elektrotherapiegerät, Zimmer Elektromedizin; 1995 für Gerätefamilie Lötstationen ERSA, Löttechnik GmbH; 1995 iF Gold Award für Cafe Frischbrühautomat Spengler; 1995 iF Gold Award für Defibrillator GS-Elektromedizinische Geräte Gmbh; 2002 für Vista Cam2 ID Design Agentur
DESIGN CENTER STUTTGART: 1987 für Tischthermometer DIEHL; 1989 für Geräte-träger „dacomobile", Knürr AG; 1994 für Waschtisch „TIZIO", Ideal-Standard; 1999 für Medizinischer Diodenlaser „Dornier Medilas D", Dornier MedizinLaser GmbH
DESIGN ZENTRUM NORDRHEIN WESTFALEN: 1996 für Duschkabine Toscana, KERMI GmbH; 1997 Universal-Gerätewagen kombiTROLL „L", Kreuzer GmbH
RED DOT DESIGN AWARD: 2004 Vakuumiergerät AMC International; 2009 LED Krankenbettleuchte RZB
DIE NEUE SAMMLUNG: Einbruchmeldezentrale BBC, Staatliches Museum für angewandte Kunst
DESIGN-INNOVATIONEN: 1991 PC Schrank PC 4600/4610, Rittal-Werk
WORLDSTAR PACKAGING AWARD USA: 1996 Verpackung Sanitär Amaturen; Artema A.S. Türkei
MATERIALICA AWARD: 2003 Rheometer, Thermo Haake

IDENTIS GMBH, DESIGN-GRUPPE JOSEPH PÖLZELBAUER
IF COMMUNICATION DESIGN AWARD GOLD: 2007 für Exponat EnBW Geothermie Cube; 2010 für Packaging Wild Bag Box; 2011 für Corporate Design Staufenstiftung
IF COMMUNICATION DESIGN AWARD: 2006 für Messeauftritt EnBW Energie Baden-Württemberg AG; 2007 für Exponat EnBW EnyCity; 2007 für Messeauftritt Nord Stream AG; 2009 für Corporate Design Gemeinschaftspraxis für Pathologie, Freiburg
IF PACKAGING DESIGN AWARD GOLD: 2011 für Packaging Wild Bag Box
IF PACKAGING DESIGN AWARD: 2011 für Staufenstiftung
REDDOT DESIGN AWARD WINNER: 2007 für Exponat EnBW Geothermie Cube; 2007 Messeauftritt Nord Stream AG; 2010 für Wild Bag Box; 2011 für Solidaritäts-Kampagne Staufenstiftung; 2011 für Packaging Staufenstiftung; 2011 für Corporate Design 50 Jahre Volkswagen Zentrum Freiburg
DDC AWARD BRONZE: 2007 für Exponat EnBW Geothermie Cube; 2010 für Packaging Wild Bag Box
CORPORATE DESIGN PREIS AUSZEICHNUNG: 2002 für Badenova; 2004 für Givit Garantie Management System; 2005 für EnBW Energie Baden-Württemberg AG; 2008 für Nord Stream AG
CORPORATE DESIGN PREIS AWARD-WINNER: 2003 für Electricité de Strasbourg
ART DIRECTORS CLUB: AUSZEICHNUNG: 2011 für Packaging Wild Bag Box
AUTOMOTIVE BRAND CONTEST: BEST OF BEST: 2011 für Kampagne „VW – 50 Jahre Mobilität"
PENTAWARDS: PLATINUM: 2010 für Packaging Wild Bag Box
PENTAWARDS: GOLD: 2011 für Packaging Staufenstiftung
LONDON INTERNATIONAL AWARDS: 2010 für Packaging Wild Bag Box
DP3D PRÄDIKAT: HERAUSRAGEND: 2007 für Exponat EnBW EnyCity; für Exponat EnBW Geothermie Cube
DIE MARKE IM MARKT: PREISTRÄGER: 2003 für Corporate Design Landesgartenschau Kehl & Straßburg
NOMINEE DESIGNPREIS DEUTSCHLAND: EnBW Energie Baden-Württemberg AG (5x); Nord Stream AG (2x); Gemeinschaftspraxis für Pathologie, Freiburg (1x); Staufenstiftung (3x); Volkswagen Zentrum Freiburg (1x); Wild Bag Box (2x)

IFP. INSTITUT FÜR MARKEN-, PACKUNGS- UND CORPORATE DESIGN GMBH
CREATIVITY INTERNATIONAL AWARD: 2010 für RESOLUTE/solicut Messerserie
IF PACKAGING DESIGN AWARD: 2011 für RESOLUTE/solicut Messerserie

INDEED INNOVATION
IF PRODUCT DESING AWARD: 5x
RED DOT DESIGN AWARD WINNER: 5x
NOMINIERT FÜR DEN DESIGNPREIS DER BRD: 4x
DEUTSCHER VERPACKUNGSPREIS
DER PROMOTIONAL GIFT AWARD
GOOD DESIGN JAPAN
DESIGN PLUS AWARD
WORLDSTAR FOR PACKAGING
HAMBURGER DESIGNPREIS

INDEPENDENT MEDIEN-DESIGN
WETTBEWERB DER SOCIETY OF PUBLICATION DESIGNER, N.Y.: Bisher über 50 Awards im international bedeutendsten Wettbewerb für Zeitschriftendesign. independent Medien-Design ist das erfolgreichste deutsche Studio in diesem Wettbewerb.
BCP BEST OF CORPORATE PUBLISHING: Seit Bestehen des Wettbewerbs 2003 bis 2010 insgesamt 10 Goldmedaillen, 30 Silbermedaillen und zwei Hall-of-Fame-Auszeichnungen.
4 REDDOT DESIGN AWARD: 1 Best of the best 2010
NOMINIERT FÜR DEN DESIGNPREIS DER BUNDESREPUBLIK DEUTSCHLAND: 2010
DEUTSCHER FOTOBUCHPREIS IN GOLD UND SILBER: 2010
LEAD AWARD: 2010 Newcomer Magazin

INTERBRAND
CORPORATE DESIGN PREIS: 2005, Lanxess - Gold Award; 2008 Lucerne Festival – Award; 2008 Dow XLA - Auszeichnung; 2008 congstar - Auszeichnung; 2008 LLB Liechtensteinische Landesbank - Auszeichnung; 2009 Usiminas - Gold Award; 2009 Schindler - Auszeichnung; 2009 LBBW - Nominierung; 2009 Walter AG - Nominierung; 2011 Actelion – Gold Award; 2011 Fürstenberg – Auszeichnung; 2011 Husqvarna - Nominierung
SCHWEIZER DESIGN PREIS: 2011 Actelion - Nominierung
IF COMMUNICATION DESIGN AWARD: 2009 Deutsche Telekom Corporate Fashion; 2009 Schindler; 2009 Troika Dialog; 2009 Usiminas; 2009 Walter AG; 2011 Husqvarna
IF PACKAGING DESIGN AWARD: 2011 Wrigley's Extra
RED DOT AWARD: COMMUNICATION DESIGN: 2006 Loewe Exhibition IFA 2005; 2009 Usiminas; 2010 Rolls-Royce; 2010 Kennen Sie Dürer?; 2011 Actelion; Fürstenberg
GUTE GESTALTUNG: 2008 congstar - Silber; 2008 Lucerne Festival - Bronze; 2010 Usiminas - Bronze; 2010 LBBW - Bronze
DESIGNPREIS DER BUNDESREPUBLIK DEUTSCHLAND: 2007 MINI Exhibition Genf Trade Fair 2006 - Silber; 2009 Lucerne Festival – Nominierung; 2009 congstar - Nominierung; 2010 Lucerne Festival – Nominierung; 2011 Usiminas – Nominee; 2011 Schindler – Nominee; 2011 LBBW – Nominee; 2011 Troika Dialog – Nominee; 2011 Walter AG – Nominee; 2011 Corporate Fashion Deutsche Telekom – Nominee; 2012 Rolls-Royce – Nominee; 2012 Husqvarna – Nominee; 2012 Kennen Sie Dürer – Nominee

K

KISKA GMBH
IF PRODUCT DESIGN AWARD: 2009 für den KTM X-Bow; 2008 für das Hilti PD4 Laser Distanzmessgerät; 2008 für das Hilti PD42 Laser Distanzmessgerät; 2008 Gold Award für den Hilti PR12 Rotationslaser
RED DOT PRODUCT DESIGN AWARD: 2009 für die AKG Miniheadphones K420 / K450
DIE GOLDENE KAMERA: 2008 für 3D Videoprojekt „Stretching the Limits – A Deeper Insight"
LIGHTING DESIGN AWARD: 2007 für Siteco Novaluna S

KORB + KORB ARCHITEKTUR KOMMUNIKATION DESIGN
AUSTRALIAN INTERNATIONAL DESIGN AWARD: 2009 SENSE
IDEA INTERNATIONAL DESIGN EXCELLENCE AWARDS: 2009 Finalist SENSE
ICFF EDITOR'S AWARD FOR BODY OF WORK: 2008 SENSE FOR HOME
DESIGN ZENTRUM NORDRHEIN-WESTFALEN: 1995 Design Innovation 95 OPTIONAL; 1997 Design Innovation 97 SPIRIT; 1999 Design Innovation 99 P.O.S.
RED DOT DESIGN AWARD: Best of the Best FRAMELIGHT 1; 2001 Produktdesign P.O.S. ELEGANCE; 2003 Produktdesign IN TWO; 2008 Produktdesign SENSE
NOMINIERT FÜR DEN DESIGNPREIS DER BRD: 2000 für STEP; 2007 für SYSTEM 24
IF HANNOVER: 1995 Preis für gutes Industriedesign OPTIONAL; 2003 Preis für gutes Industriedesign IN-TWO; 2006 Preis für gutes Industriedesign SYSTEM 24
GOOD DESIGN AWARD: 2003 Preis für gutes Industriedesign IN-TWO
IF CHINA: 2003 Preis für gutes Industriedesign P.O.S.; 2003 Preis für gutes Industriedesign IN-TWO
I.DOT ITALY: 2002 P.O.S. ausgewählt für „Italien Design on Tour"
RANKING DESIGN: 2002 10. Position in der Kategorie Office and Object Design
INNOVATIONSPREIS ARCHITEKTUR UND OFFICE 2000: 2000 AiT, ABiT und intelligent architecture SYNTHESE
ARCHITEKTUR UND WOHNEN: 1998 ausgewählt für die 125 besten Innenarchitekten und Designer
BEST OF NEOCON CHICAGO: 1998 Gewinner des Silver Award K. NET
THE CHICAGO ATHENAEUM: 1998 ausgewählt für die Ausstellung good design 98 P.O.S.
JOSEF BINDER AWARD VIENNE: 1997 Design Award SPIRIT

AWARDS

KOREFE – KOLLE REBBE FORM UND ENTWICKLUNG
CANNES: 2011 Silber – The Deli Garage Käsestifte; 2011 Bronze – STOP THE WATER WHILE USING ME!; 2010 Gold – Borkebjs Die Rückkehr der Monster
MOBIUS: 2011 Second Place – Borkebjs Die Rückkehr der Monster
NEW YORK FESTIVALS: 2010 Gold – Borkebjs Die Rückkehr der Monster; 2010 Gold – Corporate Design der The Deli Garage; 2010 Bronze – The Deli Garage Schokoleim; 2010 Bronze – The Deli Garage Esslack
CLIO: 2010 Bronze – Corporate Design der The Deli Garage
D&AD: 2011 In Book (Bronze) – STOP THE WATER WHILE USING ME!; 2010 In Book (Bronze) – Corporate Design der The Deli Garage; 2010 In Book (Bronze) – The Deli Garage Mehrzwecknudeln
FAB AWARD: 2010 FAB Award (Gold) – Corporate Design der The Deli Garage
ADC DEUTSCHLAND: 2011 Silber – STOP THE WATER WHILE USING ME!; 2011 Bronze – The Deli Garage Backsteine; 2010 Bronze – The Deli Garage Mehrzwecknudeln
ADC EUROPE: 2011 Gold – STOP THE WATER WHILE USING ME!
PENTAWARDS: 2011 Gold – The Deli Garage Lutschwerkzeug; 2011 Bronze – The Deli Garage Käsestifte; 2010 – meist ausgezeichnetste Agentur des Jahres; 2010 Platin – The Deli Garage Schokoleim; 2010 Gold – Corporate Design der The Deli Garage; 2010 Silber – STOP THE WATER WHILE USING ME!
RED DOT: 2011 red dot (Silber) – Corporate Design von Tony Petersen Film; 2010 red dot best of the best (Gold) – The Deli Garage Esslack; 2010 red dot best of the best (Gold) – STOP THE WATER WHILE USING ME!; 2010 red dot (Silber) – Corporate Design von Laid Records; 2010 red dot (Silber) – The Deli Garage Mehrzwecknudeln; 2010 red dot (Silber) – Borkebjs Die Rückkehr der Monster; 2010 red dot (Silber) – Galerie Mono KYRRD; 2010 red dot (Silber) – STOP THE WATER WHILE USING ME!
LONDON INTERNATIONAL AWARDS: 2010 Silber – Borkebjs Die Rückkehr der Monster
DDC: 2010 Silber – Borkebjs Die Rückkehr der Monster
MONTREUX: 2011 Gold – inlingua. A Story Lost in Translation
BERLINER TYPE: 2010 Gold – Galerie Mono KYRRD
EPICA: 2010 Bronze – The Deli Garage Mehrzwecknudeln
EURO BEST: 2010 Silber – Borkebjs Die Rückkehr der Monster; 2010 Bronze – Corporate Design der The Deli Garage; 2010 Bronze – The Deli Garage Schokoleim; 2010 Bronze – The Deli Garage Mehrzwecknudeln
ONE SHOW: 2011 Silber – STOP THE WATER WHILE USING ME!; 2011 Silber – Borkebjs Die Rückkehr der Monster; 2011 Bronze – Borkebjs Die Rückkehr der Monster
IF DESIGN: 2010 Gold – Borkebjs Die Rückkehr der Monster

KURZ KURZ DESIGN
IF PRODUCT DESIGN AWARD: 2009 für Xled, Steinel; 2007 für TWIN 1731, Zwilling; 2006 für sensIQ, Steinel; 2005 für atmoMAG, Vaillant; 2005 für turboMAG, Vaillant; 2003 für EasyLock, Hettich; 2002 für VED-E classic, Vaillant; 2002 für VED, Vaillant; 2001 für InnoTech, Hettich; 1996 für Una 1000, Hüppe
RED DOT DESIGN AWARD: 2011 für Palmarium, Küppersbusch; 2009 für senses, spirit of senses; 2006 für Star Z15TT, Wilo; 2003 für Merkur, damixa; 2003 für FiberT1 Automatic, Knirps; 1995 für Una 1000, Hüppe
DESIGN PLUS AWARD: 2001 für VED-E, Vaillant; 1997 für Marano, Hüppe
PLUS X AWARD KÖLN: 2008 für Xled, Steinel
INTERZUM AWARD: 2003 für EasyLock, Hettich; 2001 für InnoTech, Hettich
Q-ROUGE NRW: 2005 für Corporate Design, Dürselen
GOOD DESIGN CHICAGO: 2006 für TWIN Select, Zwilling

KW43 BRANDDESIGN
ANDY AWARD: 2003
ANIMAGO: 2003
ART DIRECTORS CLUB GERMANY: 1998, 2002, 2006, 2009
ART DIRECTORS CLUB NEW YORK: 1998, 2000, 2002
BERLINER TYPE: 2000, 2002, 2004, 2005
CORPORATE DESIGN PREIS: 2000, 2011
CREATIVITY: 2001, 2009
DESIGN-EHRENPREIS DES LANDES NRW: 2005
DEUTSCHER DESIGNER CLUB: 2005, 2006, 2008, 2009, 2010, 2011
NOMINIERT ZUM DESIGNPREIS DER BRD: 2007, 2008, 2010, 2011, 2012
DT. MARKETINGPREIS: 2003
DT. PREIS FÜR KOMMUNIKATIONSDESIGN: 1998, 2000
DT. PREIS FÜR WIRTSCHAFTSKOMMUNIKATION: 2002
EPICA AWARD: 1998
GLOBAL CORPORATE IDENTITY: 2002
IF DESIGN AWARD: 2002-2004, 2009, 2010, 2011
INTERNATIONAL MIDAS AWARD: 2002
LEAGUE OF AMERICAN COMMUNICATIONS PROFESSIONALS: 2004, 2007
LONDON INTERNATIONAL ADVERTISING AWARD: 1998, 2002, 2005, 2009
LORIE AWARDS: 1998
MOSKOW INTERNATIONAL ADVERTISING FESTIVAL: 2000
MOBIUS: 2002
NEW YORK FESTIVALS: 1998, 2000-2002
RED DOT DESIGN AWARD: 2002-2004, 2007, 2009, 2010, 2011
TYPE DIRECTORS CLUB: 1998, 2010

L

LSG SKY CHEFS CATERING LOGISTICS GMBH
RED DOT „BEST-OF-THE-BEST": 2009 für Lufthansa Economy Class Geschirr
GOOD DESIGN JAPAN: 2009 für Lufthansa Economy Class Geschirr
NOMINIERT FÜR DESIGNPREIS DER BRD: 2009 für Lufthansa Economy Class Geschirr
OBSERVEUR DU DESIGN FRANKREICH: 2009 für Corsairfly Economy Class Geschirr
"STARS OF" OBSERVEUR DU DESIGN FRANKREICH: 2009 für TAM Ainrlines Geschirr aus Zuckerrohr/ Sugarcane
NOMINIERT FÜR DESIGNPREIS DER BRD: 2010 für TAM Airlines Geschirr aus Zuckerrohr/ Sugarcane
GOOD DESIGN JAPAN: 2010 für TAM Airlines Geschirr aus Zuckerrohr/ Sugarcane
OBSERVEUR DU DESIGN FRANKREICH: 2010 für Lufthansa „Secretary" Tablett
OBSERVEUR DU DESIGN FRANKREICH: 2010 für Czech Airlines „Passion" Geschirrserie
RED DOT "HONOURABLE MENTION": 2010 für Lufthansa Business Class starter box
GOOD DESIGN JAPAN: 2010 für Lufthansa Business Class starter box
IF DESIGN AWARD: 2010 für Air Berlin Geschirrserie
GOOD DESIGN USA: 2010 für TAM Airlines Geschirr aus Zuckerrohr/ Sugarcane
GOOD DESIGN USA: 2010 für Finnair Porzellan Serie
OBSERVEUR DU DESIGN FRANKREICH: 2011 Lufthansa Metropolitan Mahlzeitenbox

M

DESIGNBÜRO WOLFGANG C.R. MEZGER
AUSZEICHNUNG BEIM BRAUN PREIS: 1980
AUSZEICHNUNG VERSCHIEDENER PRODUKTE DURCH AUFNAHME IN DIE DESIGN AUSWAHL DES DESIGN CENTER STUTTGART: 1984, 1985, 1986, 1992, 1994
MÖBELDESIGN MADE IN GERMANY: 1984
HAUS INDUSTRIEFORM ESSEN: 1985
TOP TEN, ZEITSCHRIFT ZUHAUSE: 1989
TOP TEN, AUSWAHL DESIGNZENTRUM NORDRHEIN-WESTFALEN UND MD: 1991
PRODUCT DESIGN AWARD, INSTITUTE OF BUSINESS DESIGNERS NEW YORK: 1992
IF INDUSTRIE FORUM DESIGN, HANNOVER: 1993
ROTER PUNKT FÜR HOHE DESIGNQUALITÄT VOM DESIGNZENTRUM NORDRHEINWESTFALEN: 1993, 1994
ROSCOE DESIGN AWARD, NEW YORK: 1993
NIEDERLÄNDISCHER MÖBELPREIS: Prijs voor het beste nederlandse Meubelontwerp, Amsterdam 1993
„GOED INDUSTRIEEL ONTWERP": The Foundation Goed Industrial Design, Den Haag, 1996, 1997
INTERNATIONAL INTERIOR DESIGN ASSOCIATION: Apex Award Gold, New York 1997
BEST OF NEOCON, GOLD AWARD, CHICAGO: 1998, 2002, 2008, 2011 2x
DESIGN INNOVATIONEN '99: Auszeichnung für Hohe Designqualität, Designzentrum Nordrhein Westfalen, 1999
TOP 200 FOR 2000: MD 1 / 2000
BEST OF NEOCON, SILVER AWARD, CHICAGO: 2000, 2006, 2007
GOOD DESIGN AWARD: 2000, 2002 the Chicago ATHENAEUM Museum Of Architecture And Design
BEST OF DESIGN WEEK: Design Journal, Los Angeles, 2000
RED DOT AWARD: Design Zentrum Nordrhein-Westfalen, Essen 2001
„BEST SELECTION: OFFICE DESIGN": Design Zentrum Nordrhein-Westfalen, Essen 2001
BEST OF SHOW AWARD – DESIGN JOURNAL, LOS ANGELES: 2002
ADEX PLATINUM AWARD FOR SEATING FURNITURE, USA: 2002
ADEX AWARD, BEST OF COMPETITION, USA: 2002
FOCUS BALANCE, INTERNATIONALER DESIGNPREIS BADEN-WÜRTTEMBERG: 2003
INTERNATIONAL INTERIOR DESIGN ASSOCIATION:
ACCLAIM AWARD AND BEST OF COMPETITION, LOS ANGELES: 2003
NOMINIERT FÜR DESIGNPREIS DER BUNDESREPUBLIK DEUTSCHLAND: 2004, 2008, 2009, 2010, 2011
IF PRODUCT DESIGN AWARD: 2004, 2006, 2007, 2008
DDC AWARD: 2004, 2006, 2007, 2008, 2009
IIDEX / NEOCON CANADA INNOVATION AWARDS: Silver, 2008
INTERIOR INNOVATION AWARD, COLOGNE: 2011
BEST OF NEOCON, NOMINATED FOR "BEST OF COMPETITION", CHICAGO: 2011

MEYER-HAYOZ DESIGN ENGINEERING GROUP

RED DOT DESIGN AWARD PRODUCT DESIGN: 2009 für KiBox To Go der Firma Kistler Instrumente AG; 2009 für VITA Linearguide 3D-Master der VITA Zahnfabrik H. Rauter GmbH & Co. KG; 2009 honourable mention für Gallus ICS 670 der Gallus Ferd. Rüesch AG; 2009 honourable mention für the modula wave der Kirsten Soldering AG; 2007 für Hausautomationssystem der Adhoco AG; 2004 für VITA VM Flasche der VITA Zahnfabrik H. Rauter GmbH & Co. KG; 2002 für EvoTron der HealthTronics, Inc.; 2002 für Orthora 200 der Mikrona Technologie AG; 2001 für Gallus RCS 330 der Gallus Ferd. Rüesch AG; 2001 für CombiDrum / CombiServer der Ferag AG; 1993 "Die Besten der Besten" für Schleifmaschine für keramische Inlays (Celay) der Mikrona Technologie AG
GOOD DESIGN CHICAGO ATHENAEUM: 2004 für VITA VM Flasche der VITA Zahnfabrik H. Rauter GmbH & Co. KG; 2002 für EvoTron der HealthTronics, Inc.; 2002 für Orthora 200 der Mikrona Technologie AG
NOMINIERT FÜR DEN DESIGN PREIS DEUTSCHLAND: 2011 Gallus ECS 340 der Gallus Ferd. Rüesch AG; 2011 Premion Line by SVG der SVG Medizinsysteme GmbH & Co. KG 2011 für VIRTU RR 50 der Polytype Ltd.; 2011 für VITA Vacumat 6000 M der VITA Zahnfabrik H. Rauter GmbH & Co. KG; 2004 für VITA VM Flasche der VITA Zahnfabrik H. Rauter GmbH & Co. KG
IF DESIGN AWARD CHINA: 2010 für XEVONTA der B.Braun Avitum AG; Gold 2003 in Shanghai für VITA VM Flasche der VITA Zahnfabrik H. Rauter GmbH & Co. KG
DESIGN PREIS SCHWEIZ: 2003 Anerkennung für VITA VM Flasche der VITA Zahnfabrik H. Rauter GmbH & Co. KG; 2001 Nomination für CombiDrum / CombiServer der Ferag AG; 1999 Anerkennung für Mehrphasenwebmaschine M8300 der Sulzer Textil AG; 1997 Anerkennung für Etikettenmaschine Indigo DO 330 der Gallus Ferd. Rüesch AG; 1991 Anerkennung für Schleifmaschine für keramische Inlays (Celay) der Mikrona Technologie AG; 1991 Anerkennung für CDA-Terminal der Egeli AG
FOCUS OPEN: 2010 Silber für Gallus ECS 340 der Gallus Ferd. Rüesch AG; 2010 Silber für Premion Line by SVG der SVG Medizinsysteme GmbH & Co. KG
INTERNATIONALER DESIGN PREIS BADEN-WÜRTTEMBERG: 1997 für Coriolis Durchflussmesssystem Promass der Endress + Hauser Flowtec AG
IF PRODUCT DESIGN AWARD: 2011 für VITA Vacumat 6000 M der VITA Zahnfabrik H. Rauter GmbH & Co. KG; 2011 für Gallus ECS 340 der Gallus Ferd. Rüesch AG; 2011 für VIRTU RR 50 der Polytype Ltd.; 2004 für VITA VM Flasche der VITA Zahnfabrik H. Rauter GmbH & Co. KG; 2004 für Dialog+ der B.Braun Avitum AG; 2004 für Shape Twist der SIG allCap AG; 2003 für Litho Diamond der HealthTronics, Inc.; 2001 für CombiDrum / CombiServer der Ferag AG
IF DESIGN AWARD SILVER: 2002 für Combi Twist der SIG allCap AG
CDIF CHINA PRODUCT INNOVATION DESIGN AWARD: 2003 in Gold in Shenzhen für VITA VM Flasche der VITA Zahnfabrik H. Rauter GmbH & Co. KG
DIE NEUE SAMMLUNG: 1993 Aufnahme in die Pinakothek der Moderne München für Ascom Telefonsystem
DESIGN SENSE AWARD, DESIGN MUSEUM LONDON: 2000 für Mehrphasenwebmaschine M8300 der Sulzer Textil AG

MILLA & PARTNER

ADC: 2011 balancity, Deutscher Pavillon, Expo 2010 (Silber); Die Kugel von balancity (1 x Silber, 2 x Bronze, 1 x Auszeichnung); 2009 Bronze für IdeenPark; 2008 Auszeichnung für Container für Flüchtlinge; 2006 Auszeichnung für Die Welt von Steiff, Giengen; 2006 Silber für Brockhaus Frankfurter Buchmesse; 2002 Silber für www.milla.de
ADC OF NEW YORK: 2006 Distinctive Merit, Brockhaus Frankfurter Buchmesse
ADAM AWARD: 2010 balancity, Deutscher Pavillon, Expo 2010; 2004 Sonderpreis für Themenparks: Biovision; 2001 Silber für Nautica, Pavillon des BMVBW Expo 2000
CANNES PROMO LÖWE: 2006 für Brockhaus Frankfurter Buchmesse
DDC AWARD: 2010 balancity, Deutscher Pavillon, Expo 2010; 2008 Auszeichnung für IdeenPark; 2006 Bronze für Brockhaus Frankfurter Buchmesse
EVA AWARD: 2010 balancity, Deutscher Pavillon, Expo 2010; 2007 Bronze für Container für Flüchtlinge; 2006 Gold für Brockhaus Frankfurter Buchmesse; 2004 Bronze für Siemens International Sales Meeting Sardinien; 2003 Bronze für E.ON auf der Hannover Messe Industrie; 2002 Sonderpreis für Wir Flüchtlinge in Stuttgart; 2000 Silber für Bosch Pavillon, Expo 2000; 1999 Gold für Weidmüller Messestand HMI; 1998 Gold für OCEANIS Lissabon
EXHIBITOR EXPO 2010 AWARD: 2010 Best Pavilion balancity, Deutscher Pavillon Expo 2010; Best interaction: Die Kugel von balancity
IF COMMUNICATION DESIGN AWARD: 2011 Auszeichnung für Mercedes-Benz auf der Automechanika, Auszeichnung für E.ON Multitouch-Medientisch, Auszeichnung für Die Kugel von balancity, Gold für balancity, Deutscher Pavillon, Expo 2010; 2008 Auszeichnung für E.ON auf der Hannover Messe; 2006 Auszeichnung für Brockhaus Frankfurter Buchmesse; 2004 Auszeichnung für Ausstellung Foyer Bosch Repräsentanz, Berlin; 2002 Silber für www.milla.de
IF PRODUCT DESIGN AWARD: 2004 Auszeichnung für Travego-Exponat, Messeauftritt Mercedes-Benz Nutzfahrzeuge
INTERNATIONALER DESIGNPREIS BADEN-WÜRTTEMBERG: 2005 Auszeichnung für Mercedes-Benz Nutzfahrzeuge auf der Nfz IAA
GOLDEN AWARD OF MONTREUX: 2011 Gold für balancity, Deutscher Pavillon, Expo 2010; Auszeichnung für Die Kugel von balancity
NOMINIERT FÜR DEN DESIGNPREIS DEUTSCHLAND: 2011 für E.ON Multitouch-Medientisch; balancity, Deutscher Pavillon, Expo 2010; Die Kugel von balancity; 2009 für E.ON auf der Hannover Messe; 2009 für IdeenPark; 2007 für Brockhaus Frankfurter Buchmesse; 2004 Ausstellung Bosch Repräsentanz, Berlin; 2004 für www.milla.de
RED DOT AWARD COMMUNICATION DESIGN: 2010 Gold für E.ON Multitouch-Medientisch; Auszeichnung für balancity, Deutscher Pavillon, Expo 2010; 2006 Auszeichnung für Brockhaus Frankfurter Buchmesse; 2004 Auszeichnung für E.ON auf der Hannover Messe Industrie; 2002 best of the best für www.milla.de
XAVER EVENT AWARD: 2004 Auszeichnung für Opel Signum WindowScapes, Automobilsalon Genf
BEST OF BUSINESS TO BUSINESS: 2002 Silber für www.milla.de
DEUTSCHER MULTIMEDIA AWARD: 2002 Auszeichnung für www.milla.de VOL 1

MOSKITO KOMMUNIKATION UND DESIGN

BEST OF CORPORATE PUBLISHING: Silber
RED DOT DESIGN AWARD
DESIGNPREIS DER BUNDESREPUBLIK DEUTSCHLAND: Nominierung
IF DESIGN AWARD: in der Disziplin Communication Design
BERLINER TYPE: Silber
BEST OF BUSINESS-TO-BUSINESS COMMUNICATIONS AWARD: Shortlist
INKOM GRAND PRIX: 3. Platz in der Kategorie Mitarbeiterkommunikation
BERLINER TYPE: Gold und Silber
MEDIENPREIS «DIE BESTEN KUNDENMAGAZINE»: 2. Platz in der Kategorie B2B und Innovation des Jahres
WUV CORPORATE PUBLISHING PREIS

MOYSIG RETAIL DESIGN

JANUS 2008 DE L'INDUSTRIE: für Präsentationssystem Grid 40

N

NEXUS PRODUCT DESIGN

EHRENPREIS TOP TEN DESIGN NRW: 2003
NOMINIERT FÜR DEN BUNDESPREIS FÜR PRODUKTDESIGN: 1995, 1998, 2004, 2006–2008
EHRENPREIS FÜR PRODUKTDESIGN DES LANDES NRW: 1997
DESIGN PLUS, FRANKFURT: 2003, 2009
GOOD DESIGN AWARD, THE CHICAGO ATHENAEUM: 2006, 2007
RED DOT DESIGN AWARD: 1987, 1989, 1993, 1996, 1997, 2000, 2003, 2004, 2006, 2007, 2010
RED DOT AWARD „DIE BESTEN DER BESTEN": 1997
RED DOT AWARD COMMUNICATION DESIGN: 2001
IF DESIGN AWARD: 1995, 1998, 2000, 2003, 2006, 2008
LIGHTING PRODUCT AWARD: 1997
DESIGN AUSWAHL STUTTGART: 1988
BAYERISCHER STAATSPREIS: 1989
AIT INNOVATIONSPREIS ARCHITEKTUR UND TECHNIK: 2007 und ARCHITECTURE AND HEALTH 2008
BAYERISCHER STAATSPREIS FÜR NACHWUCHSDESIGNER: 2002
DESIGNPREIS NEUNKIRCHEN: 2001
MARIANNE-BRANDT-PREIS: 2001
GOLDEN INTRAMA, BRNO: 1994
„FRISCHZELLEN"-WETTBEWERB VON „NEUEKOEPFE.DE": 2002, 1. Preis

NODESIGN

RED DOT DESIGN AWARD: 2003, 2005, 2006 3 red dot Awards; 2008 2 red dot Awards; 2009
PLAKAT GRAND PRIX SILBER: 2004
IF COMMUNICATION DESIGN AWARD: 2006, 2005 2 iF Awards; 2010
NOMINIERT FÜR DEN DESIGNPREIS DER BRD: 2006 2 x; 2007 4 x; 2009 2 x; 2010
BUCHMARKT-AWARD: 2008
GOLD MGF AWARD: 2010 Shortlist
BRONZE UND SILBER DDC AWARD: 2010 2 x
BRONZE EUROPEAN DESIGN AWARD: 2011

P

PEARL CREATIVE
DESIGNPREIS DER BUNDESREPUBLIK DEUTSCHLAND: In Silber 1 x
DESIGNPREIS DER BUNDESREPUBLIK DEUTSCHLAND: Nominiert 14 x
IF PRODUCT DESIGN AWARD: 14 x
RED DOT PRODUCT DESIGN AWARD: 14 x
GOOD DESIGN AWARD: 4 x
FOCUS INTERNATIONALER DESIGNPREIS BADEN-WÜRTTEMBERG: In Gold 1 x; In Silber 7 x
FOCUS INTERNATIONALER DESIGNPREIS BADEN-WÜRTTEMBERG PUBLIKUMSPREIS: 1 x
PLUS X AWARD: 1 x
IF MATERIAL AWARD: 1 x
MATERIALICA DESIGN + TECHNOLOGY AWARD: 1 x
CATERER AND HOTELKEEPER AWARD: 1 x
ISSA INTERCLEAN INNOVATION AWARD: 2 x
KÜCHE AWARD: 2011 1 x
DOMOTECHNIKA AWARD: 2 x
DESIGN DEUTSCHLAND CASE STUDY 2008
I.D. INDUSTRIAL DESIGN REVIEW

PETER SCHMIDT GROUP [AUSZÜGE]
BERLINER TYPE AWARD – DIE BESTEN DRUCKSCHRIFTEN: 2007 Silber für HUGO BOSS Geschäftsbericht 2005; 2007 Bronze für Linde Geschäftsbericht 2005; 2007 Bronze für Wöhner Didaktische Broschüre; 2008 Nominierung für Linde Geschäftsbericht 2006; 2008 Diplom für Peter Schmidt Group Imagebuch 2008; 2009 Diplom für Peter Schmidt Group Elephant Print No. 2; 2010 Diplom für Linde Geschäftsbericht 2009; 2011 Diplom für Linde Geschäftsbericht 2010; 2011 Nominierung für STOXX – Pressekit, Deutsche Börse; 2011 Nominierung für Peter Schmidt Group Elephant Print No. 4
CORPORATE DESIGN AWARD: 2007 Nominierung für KION; 2009 Nominierung für Wataniya Airways; 2010 Nominierung für BOSS ORANGE; 2010 Nominierung für MASA AG; 2010 Gold für Nezu Museum, Tokio; 2011 Auszeichnung für Nezu Private, Tokio; 2011 Auszeichnung für STOXX, Deutsche Börse; 2011 Nominierung für Goethe-Institut
DEUTSCHER DESIGNER CLUB GUTE GESTALTUNG: 2007 Bronze für Blat Advanced Vodka, Cogrami Canarias; 2007 Bronze für Persil International Relaunch für Henkel; 2007 Wöhner Didaktische Broschüre; 2008 GOLD für Juchheim – Die Marke; 2009 Wataniya Airways
IF COMMUNICATION DESIGN AWARD: 2007 Juchheim Die Meister „Strahlendes Glück"; 2007 Linde Geschäftsbericht 2006; 2007 GOLD für Persil International Relaunch für Henkel; 2007 Wöhner Didaktische Broschüre; 2008 HUGO BOSS Geschäftsbericht 2007; 2008 Linde CR Report 2007; 2008 Linde Geschäftsbericht 2007; 2008 Peter Schmidt Group Imagebuch 2008; 2009 BayWa Geschäftsbericht 2008; 2009 Peter Schmidt Group Elephant Print No. 2; 2009 Linde Geschäftsbericht 2008, 2009 Linde Technology 2008; 2009 Wataniya Airways – Corporate Design; 2010 Rewe Feine Welt; 2010 MASA AG – Corporate Design; 2010 Juchheim Die Meister „Valentine's Day 2010"; 2011 KION News; 2011 Goethe-Institut Imagebroschüre
IF PACKAGING AWARD: 2008 Blat Advanced Vodka, Cogrami Canarias; 2008 GOLD für Juchheim „Die Meister" Oil & Perfume Collection
RED DOT AWARD: COMMUNICATION DESIGN: 2007 GMX MultiMessenger; 2007 HUGO BOSS Geschäftsbericht 2006; 2007 Juchheim Die Meister „Strahlendes Glück"; 2007 Linde CR Report 2005; 2007 Linde Geschäftsbericht 2006; 2007 Persil International Relaunch für Henkel; 2007 Wöhner Didaktische Broschüre; 2008 best of the best für HUGO BOSS Geschäftsbericht 2007; 2008 Linde CR Report 2007; 2009 Nezu Museum, Tokio; 2009 Linde Geschäftsbericht 2008; 2010 Rewe Feine Welt; 2010 BOSS ORANGE; 2011 Karl Juchheim „White Day 2011"; 2011 Rinti Nature's Balance; 2011 Nezu Private, Tokio
ART DIRECTOR'S CLUB DEUTSCHLAND: Bronze 2009 für Blat Advanced Vodka, Cogrami Canarias
BEST CORPORATE PUBLISHING: 2009 Nominierung für Linde Technology 2008; 2011 Gold für Linde Geschäftsbericht 2009
AIGA ANNUAL DESIGN COMPETITIONS OUTSTANDING DESIGN: 2008 Peter Schmidt Group Imagebuch 2008
VISION AWARDS: 2007 Platinum für HUGO BOSS Geschäftsbericht 2006; 2007 Platinum für Linde Geschäftsbericht 2006; 2008 Platinum für HUGO BOSS Geschäftsbericht 2007; 2008 Gold Award für Linde CR Report 2007; 2008 Platinum Award für Linde Geschäftsbericht 2007; 2011 Silber für DZ BANK Geschäftsbericht 2010; 2011 Bronze für Haniel Geschäftsbericht 2010
DESIGN PREIS DER BUNDESREPUBLIK DEUTSCHLAND: 2007 Nominierung für Linde Corporate Design Relaunch 2006; 2007 Nominierung für Linde CR Report 2005; 2007 Nominierung für Linde Geschäftsbericht 2005; 2007 Shortlist für HUGO BOSS Geschäftsbericht 2006; 2007 Shortlist für Linde Geschäftsbericht 2006; 2007 Shortlist für Linde CR Report 2005

PULS PRODUKTDESIGN
IF PRODUCT DESIGN AWARD: 2008 für MultiMotion, Patientenkopfstütze, Kunde Sirona Dental Systems; Gold Award 2009 für Teneo, Dentale Behandlungseinheit, Kunde Sirona Dental Systems; 2009 für FCA, Füllclip-Automat, Kunde Poly-clip System
IF COMMUNICATION DESIGN AWARD: 2010 für Bedienerführung Teneo, Dentale Behandlungseinheit Kunde Sirona Dental Systems
NOMINIERT FÜR DEN DESIGNPREIS DER BRD: 2009 Teneo, Dentale Behandlungseinheit, Kunde Sirona Dental Systems; 2010 Bedienerführung Teneo, Dentale Behandlungseinheit, Kunde Sirona Dental Systems
RED DOT AWARD: 2010 für Sirolaser Advance, Dentallaser, Kunde Sirona Dental Systems
GOOD DESIGN CHICAGO: 2009 für CERC AC, CAD-CAM System, Kunde Sirona Dental Systems; 2009 für SiroLaser Advance, Dentallaser, Kunde Sirona Dental Systems

Q

QUADESIGN PARTNER AG
JOSEF BINDER AWARD: 1997 für Garsystem, AMC International; 1997 für oecos Büromöbelprogramm, DER HOLZHOF GmbH
DESIGN PREIS SCHWEIZ: 2001 für Patientenliege, Swissray Medical AG
GOOD DESIGN USA: 2002 für Messersystem, AMC International
GOOD DESIGN JAPAN: 2002 für Bürostuhlprogramm G63, Stoll Giroflex AG
GOLDENER KREATIVITÄTS-OSKAR: 2004 für Abfalleimer Abfallhai, Brüco Swiss AG
IF PRODUCT DESIGN AWARD: 2005 Gold Award für Rohrleitungssystem iFit, Georg Fischer AG; 2005 Gold Award für Küchenmodule „Eisinger Blocks", Franke Küchentechnik AG; 2006 für OptiFlex mobile Pulverbeschichtungs-Anlagen, ITW Gema GmbH; 2007 für J5 Kaffeevollautomat, Jura Elektroapparate AG; 2008 für Küchenlüftung EVMC 207, Wesco AG; 2008 für Küchenlüftung EVMC 211, Wesco AG; 2010 für Planario sink, Franke Italy; 2010 für J7 Kaffeevollautomat, Jura Elektroapparate AG; 2010 für Z7 Kaffeevollautomat, Jura Elektroapparate AG
DESIGN PLUS: 2005 für Rohrleitungssystem iFit, Georg Fischer AG
NOMINIERT FÜR DEN DESIGN PREIS DER BRD: 2006 für Küchenmodule „Eisinger-Blocks", Franke Küchentechnik AG; 2006 für Rohrleitungssystem iFit, Georg Fischer AG; 2009 für J5 Kaffeevollautomat, Jura Elektroapparate AG
RED DOT DESIGN AWARD: 2007 für J5 Kaffeevollautomat, Jura Elektroapparate AG; 2010 best of the best für Visualizer VZ9, WolfVision GmbH; 2011 für J9 One Touch Kaffeevollautomat, Jura Elektroapparate AG
GOOD DESIGN: 2007 für J5 Kaffeevollautomat, Jura Elektroapparate AG; 2009 für Visualizer VZ9, WolfVision GmbH
PLUS X AWARD: 2010 für KNX TouchPanel 7, für PIRIOS Bewegungsmelder, für EDIZIOdue Lichtschalter, Feller AG
INTERIOR INNOVATION AWARD: 2011 für Planario sink, Franke Italy
DESIGNPREIS DER BRD: 2012 nominiert für Visualizer VZ-9 plus3, Wolfvision GmbH

R

REALDESIGN GMBH
IF AWARD: 1991 für Portaldrehkran, Kranbau Eberswalde; 1991 für Eisenbahndrehkran, Kirow Leipzig
BUNDESPREIS PRODUKTDESIGN: 1992 für Portaldrehkran, Kranbau Eberswalde
SÄCHSISCHER STAATSPREIS FÜR DESIGN: 1994 für Ohrspülgerät, Dantschke Leipzig

RINCÓN2 MEDIEN GMBH
NOMINIERT FÜR DEN DESIGNPREIS DEUTSCHLAND: 2012
SILBER/EUROPEAN DESIGN AWARD: 2010
RED DOT DESIGN AWARD: 2007, corporate design für die Geschäftsausstattung von Kunde Creutz & Partners, Aachen
INNOVATIONSPREIS DER „INITIATIVE MITTELSTAND": 2008 für das agentureigene Content-Management-System webVanilla® Buch 2.indb 190 28.08.2009 12:41:45
ADC DEUTSCHLAND: 2000 in Gold und Silber
IAAA: 2000 in Silber und Bronze
EUROBEST: 2000 Finalist
KONTAKTER ANZEIGE DER WOCHE: 1999 Auszeichnung
CANNES FESTIVAL: 1999 Shortlist
LONDON INTERNATIONAL ADVERTISING AWARD: 1999 Finalist
EPICA: 1999 Finalist
GEWINNENDE WERBUNG: 1999 in Gold
ANDY ADVERTISING CLUB OF NEW YORK: 1999 Finalist
DIE ANZEIGE: 1999 in Bronze
JAHRBUCH DER WERBUNG: 1997 Phoenix Product Design Branchensieger
BERLINER TYPE: 1996 in Silber für Mercedes-Benz SLK-Silberfibel
EUROPEAN REGIONAL DESIGN ANNUAL: 1995 Design Excellence für VW Käfer Kalender

S

SCALA DESIGN
IF PRODUCT DESIGN AWARD: 1995 für Diamant Kernbohrgerät – HILTI DD-250-E; 1996 für Schlitzgerät – HILTI DC-S E19; 1997 für Akku Montageschrauber – HILTI SB 10; 1997 für Meißelhammer – HILTI TE 704; 1997 für Kombihammer – Hilti TE 55; 1997 für Kombihammer – HILTI TE 75 – 2011 für Universal-Werkzeughalter – Nishiumura Jig SpinChuck
INTERNATIONAL DESIGN AWARD BADEN-WÜRTTEMBERG: 1998 für Hochgeschwindigkeitsplotter HSP – Lasercomb Laser-Kombinations-Systeme GmbH; 1998 für Rotationslaser – HILTI PR 10; 1998 für Rotationslaser – HILTI PR 50; 1998 für Meißelhammer HILTI TE 905 – 2010 für Kreuzlinienlaser – NEDO Quasar 6 – 2010 für Rotationslaser – NEDO Primus 2 – 2010 für Universal-Werkezughalter – Nishimura Jig SpinChuck
RED DOT PRODUCT DESIGN AWARD: 2008 für Kombihammer – Metabo KHE 56 – 2011 für Garten- und Wellness-Liege – Scala Designware Longchair – 2011 für Dentalkompressor – Dürr Dental Tornado 2 – 2011 für Speicherfolienlesegerät – Dürr Dental VistaCan mini plus – 2011 für Universal-Werkzeughalter – Nishimura Jig SpinChuck – 2011 für Kreuzlinienlaser – NEDO Quasar 6 – 2011 für Rotationslaser – NEDO Primus 2

MARIUS SCHREYER DESIGN
IF PRODUCT DESIGN AWARD: 1997 - Aufzugswerke Schmitt + Sohn GmbH & Co. "Elevator Systems"
IF PRODUCT DESIGN AWARD: 2008 - Aufzugswerke Schmitt + Sohn GmbH & Co. „Color Glas Aufzüge"
NOMINIERUNG DESIGNPREIS 2009 DES BUNDESMINISTERIUM FÜR WIRTSCHAFT UND TECHNOLOGIE: - Aufzugwerke Schmitt + Sohn GmbH & Co. „Color Glas Aufzüge"

SIGN KOMMUNIKATION GMBH
Auszug (seit 2004):
IF COMMUNICATION DESIGN AWARD: 2009 für Magazin „Hear the World 9"; 2007 für Magazin „Hear the World", Buch „Bathrooms", Bücher „the design annual"; 2006 Gold Award für Buch „Switch"; 2006 für Buch „Blanko", „100 Jahre e15", Katalog „e15"; 2005 für Buch „20 Jahre serien.lighting", Buch „Office Solutions"; 2004 für Buch „Blockade"
RED DOT DESIGN AWARD: 2009 „best of the best" für „Sakura"; 2009 für „Dossier / Claus Richter", Buch „B / Lack", Buch „Flight"; 2007 für Katalog „e15"; 2006 für Buch „Blanko"
BERLINER TYPE: 2008 Diplom für Magazin „Switch"; 2005 Diplom für Buch „Blanko"
BEST OF CORPORATE PUBLISHING (BCP): 2009 Silber für Magazin „Switch"; 2008 Silber für Magazin „Switch"; 2007 Gold für Magazin „Hear the World"; 2005 Silber für Magazin „Stylepark"
TDC NY 28: 2007 „Certificate for Typographic Excellence" für Signage „Touchy-feely", Buch „Blanko"
TOKYO TDC: 2007 Buch „Switch", Buch „Blanko"; 2006 Buch „A word is worth a thousand pictures"; 2005 Buch „Barock 2004"; 2004 Buch „Logotypographic", Buch „Blockade", Poster „Stylepark", Buch „Furnitured Ways"

UWE SPANNAGEL™
RED DOT: 2011 für die Küchenarmatur Culina von Blanco
IF: 2011 für die Duschbadewanne Stairway von Repabad
NOMINIERT FÜR DEN DESIGNPREIS DER BRD: 2010 Badewanne Easy In 170/180 der Firma Repabad
IF PRODUCT DESIGN AWARD: 2009 für die Duschbadewanne Easy In von Repabad; 2008 für die freistehende Badewanne Ovalis für Repabad; 2003 für den LCD Fernseher TV-Familie von 23–50 Zoll; 1996 für Fast Security Softwareschutz-Adapter Hardlock Twin
DESIGN PLUS AWARD: 2009 für die Duschbadewanne Easy In von Repabad; 2008 für das Luxus-Dampfbad Aspen von Repabad; 2005 für das Küchenplanungsprogramm Steelart der Firma Blanco
RED DOT DESIGN AWARD: 2009 für die Einbauspüle Kristall von Blanco; 2004 für den Plasma Fernseher MD 40333 von Medion; 2003 für den Medion TFT Display MD 9404 QB
NOMINIERT FÜR DEN DESIGNPREIS DER BRD: 2006- Keramikdampfbad Aspen der Firma Repabad
GOOD DESIGN CHICAGO: 2004 für den Medion PC für den Massenmarkt

STRUPPLER INDUSTRIEDESIGN
NOMINIERUNG FÜR DEN DESIGNPREIS DER BRD: 2009 für e-mood; 2007 für Relations; 2007 für F45 Elmo; 2006 für Bagnotherm; 2004 für ZikZak – Steelcase
IF PRODUCT DESIGN AWARD: 2008 für das Badmöbelprogramm e-mood – Duravit; 2008 für die Formatkreissäge WA 80 – Altendorf; 2007 iF Gold Award für die Formatkreissäge F45 Elmo – Altendorf; 2006 für den Badheizkörper Bagnotherm; 2004 für ZikZak – Steelcase
RED DOT DESIGN AWARD: 2007 für Relations – Sedus Systems; 2005 für den Badheizkörper Bagnotherm; 2002 „best of the best" für ZikZak – Steelcase
NEOCON GOLD AWARD: 2011 für das Tischsystem Haworth Kiron; 2006 für den Bürostuhl Mitos – Interstuhl
BEST OFFICE SELECTION: 2003 für den Bürostuhl Mitos
AUSSTELLUNG DES BÜROMÖBELSYSTEMS FRISCO: 2000 im MOMA, NY

STUDIO LAEIS
NOMINIERT FÜR DEN DESIGNPREIS DER BRD: 2009 für Fachanzeige „Natürliche Kaufunktion"; 2007 für Anzeigenkampagne „VITA Zähne" und Fachanzeige „Auf die Gerüste! Fertig! Los!"
IF COMMUNICATION DESIGN AWARD: 2007 für Fachanzeige „Natürliche Kaufunktion"; 2005 für Anzeigenkampagne „VITA Zähne"
RED DOT DESIGN AWARD: 2005 für Fachanzeige „Auf die Gerüste! Fertig! Los!"
PRINTERS CLUB AWARD: 2005 für Bildband "Motivation"

HEINRICH STUKENKEMPER INDUSTRIAL DESIGN TEAM
RED DOT DESIGN AWARD: 2001 für Bleistift grip 2001, Faber-Castell; 2004 für Schreibgeräte emotion Softlack, Faber-Castell; 2005 für Serviersystem, Rösle; 2008 für Design bleistift, Faber-Castell; 2010 Schreibgeräte Faber-Castell Intuition
IF PRODUCT DESIGN AWARD: 1991 für Rollstuhl Genius 522, Meyra; 1995 für Rollstuhl Eurostar, Meyra; 1997 für Rollstuhl Optimus, Meyra; 2001 für Bleistift grip 2001, Faber-Castell; 2007 für Vorlege-Serie, Rösle; 2008 für Radierer sleeve, Faber-Castell; 2011 Schreibgeräte Faber-Castell Loom
DESIGN CENTER STUTTGART: 2000 für Bleistift grip 2001, Faber-Castell
DESIGN PLUS AWARD: 1994 für Bleistifte und Cassette, Graf von Faber-Castell; 1995 für Radierer und Spitzer UFO, Faber-Castell
GOOD DESIGN AWARD: 2007 für Ambition Cocos, Faber-Castell
NOMINIERT FÜR DEN DESIGNPREIS DER BRD: 2006 für Serviersystem, Rösle; 2007 für emotion Edelharz, Faber-Castell; 2008 fürVorlege-Serie, Rösle; 2009 für Ambition Cocos, Faber-Castell; 2009 Designbleistift, Faber-Castell; 2009 Radierer sleeve, Faber-Castell

SYNAPSIS DESIGN GMBH
INTERNATIONALER DESIGNPREIS BADEN-WÜRTTEMBERG FOCUS DIALOG SILBER: 2004 für Maxium, HF-Chirurgiegerät, KLS Martin GmbH & Co.KG
IF PRODUCT DESIGN AWARD: 2009 für miniTwin4, Lichtgitter, SICK AG ; 2006 für Curis, RF-Chirurgiegerät, SUTTER Medizintechnik; 2005 für M4000, Lichtgitter, SICK AG; 2005 für UE403, Elektronikbox, SICK AG
RED DOT DESIGN AWARD: 2009 für miniTwin4, Lichtgitter, SICK AG; 2009 für GM32, Abgasmessgerät, SICK Maihak GmbH
NOMINIERT FÜR DEN DESIGN PREIS DER BRD: 2006, 2005

SYZYGY
ADC DEUTSCHLAND: Auszeichnung Digitale Kampagnen für „Pritt Paper Gang", Auszeichnung Events Craft Dramaturgie für „ADC Awards Show 2010" (2011); Auszeichnung für Digitale Medien Craft – Motiondesign „Jägermeister.de" (2010); Auszeichnung für Microsite „Mercedes-Benz Viano: Der beste Platz für Helden"(2009)
ANNUAL MULTIMEDIA: Auszeichnung für „ZDFmediathek"(2011); Auszeichnung für „jägermeister.de" , Auszeichnung für Jägermeister Hirschkulurerbe" (2010); Auszeichnung für Bannerkampagne „Bird of prey"; Microsite „Mercedes-Benz Viano: Der beste Platz für Helden" (2009); Auszeichnung für Rotwild-Banner „Downhill" (2008)
CANNES CYBER LIONS: Shortlist in Interactive Tools für „ZDFmediathek" (2010); Bronze für Rotwild-Banner „Downhill" (2008)
DDC GUTE GESTALTUNG: Gold Digital Media für „CHANEL N°5 Nachtzug, Bronze Digital Media für „ZDFmediathek", Bronze Digital Media für „Pritt Paper Gang" (2011); Award für „jägermeister.de" (2010); Bronze für Microsite „Mercedes-Benz Viano: Der beste Platz für Helden" (2009)
DMMA ONLINESTAR: Shortlist für „ZDFmediathek", „o2 Surface", „Pritt Paper Gang" (2010); Bronze Sonderformat für „Jägermeister Hirschkulturerbe" (2009); Bronze für Microsite „Mercedes-Benz Viano: Der beste Platz für Helden" (2009)
IF COMMUNICATION DESIGN AWARD: Auszeichnung Online/Offline Applications für Surface: FUJIFILM oder-it ulitmate (2011); Auszeichnung für „ZDFmediathek", „o2 Surface", Gold Award für Mercedes-Benz Viano; in Kategorie Screendesign: Website „uniquedigital GmbH" und Microsite (2009); „Mercedes-Benz Viano: Der beste Platz für Helden"; in Kategorie Animation: Trailer„DARWIN" und Microsite „Mercedes-Benz Viano: Der beste Platz für Helden"(2009)
NEW MEDIA AWARD: Bronze Online für „CHANEL N°5 Nachtzug (2010)
THE NEW YORK FESTIVAL: Finalist Certificate in Digital & Interactive Competition für FRIJJ Swap Soccorettes (2011); Bronze World Medal in Art/Technique: Interactive / Animation und 4x Finalist Certificates in verschiedenen Kategorien für "jägermeister.de"; Finalist Certificates für „CHANEL N°5 Night Train" (2010); Finalist Certificates für Best consumer-targeted website:Microsite „Mercedes-Benz Viano: Der beste Platz für Helden"; Best design: Microsite, „Mercedes-Benz Viano: Der beste Platz für Helden"; Best use of sound / music: Microsite, „Mercedes-Benz Viano: Der beste Platz für Helden"; Banner „Bird of prey" (2009)
HORIZON INTERACTIVE AWARDS: Gold in Integrated Marketing für FRIJJ Swap Soccorettes (2011); 2 Mal Gold, jeweils 1 Mal Silber und Bronze; Gold für Website HSBC Private Bank; Gold für Website „Dolce & Gabbana"; Silber für Website Mazda 2; Bronze für Bannerkampagne „HSBC" (2009)
GOLDEN AWARD OF MONTREUX: 2008 Shortlist für Rotwild-Banner „Downhill"
ONLINE STAR: 2008 Bronze für Rotwild-Banner „Downhill"
EPICA: 2008 Bronze für Microsite „Mercedes-Benz Viano: Der beste Platz für Helden"

MOBIUS AWARDS: 2008 First Place für Microsite „Mercedes-Benz Viano: Der beste Platz für Helden"
THE FWA: Site of the Day [Januar 2010] für "jägermeister.de"; Site of the Day [Oktober 2008] für Microsite „Mercedes-Benz Viano: Der bestePlatz für Helden"
JAHRBUCH DER WERBUNG: 2009 diverse Auszeichnungen für Bannerkampagne „Sticky!" (Pritt); Bannerkampagne „Bird of prey"; Microsite „Mercedes-Benz Viano: Der beste Platz für Helden"; Bannerkampagne „Natural born schredder" (Dt. Post)
ONE SHOW INTERACTIVE: Merit Award in Craft: Interface Design für "o2 Surface: Natural User Interface goes Buisness" (2010)
RED DOT COMMUNICATION DESIGN AWARD: Auszeichnung "red dot: best of the best" für "ZDFmediathek" (2010)
WEBBY AWARD: Official Honoree in Online Campaigns für „Pritt Paper Gang" (2011); : Official Honoree in Food and Beverage für "jägermeister.de" (2010)

T

TEAGUE/SIGNCE
RED DOT DESIGN AWARD: 2005 für WACOM Intuos3 Grafiktablett; 2007 für Bamboo Grafik Stifttablett; 2007 für Leica Geosystems Lino Kreuzlinienlaser; 2007 für Grundig FineArts LCD TV; 2008 für Bamboo Fun Grafik Stifttablett; 2008 für Leica Geosystems Disto D3 Laser Distanzmesser; 2009 für Grundig Vision 9 LCD TV; 2009 Melitta Stage Filterkaffeemaschine
IF PRODUCT DESIGN AWARD: 2011 für AKG K840 KL Wireless headphones; 2011 für Vodafone TV Remote; 2011 für WMF PickUp Einkaufskorb; 2008 für Vodafone 720 3G flip phone; 2008 für Grundig Audiorama Kugellautsprecher; 2009 für Leica Geosystems Roteo Rotationslaser
GOOD DESIGN AWARD: 2007 für Bamboo Grafik Stifttablett
NOMINIERT FÜR DEN DESIGN PREIS DER BRD: 2009 für Bamboo Fun Grafik Stifttablett
IDEA DESIGN AWARD: 2005 Gold Award für WACOM Intuos3 Grafiktablett; 2008 Bronze Award Bamboo Grafik Stifttablett; 2009 Gold Award für Nymphenburg Porzellan Environment; 2008 Finalist für Grundig Audiorama; 2008 Finalist für Grundig FineArts

TINZ.*DDC* / T.V.T SWISSCONSULT GMBH
Mehrfache Design-Auszeichnungen
HIF-DESIGN-PREIS, DESIGN-CENTER STUTTGART, CONSUMER ELECTRONIC & DESIGN-AWARD, IF-PRODUCT DESIGN AWARD, PLATIN DESIGN-AWARD, ÖSTERREICHISCHER STAATSPREIS FÜR DESIGN, CHICAGO-DESIGN-AWARD, REDDOT DESIGN AWARD, TOP 100 UNTERNEHMEN IN BADEN-WÜRTTEMBERG, TOP 100 UNTERNEHMEN IN DEUTSCHLAND, ECON-DESIGN-AWARD DER BESTEN 200 AGENTUREN IN EUROPA

TRICON DESIGN AG
NOMINIERT FÜR DEN DESIGNPREIS DER BRD: 2010 für Produkt „Fahrradträger euro-select"; 2009 Nominierung für Produkt „Opal Warnbalken"
RED DOT DESIGN AWARD: 2009 für Produkt „Fahrradträger euro-select"; 2007 für Produkt „Glacier Express – Panorama-Reisezugwagen"; 2000 für Produkt „Fluggastsitz FAST PRIMO; 2000 für Produkt „Kunststoffsitzschale Pino"; 1997 für Produkt „Fahrgastsystem Wing"
IF PRODUCT DESIGN AWARD: 2009 für Einreichung Produkt „Vio Fußschalter"; 2007 für Produkt „Glacier Express – Panorama-Reisezugwagen"; 2006 für Produkt „Reisebussitz Grand Tourismo"; 1997 für Einreichung Produkt „Fahrgastsystem Wing"
INTERNATIONALER DESIGNPREIS BADEN-WÜRTTEMBERG FOCUS SICHERHEIT: 2007 für Produkt „Opal Warnbalken"

V

VISUPHIL DESIGN STUDIOS
ECON AWARD NOMINEE 2011
NOMINIERUNG FÜR DEN DESIGNPREIS DEUTSCHLAND 2011
ECON AWARD NOMINEE 2010
GOOD DESIGN AWARD 2009
ECON AWARD NOMINEE 2009

W

WALBERT SCHMITZ
IF COMMUNICATION DESIGN AWARD 2001; für Materna auf der CeBIT
ADAM AWARD DER AUSGEZEICHNETEN MESSEAUFTRITTE; 2002 Bronze für SHARP auf der IFA 2001
ADAM AWARD DER AUSGEZEICHNETEN MESSEAUFTRITTE: 2004 Silber für Fujitsu Siemens Computers auf der CeBIT 2004
ADAM AWARD DER AUSGEZEICHNETEN MESSEAUFTRITTE: 2005 Bronze für Grohe auf der ISH 2005
RED DOT AWARD: 2006 für Fujitsu Siemens Computers auf der CeBIT 2004
DESIGNPREIS DER BUNDESREPUBLIK DEUTSCHLAND: 2006 nominiert für Fujitsu Siemens Computers auf der CeBIT 2004
ADAM AWARD DER AUSGEZEICHNETEN MESSEAUFTRITTE: 2007 Bronze für WOLF-Garten auf der gafa 2006
ADAM AWARD DER AUSGEZEICHNETEN MESSEAUFTRITTE: 2008 Gold für Bayer MaterialScience auf der K 2007
RED DOT AWARD: 2008 für Bayer MaterialScience auf der K 2007
DESIGNPREIS DER BUNDESREPUBLIK DEUTSCHLAND: 2009 nominiert für Bayer MaterialScience auf der K 2007
DESIGNPREIS DER BUNDESREPUBLIK DEUTSCHLAND: 2009 nominiert für WOLF-Garten auf der gafa 2006
EXHIBIT DESIGN AWARDS: 2009 Gold für Bayer MaterialScience auf der K 2007
RED DOT AWARD: 2011 für TOTO auf der ISH 2011

REGELINDIS WESTPHAL GRAFIK-DESIGN
IMCA AWARDS: 2007 Bronze in der Kategorie Exhibition Campaign für Albert Einstein. Ingenieur des Universums
DEUTSCHER FOTOBUCHPREIS: 2011 Silber in der Kategorie Fotolehrbücher für BFF Handbuch Basiswissen

WHITE-ID
DEUTSCHER DESIGNPREIS IN GOLD: 2011
DEUTSCHER DESIGNPREIS NOMINIERT: 2010, 2012, 2007, 2008
IF DESIGN AWARD WINNER: 2002, 2003, 2009
RED DOT DESIGN AWARD WINNER: 2006, 2007
FOCUS OPEN SILBER: 2x in 2009, 2007
DEUTSCHER DESIGNER CLUB SILBER: 2010
DESIGN PLUS MATERIAL VISION WINNER: 2011

WIEGE ENTWICKLUNGS GMBH
IF PRODUCT DESIGN AWARD
RED DOT DESIGN AWARD
DESIGNPREIS DER BRD
FOCUS DESIGN AWARD
GOOD DESIGN AWARD
INNOVATIONSPREIS ARCHITEKTUR UND OFFICE
ADAM AWARD
NEOCON BEST OF COMPETITION
UNIVERSAL DESIGN AWARD

Z

ZWÖLFTON DESIGN
IF COMMUNICATION DESIGN AWARD: 2008 / Screendesign www.zwoelfton.com
NOMINIERT FÜR DEN DESIGNPREIS DER BRD: 2009 / www.zwoelfton.com
AUSGEWÄHLT IM ANNUAL MULTIMEDIA: 2009 / www.zwoelfton.com
AUSGEWÄHLT IM ANNUAL MULTIMEDIA: 2011 / www.come-closer.net, www.audiluma.de

formabo.de

DESIGN LESEN!

IMPRESSUM — IMPRINT

HERAUSGEBER UND VERLAG/EDITOR AND PUBLISHER
Birkhäuser GmbH, Basel, Switzerland
Part of ActarBirkhäuser

VERLAGSLEITER / CHIEF UNIT MANAGER
Dr. Ulrich Schmidt

PROJEKTLEITUNG / PROJECT MANAGEMENT
Katharina Kulke

COVER DESIGN
David Lorente

GRAPHIC DESIGN & BOOK PRODUCTION
ActarBirkhäuserPro
www.actarbirkhauserpro.com
Barcelona - Basel

ESSAYS
© form-The Making of Design
www.form.de

ÜBERSETZUNG / TRANSLATION
Jeremy Gaines, Frankfurt

Bibliographic information published by the German National Library
The German National Library lists this publication in the Deutsche
Nationalbibliografie; detailed bibliographic data are available on the
Internet at http://dnb.d-nb.de.

This work is subject to copyright. All rights are reserved, whether
the whole or part of the material is concerned, specifically the
rights of translation, reprinting, re-use of illustrations, recitation,
broadcasting, reproduction on microfilms or in other ways, and
storage in databases. For any kind of use, permission of the
copyright owner must be obtained.

DISTRIBUTION
ActarBirkhäuserD
www.actarbirkhauser-d.com
Barcelona - Basel - New York

Roca i Batlle 2
E-08023 Barcelona
T +34 93 417 49 43
F +34 93 418 67 07
salesbarcelona@actarbirkhauser.com

Viaduktstrasse 42
CH-4051 Basel
T +41 61 5689 800
F +41 61 5689 899
salesbasel@actarbirkhauser.com

151 Grand Street, 5th floor
New York, NY 10013, US A
T +1 212 966 2207
F +1 212 966 2214
salesnewyork@actarbirkhauser.com

© 2012 Birkhäuser GmbH, Basel
P.O. Box, 4002 Basel, Switzerland
Part of ActarBirkhäuser

Printed on acid-free paper produced from chlorine-free pulp. TCF ∞
Printed in Spain

VOLUME 1 INDUSTRIAL & EXHIBITION DESIGN
ISBN 978-3-0346-0764-3

VOLUME 2 GRAPHIC DESIGN, CORPORATE & MULTIMEDIA DESIGN
ISBN 978-3-0346-0763-6

SET [VOLUME 1 & 2]
ISBN 978-3-0346-0762-9

9 8 7 6 5 4 3 2 1   www.birkhauser.com

KOREFE
KW43 BRANDDESIGN
MEDIENDESIGN
MEYER-HAYOZ DESIGN ENGINEERING GROUP
MOSKITO KOMMUNIKATION UND DESIGN
MOYSIG RETAIL DESIGN GMBH
MUTHMARKEN
NODESIGN
PETER SCHMIDT GROUP
POLYFORM
PROFORMA
PURE COMMUNICATIONS
RINCÓN2
BÜRO SIEBER
SIGN KOMMUNIKATION GMBH
STUDIO LAEIS
STUDIO 38 PURE COMMUNICATION GMBH
SYZYGY
TRAWNY / QUASS VON DEYEN
VISUPHIL© DESIGN STUDIOS
BÜRO FÜR GESTALTUNG WANGLER & ABELE
REGELINDIS WESTPHAL GRAFIK-DESIGN
ZWÖLFTON DESIGN

ABERHAM
ALLDESIGN
BAGGENDESIGN
BEAU BUREAU DESIGN
LOTHAR BÖHM
RUD NOLTE VISUELLE KOMMUNIKATION UND BERATUNG
BRANDTOUCH
BRÖSSKE, MEYER & RUF GMBH
BURKARDT | HOTZ
BÜRO BENSELER
BÜRO GROTESK
CHRISTIAN WEISSER AGENTURGRUPPE
C&N DESIGN-AGENTUR GMBH
CREDO CONCEPT. COMMUNICATION
CYCLOS DESIGN
DESIGNSHIP
DISEGNO GBR
ELBEDESIGNCREW
IFP
IDENTIS
INDEPENDENT MEDIEN-DESIGN
INTERBRAND
JUNGEPARTNER
KISKA